THiNKi
skills

ages
7-9

CREDITS

Author
Georgie Beasley

Editor
Irene Goodacre

Assistant Editor
Barbara Newby

Series Designers
Rachael Hammond
Joy Monkhouse

Designer
Rachael Hammond

Illustrations
Robin Edmonds

Cover image
© Digital Vision and © Dynamic Graphics

HarperCollins Publishers Ltd for the lyrics only from 'The ghost train' from *The Multi-Coloured Music Bus* by Peter Canwell © Peter Canwell (HarperCollins).
Jan Holdstock for use of the lyrics only to 'Country Life' by Jan Holdstock from *Flying a Round: 88 Rounds and Partner Songs* edited by David Gadsby and Beatrice Harrop © 1980, Jan Holdstock (1980, A & C Black).
John Rice for the use of 'Dog Talk' by John Rice from *Twinkle, Twinkle Chocolate Bar* edited by John Foster © 1991, John Rice (1991, Oxford University Press).

Material from The National Curriculum © Crown copyright. Reproduced with the permission of the Controller of HMSO and the Queen's Printer for Scotland.

Material from the National Literacy Strategy *Framework for Teaching* and the National Numeracy Strategy *Framework for Teaching Mathematics* © Crown copyright. Reproduced under the terms or HMSO Guidance Note 8.

Published by Scholastic Ltd,
Villiers House,
Clarendon Avenue,
Leamington Spa,
Warwickshire CV32 5PR

www.scholastic.co.uk

Text © 2004 Georgie Beasley
© 2004 Scholastic Ltd

Designed using Adobe Indesign

Printed by Bell & Bain Ltd, Glasgow

67890   67890123

British Library Cataloguing-in-Publication Data
A catalogue record for this book is available from the British Library.

ISBN 0-439-98340-1

CONTENTS

INTRODUCTION 5

INFORMATION-PROCESSING SKILLS 7

REASONING SKILLS 34

ENQUIRY SKILLS 61

CREATIVE THINKING SKILLS 87

EVALUATION SKILLS 111

CROSS-CURRICULAR PROJECTS 134

INTRODUCTION

Thinking Skills is a series of books which outlines detailed lesson plans for developing children's thinking and helping them to develop key skills of learning. The series gives ideas on how to incorporate the teaching of thinking skills into current curriculum teaching by making changes to the way activities are presented.

There are five thinking skills identified in the National Curriculum 2000 document:
⊙ information-processing skills
⊙ reasoning skills
⊙ enquiry skills
⊙ creative thinking skills
⊙ evaluation skills.

Teachers are probably most familiar with information-processing skills, and they are used to planning and developing activities to develop these skills in maths and science. Similarly, evaluative thinking skills are usually developed well in gymnastics, dance, music, and design and technology lessons, when children are encouraged to evaluate the quality of their own and others' performances, or the quality of their models and other artefacts, and to consider ways to make any improvements. The aim of this series of books is to find contexts in all subjects to develop all types of thinking skills.

ABOUT THE BOOK

Where appropriate, this book follows the National Literacy and Numeracy strategy objectives and the QCA Schemes of Work for all National Curriculum subjects.

The activities in this book identify exactly how to develop each thinking skill within specific units of work. They also show clearly how to adapt familiar activities to make sure that suitable emphasis is given to developing children's thinking. Sometimes, an activity identified in a QCA scheme is planned with specific focus to its organisation, so that it will support the development of children's thinking. Sometimes, specific questions are outlined that encourage children to identify why a particular activity is being done.

There are many specific learning styles and strategies that encourage children's thinking, including those to develop memory, thought sharing, concept mapping and exchanging ideas. Very often, a lesson activity can be organised in a different way to allow children to organise their own thoughts and work. This will encourage thinking, rather than over-directing knowledge. For example, the activity in the Enquiry skills chapter 'What can I find out?' (page 72) helps children to identify their own questions in order to start to structure independent research. This will help them to define the problems they are likely to meet, decide whether the information they have collected is relevant to their studies, and plan and carry out independent research into other topics and themes. Too often, children are told to find out about a particular topic without being helped to think for themselves what the process of researching may be.

QUESTIONING

We all think in a different way, and the first thing to remember about asking questions is that children of the 7–9 age range are most definitely not thinking the same things as you are! Questions that encourage children to guess what the teacher is thinking are the worst kind to ask. Instead, open-ended questions help you to find out not only what the children are thinking, but also what they already know.

There are different kinds of questions that can be asked to encourage and actively develop children's thinking. The skill of questioning isn't always getting the question right, but being able to respond to the children's answers with another suitable question. This way, you are not giving the children a right or wrong answer, but using questioning to direct their thinking to the correct answer. This will enable the children to think their way to the correct answer by themselves, and for you to iron out any misconceptions that they may have.

THE ORGANISATION OF THE BOOK

There are six chapters in this book. The first five focus on developing each of the five types of thinking. Chapter 6 includes two thinking-skills projects – 'Shipwrecked' and 'A school library'. These projects are intended to develop all the thinking skills in a themed cross-curricular way. Teachers may wish to save these projects to the last half-term, but in order to complete the project children will be required to work over a longer period of time than is required for the other activities in the book. The first project can extend over the whole half-term, while the activities in 'Hansel and Gretel' are planned to be completed over a week or a fortnight.

Each chapter begins with a short explanation of the thinking skill being focused on and is followed by two sections of activities – to introduce then extend skills – each section covering most if not all of the curriculum subjects. Each section has a quick-reference grid for teachers to see what the activities contain and quickly evaluate which fit easily into their own schemes of work.

The first section introduces thinking in short activities. These contain a learning objective specific to the activity and related to QCA Schemes of Work or the Literacy or Numeracy Strategies. A 'Thinking objective' outlines the particular thinking skill that the children will be developing in the activity. This is expanded under 'Thinking skills', which detail how the activity will bring out the thinking skills in line with the learning objective. A useful resource list is provided along with a detailed explanation of how to conduct the activity. These detailed activities have been designed to encourage and develop the children's thinking skills through practical investigation and enquiry. They are structured to encourage the children to ask why that particular activity is being carried out. Particular emphasis is placed on 'how' the children will learn – the way the learning is organised and the involvement of the children in this process – rather than the 'what'. Suggestions for questions to spark discussion and encourage the children to pose questions for investigation themselves are a focus of the activities.

The second section contains extended activities which, in addition to those sections outlined above, also contain a differentiation section with suggestions for how lower attaining children can be supported and the thinking of higher attaining children can be extended. The 'Where next' section gives ideas on how teachers can consolidate, practise, reintroduce or extend the particular activity and thinking skill. There is assessment advice on how to gauge the children's success in thinking through a problem or planning an investigation. 'Learning outcomes' relate to the 'Thinking objectives', expanding on them to describe what the children have achieved and can now do.

INFORMATION-PROCESSING SKILLS

INTRODUCTION

Information processing is about being able to collect, sort, organise and interpret a range of information to support learning in all subjects. By learning to process information in different ways, children begin to make sense of the world in which they live. By the age of seven they should be encouraged to decide for themselves where they should look for information, and how to collect it. They should also decide on ways to present the information, by sequencing, sorting or classifying, facilitating its analysis and interpretation, and identify for themselves what they have learned.

Information processing is more than presenting data in different forms. It also involves deciding whether information is useful for a particular purpose. Organising information in certain ways can also support memory development and help to make links and define relationships between different bits of information. Information can be found in the form of data, facts and knowledge.

Data is collected in maths, science, history, geography, ICT and design and technology. Most data is recorded in graphical form through tables, pictograms, bar charts and sets.

Facts are found to support work in most subjects, including history, geography, music, art and design and RE. For instance, in history, timelines are a useful way to organise facts by sequencing. This allows children to understand the passing of time, and the way that the past can be separated into different historical periods, thus helping them to develop the skill of chronology.

Use of analysis leads to a deeper understanding of the purpose and meaning of the information that has been collected.

ICT is used throughout this chapter to present data in a range of different forms, as well as being used for a variety of research activities, locating and collecting facts and knowledge. Activities show how computers and other ICT equipment can be used to support learning in many subjects. Information processing helps children to develop the learning process and equips them with skills that can be applied throughout their school career. Encouraging children to process information more independently enables them to develop their thinking too.

The key to information processing is opening children's naturally inquisitive minds. *What are we trying to find out, and for what purpose?* is the usual question, but we need to take children beyond that for them to appreciate that information often gives us more than one answer, and may raise further questions. By adjusting the organisation of existing lessons and activities, and identifying suitable questions that oblige children to consider carefully what they are doing and why, they will process the information as a natural part of learning. This means that you must learn to step back, giving children time to organise the learning themselves and develop their ideas, rather than directing them towards the lessons' objectives. By giving children this freedom, they will begin to note when they can use these processes in other learning, and this will accelerate learning in the long term.

The learning in the lessons in this chapter is organised so that the children begin to think for themselves about what they are doing and how they will do it. They are also encouraged to explain what they are doing so that their thinking can be assessed. You can move things forward by asking relevant and open questions to shift the direction of the work or consolidate the children's ideas.

Skills in the following areas all form part of information processing:
- sequencing
- pattern and relationship
- sorting, matching and classifying
- locating and collecting
- comparing and measuring
- analysing.

INTRODUCING INFORMATION-PROCESSING SKILLS

Subject and QCA unit, NLS or NNS objective	Activity title	Thinking objective	Activity	Page
English. NLS objective: To practise correct formation of basic joins	Joined-up writing	To analyse	Analysing how letters are joined are made and use this information to remember how to join letters as a result.	9
Maths. NNS objectives: To classify and describe 3-D and 2-D shapes; to classify polygons	Environmental shapes	To locate, sort and classify shapes according to their properties and uses	Finding shapes in the local environment and understanding how they have been used.	9
Science. QCA unit 3A: Teeth and eating	Toothy grin	To sort and classify foods	Sorting foods into sets according to whether they help with growth or energy.	11
History. QCA unit 8: What were the differences between the lives of rich and poor people in Tudor times?	Rich or poor	To sort and classify ideas	Comparing the lives of rich and poor people in Tudor times.	12
Geography. QCA unit 7: Weather around the world	World weather	To locate and collect types of weather; to match weather to activities	Collecting weather statistics from around the world and matching them to activities people do when on holiday.	12
Design and technology. QCA unit 4D: Alarms	Automatic appliances	To analyse appliances; to locate, collect and match switches to appliances	Collecting different types of switches and matching them to the appliances that they work.	13
ICT. QCA unit 4E: Modelling effects on screen	Procedure sequences	To sequence instructions	Writing sequences to repeat shapes to make a procedure.	14
Art and design. QCA unit 3B: Investigating pattern	Patterns	To collect and match patterns and designs	Finding and matching patterns from the local and natural environment.	15
Music. QCA unit 8: Ongoing skills	Peaceful countryside	To analyse the structure of a song	Analysing the structure of a song to help children understand when their singing part is coming up.	16
RE. QCA unit 3D: What is the Bible and why is it important for Christians?	Books of the Bible	To locate books in the Bible	The children will use the contents page to locate different books and stories in the Old and New Testaments.	16
PE. QCA unit: Striking and fielding games – unit 1	Throwing skills	To sequence	Sequencing actions for sending large and small balls in different ways.	17

Joined-up writing

SUBJECT: ENGLISH. NLS OBJECTIVE: TO PRACTISE CORRECT FORMATION OF BASIC JOINS.

Learning objective
To revise or learn basic diagonal and horizontal joins.

Thinking objective
To analyse letter joins.

Thinking skills
In this activity the children will analyse how letters are joined. They will consider where each letter starts, the direction in which it goes, where it ends and whether they have to add a dot or a cross to finish it off. They will think about whether it is tall (has an ascender), or has a tail (a descender) and will consider the proportion of each letter. They will then analyse how and where each letter joins to others and use this information to examine their own handwriting to judge whether it is correctly formed and joined. This self evaluation will give them useful insight into their own learning and help them to identify for themselves what they need to do next to improve – a National Curriculum key skill.

What you need
A whiteboard and a pen; handwriting books and pencils or handwriting pens; coloured pens; sets of cards with the letters of the alphabet written in cursive style.

What to do
Write the letter *a* on the board, making sure that the children know how to form this correctly. Write *a* again, but this time join it to another letter. Ask the children to think about why the letter *a* always joins with a diagonal join. Try to reach agreement that this is because it finishes with a diagonal line, the direction of its final upstroke. Look at some of the letters that the letter *a* may join, such as *i, m, n, p* or *r*, which all start with a downstroke, in a 'top to bottom' direction, after the join from the *a*. Practise these joins together.

Next, or in a later lesson, look at other letters that *a* may be joined to – letters with ascenders and descenders, such as *b* or *p*, or letters such as *c, d, g* or *q* that start in an anticlockwise direction. Analyse the fact that the joins are always diagonal because they are following the letter *a*, which finishes with a diagonal stroke. Look for other words that contain

the letter *a* and note the letter it is joined to. Ask, *Are there any letters that do not join to 'a' at all?*

Organise the children into groups and give each group a set of cards with the letters of the alphabet written in cursive style. Ask them to consider the letters and sort them according to whether they have a diagonal join. Label the sets and note that the letters that have a diagonal join all finish with a diagonal upward stroke. Let the children create their own writing patterns linking any letter that has a diagonal join with another of their choice. If these patterns are completed in coloured pen they can be used to make a display labelled with the analysis of how they are joined and why.

Repeat the process for letters with horizontal joins, for example those with a cross such as *f* and *t*, as well as *o, s, v, w* and *z*. Reinforce the analysis by talking about why these letters have diagonal and horizontal joins and link this to the way the letter finishes each time. Use the analysis to identify whether there are more diagonal or horizontal joins, and whether there are some letters that do not join naturally, such as *x*. Ask, *Why is 'x' not a natural joiner?* Link this to the direction in which this letter finishes.

Give the children a handwriting target, asking them to remember to join the letter of the week correctly in all their writing. Include this as an objective in writing activities, telling the children that you will be looking out for a particular join each week. Each time they finish a piece of written work, encourage them to mark their own handwriting, noting whether they have joined all the letters they have learned so far correctly. Reward them in some way for remembering and achieving the agreed targets.

Environmental shapes

SUBJECT: MATHS. NNS OBJECTIVES: TO CLASSIFY AND DESCRIBE 3-D AND 2-D SHAPES; TO CLASSIFY POLYGONS USING CRITERIA SUCH AS NUMBER OF RIGHT ANGLES, WHETHER THEY ARE REGULAR, SYMMETRY PROPERTIES.

Learning objective
To identify and describe the properties of 3-D and 2-D shapes.

Thinking objective
To locate, sort and classify shapes according to their properties and uses.

THINKING SKILLS

The children will locate shapes in their immediate environment and think about how they have been used, for example cuboids for bricks, triangular prisms for roof shapes and cylinders for drainpipes. They will consider why these particular shapes have been chosen, and begin to appreciate that the reasons are based on their properties. For example, a triangular prism has a flat face to provide a stable base, and a triangular face to provide a point at the top so that water can run off. Cuboids have been chosen for bricks because they build into stable structures; cylinders have no corners for debris to get stuck inside. They will think about the similarities and differences between the shapes in order to sort them into sets according to observable attributes. They will use the information to locate and name any given shape, thinking about the number of faces, edges, corners and right angles, the shape of the faces, whether they are regular or irregular and whether they are symmetrical, if appropriate.

WHAT YOU NEED

A collection of 2-D and 3-D shapes of different sizes; sorting rings; double-sided sticky tape or Blu-Tack; whiteboard and pen.

WHAT TO DO

Go outside into the playground and name all the shapes you can see, 2-D and 3-D. Point out unusual shapes as well as those with which the children are familiar, such as triangular prisms (roof tops), pyramids (church spires), cone-shaped trees and bushes, and hexagonal prisms (church steeples). Talk about why these shapes are suitable for the uses to which they are being put: *A triangular prism is useful for roofs because it has a flat rectangular bottom to fit the shape of the walls and the water can run down the sloped faces.* Record all the shapes you can see.

Go back into school and write the names of all the shapes you have found on the board. Link the flat 2-D shapes with the solid 3-D shapes they help to make up. For example, the rectangle will join with the cuboid and rectangular prism, the triangle with the pyramid and triangular prism, and so on.

Choose one of the shapes and ask the children to describe it using mathematical vocabulary. Start with the flat shapes and talk about the number of sides and corners, whether there are any right angles and whether the sides have equal or different lengths. Next, describe the solid shapes in the same way. Complete a chart, detailing for each shape the number of faces, edges and corners and whether it has flat or curved faces.

You could extend this activity for higher attaining children by asking them to consider the number of right angles, whether the shape is symmetrical, and why.

Invite the children to think of criteria for sorting the shapes. Initially, they will probably suggest observable differences, such as the shape of the faces, the number of edges, faces, sides and right angles and whether they are regular or symmetrical. Encourage them to extend their thinking to other, non-observable similarities and differences. Ask, *How well would they build and fit together? How suitable would they be for decorative purposes, for example a pot for a garden plant?* Ask the children how they would sort the shapes to find the answers to the following questions:

◉ *Which shape has nine straight sides, six corners and five faces?*
◉ *Which shape has two triangular and three rectangular faces?*
◉ *Which shape has one curved edge, no corners and two faces?*
◉ *Which shape has twelve straight sides, eight corners and six faces?*
◉ *Which shape has eighteen straight sides, twelve corners and eight faces?*
◉ *Which shapes are regular?*
◉ *Which shapes have no right angles?*
◉ *Which shapes are symmetrical?*
◉ *Which shapes have 24 right angles?*

To find the answer to the first question, the children can sort the shapes according to whether they have fewer or more than five faces. They will then be left with those that have five faces and can check the numbers of straight sides and corners to find the shape they are seeking. Let them identify criteria for sorting the shapes to find the answers to the other questions themselves. Challenge them to think of a shape and identify questions they can ask each other.

Try sorting the shapes by whether they have straight edges and whether they have more or fewer than, or exactly six faces. Then try sorting them into sets of shapes with square, triangular, rectangular or circular faces. You may need to prompt the children to try using these criteria before encouraging them to develop their own sorting ideas.

You can differentiate your choice of shape and questions to match the learning needs of individuals and groups of children.

Finally, set up a chart with the descriptions down one side and challenge the children to match the correct shapes to the descriptions. Let them use double-sided sticky tape or Blu-Tack to attach the actual shape to the correct description.

Extend the thinking challenge by sorting using a Carroll diagram. Use criteria such as:

◉ straight/not straight sides; more than/fewer than three faces
◉ triangular/not triangular; fewer than/more than six faces.

Ask the children to identify what they have learned from this method of sorting (shapes with curved sides usually have fewer than three faces; triangular-faced shapes usually have fewer than six faces). Ask them to give a possible reason, and note those who can see a relationship between the number of sides and corners of a triangle. The children will start to realise that they can make generalisations about the shapes: *The number of straight edges on a prism is always a multiple of three. All pyramids have an even number of edges. A prism has two more faces than the number of edges of the end faces. A pyramid has one more face than the number of edges on the base face.*

TOOTHY GRIN

SUBJECT: SCIENCE. QCA UNIT 3A: TEETH AND EATING.

LEARNING OBJECTIVE
To learn that some foods contain sugar and this can be harmful to our teeth.

THINKING OBJECTIVE
To sort and classify foods.

THINKING SKILLS
The children will look at information provided on the labels of empty food containers and use this to classify foods that provide energy and others which are foods for growth. They will then look carefully at the foods that provide energy and classify these according to whether or not they contain sugar. They will use the information collected to form conclusions about these different foods and note that some are more harmful to our teeth than others.

WHAT YOU NEED
A large collection of different types of food containers and/or labels (try to include some that contain sugar, carbohydrates, protein, fat and

vitamins); large sheets of paper and pens; two enlarged contents labels from food items, one which provides for growth (probably a non-processed fish or meat product) and a second which provides energy (perhaps a tin of baked beans or a packet of biscuits).

WHAT TO DO
Talk to the children about the foods that they eat. Look at some of the food labels and containers and discuss the foods that these once contained.

Look at the enlarged contents label of the food for growth – this will contain mostly protein and vitamins and little or no carbohydrate or sugar. List its ingredients, drawing the children's attention to the protein and vitamin content. Tell them that protein and vitamins help us to grow, and name some other foods that assist healthy growth and are mainly proteins and vitamins.

Next, show them the contents label of the energy food, which will contain carbohydrate and/or sugar. Ask the children to suggest what this food is for. Tell them that carbohydrates and sugars are mainly energy givers. Name other foods that give us energy and are, therefore, mostly sugars and carbohydrates.

Divide the children into groups and give each group a good selection of food labels or containers. Ask them to sort these into two sets: growth foods (those that contain mostly protein) and energy foods (those that have more carbohydrates and sugars). When they have finished, discuss what they have placed in each set and why. This will give you an opportunity to check that they have understood.

Put the growth foods to one side and look first at the set of foods that give energy. Ask the children, *What do you notice about the amount of sugar in this group of food items? Do they all contain sugar? Which ones do not?* Sort them into two subsets, according to whether they contain sugar or not.

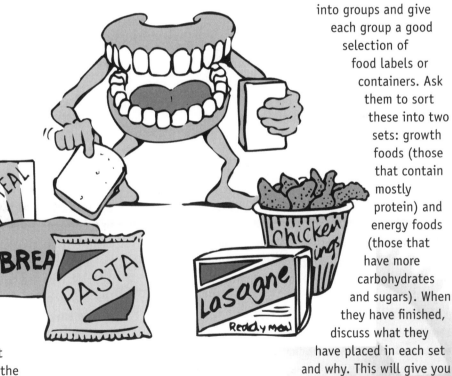

When you have sorted out those which contain sugar, order them from the most to the least sugar content. Use a decision tree classification system to decide which foods cause most harm to the teeth. Use questions such as *Does it contain more than 5 grams, 10 grams, 15 grams of sugar?* so the children can classify into *yes* or *no* groups. Ask the children which food they think would be most harmful, and then explain that although the one with most sugar is probably the most harmful, they all cause damage to teeth because they all contain sugar. Ask the children to process the information. *What is the purpose of sweetened foods if they are harmful to our teeth and we can get sugar from other foods?*

For homework, challenge the children to find sugar-free options for items that are usually sweetened, such as sugar-free drinks, baked beans or sauces, by looking on the labels to note the absence of sugar.

Rich or poor

SUBJECT: HISTORY. QCA UNIT 8: WHAT WERE THE DIFFERENCES BETWEEN THE LIVES OF RICH AND POOR PEOPLE IN TUDOR TIMES?

Learning objective
To assess the children's perceptions of wealth and poverty.

Thinking objective
To sort and classify ideas.

Thinking skills
In this activity the children will be sorting the characteristics of rich and poor people in modern and Tudor times. They will use this information to think about their lives today and what they mean by 'rich and poor' or 'wealth and poverty'. They will then relate these ideas to Tudor times to consider what life was like then for both categories of people.

What you need
Large sheets of paper and pens; whiteboard and pen; a range of resources, including pictures and books, that reflect life in Tudor times.

What to do
Tell the children that they are going to think about what it means to be rich or poor. Begin by defining the two words, perhaps by writing down the definition from a class dictionary. Note that *rich* usually means someone who has lots of money and possessions, while *poor* means people who have very little money and very few possessions. Do not get into a debate about personal wealth, as this can be a sensitive issue for some children.

Tell the children that you want them to consider what it was like to be rich or poor in Tudor times. They should work in small groups and list all the characteristics of rich and poor people's lives in Tudor times. Provide a range of evidence to prompt the children's ideas. You could give each group a different aspect to work with, such as the places people lived in town and country settings, and the way they filled their work and leisure time.

After about ten minutes, gather the children together and note all the points that the groups have thought of. Question the children about their perceptions and tell them that later lessons in this history topic will show them whether these perceptions are correct.

Over the next few history lessons, let the children work in their groups to think further about their understanding of wealth and poverty. This will provide them with a base for future research into what they think different aspects of life were like for rich and poor people in Tudor times.

World weather

SUBJECT: GEOGRAPHY. QCA UNIT 7: WEATHER AROUND THE WORLD.

Learning objective
To collect weather statistics from around the world.

Thinking objectives
To locate and collect types of weather; to match weather to activities.

Thinking skills
The children will identify different activities that people enjoy doing on holiday. They will also collect weather statistics from around the world and match these to the kinds of activities people like to do when they are on holiday. They will then use all this information to match the countries with the most suitable weather to the holiday activities identified.

What you need
Access to the Internet; holiday brochures and newspapers with good information about world weather; whiteboard and pen; paper and writing material; map of the world.

WHAT TO DO

Talk about the children's recent holiday activities, either in Britain or abroad. Ask them, *What was good about this activity? Did you do it outside or inside? Did it matter what the weather was like? How important was this to your enjoyment?*

Collect the children's ideas about all the different kinds of activities people like to do when they are on holiday. If necessary, put them into pairs to locate and collect all the activities that brochures suggest people can do while they are on holiday. Make a list of these, for example skiing, water-skiing, sailing, rock climbing, walking, swimming, sun bathing, visiting theme parks, eating, sightseeing, and so on, marking with an asterisk all the activities that rely on the weather. For example, for skiing you need snow, while for water sports a fine warm day would be preferable, and it would be good to visit a rainforest when it is not pouring with rain. This will challenge higher attaining children to consider climate and the difference between tropical and temperate regions.

Give each child a sheet of paper. Ask them to choose several holiday activities and list these down one side of their paper. Explain that they should carry out research on weather from around the world to locate countries which have weather suited to these activities. Allow the children to use the Internet and newspapers to research current weather and to look in holiday brochures to check weather types and temperature at different times of the year.

Discuss the children's findings, locating the different countries on a map. Ask, *What did you notice about places that are suitable for skiing? What about sunny places? Where would you find rainforests? What creatures will you see here in the wet and dry seasons? Will there be the same ones? Are there any places suitable for all types of holidays? For which activities is the British weather most suitable? Are there some activities for which it is suitable only at certain times of the year?*

Use the information to ask and answer questions together to find out patterns in weather conditions around the world.

AUTOMATIC APPLIANCES

SUBJECT: DESIGN AND TECHNOLOGY. QCA UNIT 4D: ALARMS.

LEARNING OBJECTIVE
To learn about the many types of switches used to operate everyday appliances.

THINKING OBJECTIVES
To analyse appliances; to locate, collect and match switches to appliances.

THINKING SKILLS
The children will collect a range of appliances to analyse how they work, and the different kinds of switches used to operate them. They will then collect the range of switches they have identified and match them to different types of operation.

WHAT YOU NEED
Pictures of appliances which are operated by a switch; a circuit with a bulb or buzzer with a switch made from foil; several large sheets of paper and pens; whiteboard and pen.

WHAT TO DO
Remind the children how they made electrical circuits in science. If necessary, make these again and talk about how a circuit needs to be complete if it is to work. Use a simple foil switch to show how the components must be pushed together to make the bulb light up. Then show the children what happens when the circuit is broken – when the switch is pulled apart, the light goes out.

Ask the children to name all the things they can think of that are worked by a switch. As they make suggestions, list these on the board, classifying the type of switch as you record them, under the headings Push, Pull, Turn and Slide. Point out to the children what you are doing and discuss briefly the different types of switches.

Explain that you are analysing the information by classifying the appliances based on the type of switch that is used in each one. For example, *This washing machine has a switch that works when the knob is pulled out. The CD player has a slide switch, some radios have switches that turn and the television has a push switch*. Review the types of switches you have thought of so far.

Now tell the class about switches that you have not already considered and explain briefly how they work. For example, *These items have switches that use sensors to detect when someone or something is approaching and turn on a device*. Ask the children to think of appliances that might use these switches. A burglar alarm has a switch that works when the circuit is broken, when it senses someone approaching. This usually uses a tilt switch to make it work. Identify other things that use similar types of switch, such as a car park barrier or automatic doors.

Now give each group of children a sheet of paper divided into five. Ask them to put five heading on it: Push, Pull, Slide, Turn and Tilt. Ask the groups to collect pictures of (or list) as many appliances as they can, and to analyse how they work by identifying the type of switch each one uses. Ask them to record the name of the appliance in what they think is the correct section. Collate all the groups' ideas on a large sheet of paper. Pay particular attention to developing the uses of the tilt switch, as these will be less familiar to the children.

Procedure sequences

Subject: ICT. QCA unit 4E: Modelling effects on screen.

Learning objective
To learn to write a sequence to make a procedure, and repeat procedures to make a pattern.

Thinking objective
To sequence instructions.

Thinking skills
The children will think about the instructions they need to write a sequence to make shapes, and how to repeat these to make a procedure. By turning the procedure they will learn how to produce different patterns.

What you need
A computer with Logo software or a floor turtle with a pen inserted and a large sheet of paper; a piece of chalk.

What to do
This activity can be done with a floor turtle and/or on a computer screen to suit children's previous experience. To remind you or the children of the procedures, print out the directions from the index in the Help section of the program.

Seat the children in a circle and ask for a volunteer to be a robot. Ask the rest of the class to give a series of instructions to make the 'robot' move in a square shape. Remind them to use mathematical language and to give the angle of turn in degrees, for example *Turn right or left ninety degrees*. The 'robot' must follow the instructions to make the square shape, drawing the route taken with a piece of chalk on the classroom floor. Repeat the activity to draw other shapes.

Go to the computer, remembering to activate the 'pen down' tool, and show the children how to use Logo software to write a sequence that will draw a square or another shape on the screen. Remind the children how they did this with Roamer during Key Stage 1. If they do not remember, or do not have experience of this activity, show them now. Put a pen through the central hole and direct Roamer to move in a square around a large piece of paper. Note the square that has been drawn. If you use Roamer World, you can transfer the same instructions to the computer screen (remembering again to use the 'pen down' tool). Reinforce that the pen needs to be down to mark the drawing and show the children what happens if you forget to put the pen down – no square! Point out that this can have its uses if you want to move the turtle to another place to start a second shape without joining this to the first shape.

Play around, drawing different shapes with the children watching and noting how to do this. Show them that you can save the sequence as a procedure, giving it a name. Then show that when this name is entered, the matching shape is drawn automatically on the screen. Let the children work in pairs to write instructions for a shape of their choice and to save this as a procedure. They could do more than one if there is time.

Choose one of the procedures they have created and extend the activity by showing them how they can repeat this procedure a number of times. Do this a few times and watch how the shape is drawn over again on top of itself. Ask the children, *How might we draw the second shape so that it is not on top of the first? Can we turn it so that it is drawn in a different place, in a different position or rotation?* Write the number of repeat, the procedure name and the angle of turn. Draw the new procedure on screen, giving it a new name if appropriate, for example 'star'. Tell the computer to draw 'star' and watch the shape appear, as if by magic.

Explain to the children that they have identified different sequences of instructions, which are telling the computer to do very precise things.

During later lessons, let the children explore new sequences and procedures to create many different types of pattern. Let them investigate 'pen up' and 'pen down' to experiment with different effects.

PATTERNS

SUBJECT: ART AND DESIGN. QCA UNIT 3B: INVESTIGATING PATTERN.

LEARNING OBJECTIVE
To collect different patterns and designs to inform ideas.

THINKING OBJECTIVE
To collect and match patterns and designs.

THINKING SKILLS
The children will collect geometric patterns usually seen in nature, in the environment, in school and at home (as patterns on wallpaper, crockery, and so on). They will reproduce these patterns using paper, paint, prints or computer stamps to make matching designs of their own.

WHAT YOU NEED
Collections of crockery, rolls of wallpaper, curtains and other fabrics (with a range of colour combinations) that have patterns repeated at intervals, perhaps transformed, rotated or reflected (70s-type designs are usually suitable, as are ones with designs taken from nature, such as flowers and leaves); large sheets of paper and adhesive; paint or computer stamps; access to a photocopier.

WHAT TO DO
Look together at your collection of objects and identify some of the patterns. Look particularly for patterns that are made from a repeated shape –

geometric shapes, leaves to make a fern, spirals to make a curved pattern, flowers to make floral designs, or anything else that has a repeating shape or design. Ask the children which they like best and why: *Is it because of the colours? Is it the way the pattern is repeated? How often is the pattern repeated? How many colours are used?*

Choose one design and look at it in detail. Question the children closely about what they observe, and make a note of their comments. Ask, *How many colours are there? Is the pattern repeated exactly, or is it transformed, at a different angle, smaller or larger, rotated or reflected?* Choose a different pattern and work through the process again, noting the same things. Find the designs that match on the patterns and note how often they are repeated.

Invite the children to work in groups to collect all the designs they like from wallpaper or wrapping paper by cutting out samples and sticking them to a large sheet of paper to create their own patterns.

When they have done this, they should think about which patterns they would keep the same and which ones they would adapt or change. This could be achieved by varying one or more colours, rotating the repetitions slightly, or altering the size to make some patterns larger and others smaller.

Now ask the children to design their own pattern for crockery, or tiles for a kitchen or bathroom with individual designs, or curtains for a bedroom by repeating one or more designs. Initially, they should create this in outline only so that they can photocopy it several times to make enough black and white copies to cover a small sheet of paper. They can then use this to design an individual or paired pattern for the curtain designs, or a template for an individual design for the tile or crockery.

Show them how to use the enlarge or reduce facility on the photocopier to change the size of some of their patterns to add variety. Alternatively, they could use a stamp facility on a computer program to print out sheets of coloured designs of the same or different sizes. Invite the children to work individually, or in pairs, to use their photocopied or computer-generated design to create their own pattern by repeating it at identical intervals on a large sheet of paper. They should then decide on the colours they will use, thinking carefully about colours that would be suitable for the environment where the item would be used or displayed. Encourage them to use only two or three colours.

Let the children use the finished designs to cover a paper plate, cup or dish, white tiles or plain fabrics with their patterns.

PEACEFUL COUNTRYSIDE

SUBJECT: MUSIC. QCA UNIT 8: ONGOING SKILLS.

LEARNING OBJECTIVE
To recognise simple structures (of songs).

THINKING OBJECTIVE
To analyse the structure of a song.

THINKING SKILLS
The children will analyse how a song is structured and use the information to recognise when to sing their own part.

WHAT YOU NEED
A copy of 'Country Life' by Jan Holdstock from *Flying a Round* (A and C Black); the words and music of the song copied onto a large sheet of paper or photocopied onto an OHP transparency.

Country Life
Oh, how peaceful living in the country,
Far away from the noisy town.
Oh, how peaceful living in the country,
Here's a place to settle down.

Cock-a-doodle-doo!
Cock-a-doodle-doo!
Six in the morning,
Up with you!

All through the day hee-haw
And at night I'll hee-haw once more!

Moo, moo, moo!
Goodnight to you!

WHAT TO DO
Perform the whole song once to the children, from beginning to end, and ask them what it is about. Start with the chorus, sing each animal part through twice, and sing the chorus again to end the song.

Talk about how the chorus sets the scene of the song and identify how each different animal has its own part. Ask the children, *Why do you think I sang each of the animal parts through twice?* In order to explain this, compare the length of the opening part with the lengths of the animal parts and note that the animal parts are four bars in length, while the opening part is twice as long with eight bars.

Teach the song to the children, encouraging them to come up with ideas to add variation and contrast to the different parts, such as singing the cow part legato, the cockerel part staccato and emphasising the *hee-haw* words by singing them with definition and more loudly in the donkey part.

Identify the two parts of the song on the written copy. Invite half the class to sing the chorus, and the other half to sing each animal part twice through, one after the other as a two-part partner song. Swap over so that all the children have a turn at each part. Ask, *Was that easy or hard?*

Divide the class into three groups. Tell them they should sing the chorus in unison, then allocate each group an animal part (2, 3 or 4) to sing through twice, one after the other. Check their understanding of the song's structure by asking them why they are singing it through twice. When they are very familiar with the parts, challenge them to sing the three animal parts at the same time. The first group should sing their part (part 2) through once to set the tempo before the other groups join in with parts 3 and 4, one after the other until they are all singing together. The children can sing their parts for as long as you like, but four times altogether will provide enough fun, and keep the overall structure.

Perform the song together with a structure identified thus:
- Part 1 – all children in unison.
- Parts 2, 3 and 4 together – sung in groups twice through.
- Part 1 – all children in unison.

Discuss how identifying and analysing the structure of the song has helped them to remember the sequence of the performance.

BOOKS OF THE BIBLE

SUBJECT: RE. QCA UNIT 3D: WHAT IS THE BIBLE AND WHY IS IT IMPORTANT FOR CHRISTIANS?

LEARNING OBJECTIVE
To learn that the Bible has two Testaments that each contain many books.

THINKING OBJECTIVE
To locate books in the Bible.

THINKING SKILLS
The children will learn about the Old and New Testaments and use the Contents page to locate books in each of these.

WHAT YOU NEED
Several copies of the same type of Bible (enough for each child or for one between two), which contains an Index and Contents page.

WHAT TO DO

Look at the Bibles as a class or in groups, and talk about the different books that make it up. Locate the first book of the Old Testament, Genesis, and read the first verse. Ask, *What does this remind you of? Do you remember the story of the Creation?*

Explain that 'Genesis' means 'beginning' and that it tells the story of the Creation, before telling stories about other characters the children may know.

Locate the Contents page and look at the list printed there. Explain that these are the different books of the Bible. Show where the New Testament starts and explain to the children that this begins around the time when Jesus was born. Clarify that the Old Testament tells the stories that happened before Jesus was born, while the New Testament relates stories that happened after he was born.

Choose a book from the Old Testament and ask the children to find it first in the Contents page, then in the Bible. Repeat this for other Old Testament books, then move on to books of the New Testament.

In later lessons, give the children verse references where they can find stories about people with whom they are familiar. If Bible stories are told in lessons or assembly, encourage the children

to find where these are located in the Bible, paying particular attention to whether they are found in the Old or New Testament.

THROWING SKILLS

SUBJECT: PE. QCA UNIT: STRIKING AND FIELDING GAMES – UNIT 1.

LEARNING OBJECTIVE

To develop the range and consistency of throwing skills.

THINKING OBJECTIVE

To sequence.

THINKING SKILLS

The children will sequence the way they execute a throw and use this information to improve their throwing skills. They will consider the sequence of the throw and note how this helps them to extend the accuracy and distance of the different throws.

WHAT YOU NEED

A selection of balls of different sizes.

WHAT TO DO

Take the children outside and challenge them to throw a small ball as far as they can. Ask, *Will it travel farther with an underarm or overarm throw? Why does it travel farther with this kind of throw? Is it because you are used to throwing in this way?* Ask the children to practise throwing the balls overarm to try to gain more distance. Encourage them to think carefully about how they complete the action, and at the sequence of their throwing action. Ask, *What do you do first? How do you balance your body before you throw? In which direction do you bring your arm forward? From where do you push the throw? Where does your hand finish at the end of the throw? If your hand finishes pointing upwards, in which direction does the ball travel? If your arm is pointing at the ground, where does the ball go? Where should the arm be pointing if you want to send it a long way? When should you release the ball?*

Let the children practise the sequence with both underarm and overarm throws, and try to decide which method sends the ball farther, and why. Ask, *How does knowing the sequence help improve your techniques for each throw?*

This activity can be repeated to define the sequence for striking accurately with different types of equipment, in order to improve the children's different skills and techniques when using them.

EXTENDING INFORMATION-PROCESSING SKILLS

Subject and QCA unit, NLS or NNS objective	Activity title	Thinking objective	Activity	Page
English. NLS objective: To write new or extended verses for performance based on models of 'performance' and oral poetry reading	Smelly dog	To analyse pattern and relationship	Reading a poem and analysing the pattern and relationship between the verses before replacing some words with ideas of their own which fit the same pattern.	19
Maths. NNS objective: To identify 2-D and 3-D shapes	Lorry maths	To locate information	Locating a range of mathematical information based on observation of lorries and analysing this to help learn about numbers and shapes.	20
Science. QCA unit 3E: Magnets and springs	Magnets and metals	To sort and classify objects	Classifying magnets to understand magnetic properties of metals.	22
History. QCA unit 9: What was it like for children in the Second World War?	Children at war	To locate areas	Collecting information about children during the Second World War and how they were affected.	23
Geography. QCA unit 9: Village settlers	Settle down	To collect and analyse information	Looking at the lifestyle in a rural settlement.	25
Design and technology. QCA unit 3A: Packaging.	Christmas 3-D boxes	To analyse packaging	Looking at a collection of different shaped packaging and analysing how it was made.	27
ICT. QCA unit 4D: Collecting and presenting information	Swinging sixties	To collect, sort and analyse information	Collecting information to put into a database that the computer can then sort.	28
Art and design. QCA unit 4A: Viewpoints	Sights for your eyes	To collect and sort images	Photographing views from different angles.	29
Music. QCA unit 10: Play it again	Ostinato rhythms	To sequence and locate ostinato rhythms	Locating repeating rhythms in a song.	30
RE. QCA unit 3A: What do signs and symbols mean in religion?	Memories are made of this	To collect and sort signs and symbols	Looking at signs and symbols in the local environment and identifying what they mean.	31
PE. QCA unit: Invasion games – unit 2	Football dance	To match ball skills to a piece of music	Creating a footballing sequence to a piece of pop music.	32

Smelly dog

Subject: English. NLS objective: To write new or extended verses for performance based on models of 'performance' and oral poetry reading.

Learning objective
To write new verses to a given format.

Thinking objective
To analyse pattern and relationship.

Thinking skills
The children will work as a class with you to analyse the pattern and relationship in a poem. You will then model how to think of a new verse based on this structure. They will finally work independently or in pairs to think of a new verse.

What you need
'Dog Talk' by John Rice, published in *Twinkle, Twinkle Chocolate Bar* compiled by John Foster (Oxford), or any poem with the same repeating structure; a whiteboard and pen; large sheets of paper and pens.

Dog Talk
Pebbles and shells
Water down wells
Churches and bells
Your dog smells.

Sand and waves
Bats and caves
Rants and raves
My dog behaves.

Beetles and slugs
Fleas and rugs
Kisses and hugs
Your dog's got bugs.

Keys and locks
Feet and socks
Eagles and hawks
My dog talks!

What to do
Read the poem together and enjoy the humour. Talk about the content and ask the children what the poem is about. Agree that it is about two dogs, what they look like and the way they behave. Note how the poet's dog does clever things, while the comments about the other dog in alternate verses are much more negative.

Start by looking together at the first verse. Ask, *What do you notice about the last words of each line?* Agree that they all rhyme. Check whether this pattern is repeated in the other three verses. The last verse is slightly different, as the first two and the last two lines have more secure rhymes. The children should be able to point this out.

Explain to the class that you want to write some new verses for the poem. Ask, *How would you need to start a verse?*

Talk about the best way to approach the task. Ask, *Is it easier to think of the first line first?* If the children are not sure about this, suggest that they might want to begin with the last line, using this as a starting point to think of other rhyming words to go with the last word. Agree that the first two words of the last line should be *My dog* or *Your dog*, depending on whether they are writing a verse about their own or someone else's dog. Invite the children to think of how they could finish this line. For example, they could use: *My dog wags his tail*, *My dog sniffs*, or *My dog's got hair*. Together decide on a last line for a class verse and write this on the board.

Ask the children to think about what to do next. Identify words that rhyme with the last word of your new verse and write them at the end of the first three lines. Then think of a word to pair with each line ending. Read the new verse together, for example:

Letters and mail
Bucket and pail
Boats with a sail
My dog wags his tail.

Invite the children to work together in groups, in pairs or independently to write one verse to add to the poem. Give them large sheets of paper and pens so that they can display their verses on the board for the class to share. Staple all the finished verses together into a class poem.

Differentiation
Give less able children a copy of the third verse and ask them to find new words to rhyme with *bugs*. They should also replace some of the other words with their own ideas.

For example:

> Cups and mugs
> Kettles and jugs
> Sinks and plugs
> Your dog's got bugs.

More able children should be encouraged to think of phrases with connectives other than *and*. They may like to have a go at writing two verses.

WHERE NEXT

Find other poems with a similar structure for the children to adapt, such as 'When the wind blows' by John Foster, and 'Come-day Go-day' by Barrie Wade in the same book.

Write a poem in the same style for a different animal of the children's choice.

ASSESSMENT

Read the children's verses and note who has managed to follow the structure. These children will have analysed the poem correctly. Let the children carry out peer assessments first by evaluating how well the verses follow the same structure. Encourage them to start positively. For example, *I would like to present Laura's work to you. She has used some imaginative vocabulary to write an alternative verse for her dog, which shows how clever he is...* and so on. Model the process for the children if necessary.

LEARNING OUTCOMES

Once the children have analysed the poem, most will be able to write another verse following the same structure. Many will extend their skills to writing an entire poem in the same style, while others will be able to think of new rhyming words to write a new third verse for the poem.

FURTHER ENGLISH CHALLENGES

On the beach

Read the poem 'On the Beach' by Michael Rosen, published in the same book, and write an alternative ending to the first and subsequent verses. The children will need to analyse the structure of the poem to discover where to add the rhyme. Encourage them to follow the structure by starting their verse with a different person and including several things they may be doing. In this poem, they need to make the second and fourth lines rhyme, for example:

> There's a postman over there
> and he's walking on the prom,
> watching people paddling and
> chatting to his good friend Tom.

Other poems can be used as long as the children are able to analyse and follow the structure when writing their own verses.

Alphabetical rhymes

Ask the children to analyse the structure of 'An alphabet has horrible habits' by Colin West and also published in *Twinkle, Twinkle Chocolate Bar*, for its use of vocabulary and overall style. Ask them to follow the same structure to write a group poem. They should decide who will write which part and divide the poem into several sections so that different individuals write a small section each before putting the whole poem together.

LORRY MATHS

SUBJECT: MATHS. NNS OBJECTIVE: TO IDENTIFY 2-D AND 3-D SHAPES.

LEARNING OBJECTIVES

To identify 2-D and 3-D shapes; to identify odd and even numbers and numbers greater or less than 10 and 100.

THINKING OBJECTIVE

To locate information.

THINKING SKILLS

It is important for children to acquire the ability to locate and gather information from picture sources. This activity focuses on mathematical information about a lorry, but the children will be able to transfer the skills they use here to other activities, where they need to infer meaning in stories or notice details and decide if these are of any importance to their learning. This activity has strong links with the children's developing observational skills.

WHAT YOU NEED

Pictures or photographs of lorries that clearly show the number of wheels and the number plate; a whiteboard and pen; 3-D shapes and boxes, or paper and drawing, painting or colouring materials.

WHAT TO DO

As a whole-class group, show the children a picture of a lorry and draw their attention to the shapes of the cab, containers and wheels. Ask the children what shapes they can see, encouraging them to note the flat or 2-D shapes and note how these build into solid or 3-D shapes. Record these on the board. Ask, *Are the shapes we have listed two- or three-dimensional?*

Can you see the two-dimensional shapes that make up the three-dimensional ones?

Ask the children to count the number of wheels. Ask, *What do you notice about the number? Does it have an odd or an even number of wheels? Is the total number greater or less than 10?* Look at the number plate or, if that is not possible, make one up. Ask the children to decide whether these numbers are odd or even, greater or less than 100.

Repeat the activity with another lorry picture, asking the children to locate the same information about shape and number. Continue until you are sure that the children are familiar with the process of finding this information.

Now split the class into groups, provide a collection of 3-D shapes and boxes, and invite the children to make their own models of lorries. Tell them to think about the information they've collected from the pictures of lorries and to base their models on this learning. Remind them to add the correct number of wheels in the correct positions and encourage them to add any other details they want, such as a number plate. Alternatively, the groups could draw and paint a picture of a lorry using shape templates.

Use the finished models or pictures of lorries to ask the children number puzzles, such as *If one lorry can hold 60 boxes, how many boxes can two lorries hold? Does this lorry have more or fewer wheels than this one?*

DIFFERENTIATION

Work with low attainers to develop number stories based on what they can see. For example, *If the lorry has ten wheels on one side and the same number on the other, how many wheels are there altogether?* Encourage higher attaining children to think of

	odd	even
< 200	Y173 GGB T141 ACB	X94 ELB
> 200	Y805 XCV	C926 SCB

problems with two or three steps and to include multiplication and division, such as *Two lorries went out one day to deliver three crates of bananas each. If each crate holds ten boxes, how many boxes of bananas did they deliver altogether? How many lorries would you need to deliver 79 boxes?*

WHERE NEXT
Carry out a traffic survey focussed on finding out whether more lorries pass the school at certain times of the day than at others. Record this as a class pictogram or graph, using computers if possible.

ASSESSMENT
Make a list of the shapes that Year 3 and 4 children should know. Record whether the children can now locate, recognise and identify the names of these shapes. Note the children who can apply the information they have collected from the picture of the lorry to the detail of their own model or picture.

LEARNING OUTCOMES
The children will learn to locate a range of mathematical information and use it to reproduce pictures and models of the same type.

FURTHER MATHS CHALLENGES
Symmetrical vehicles
Draw lines of symmetry on photographs of front views of lorries. Include some that are drawn vertically, horizontally and diagonally. Ask, *Are they all vertical? Can you find any that are horizontal?* (For example, the number plate or the wing mirror.) Look at a side view. Ask, *Can you see any lines of symmetry here?* Look at other different components of the lorry, including the wheels, and draw the lines of symmetry. Note the range of shapes and the number of lines of symmetry. Ask, *Which shape has most lines of symmetry? Can you count how many lines of symmetry there would be on a circle, or is this just too difficult?* Relate this to pictures of shapes by giving the children pictures of 2-D and 3-D shapes and asking them to draw in as many lines of symmetry as they can.

Number plates
Ask the children to look at number plates of different lorries, either recording these from (safe) observation of a nearby road or by looking at pictures. Challenge the children to find the number plate with the biggest and smallest number. The children could sort the number plates into sets according to different criteria, such as odd and even numbers, numbers greater or less than 200, 300 and so on, or multiples of 2, 5 and 10. For example, the number plate Y805 XCV shows a number bigger than 300, odd and a multiple of 5. When the numbers have been sorted

according to the criteria, ask the children to think of a collective description for each one. For example, *All these numbers are greater than 50 and are even.*

MAGNETS AND METALS

LEARNING OBJECTIVE
To learn that magnets are attracted to metals that contain iron.

THINKING OBJECTIVE
To sort and classify objects.

THINKING SKILLS
In this activity the children will revisit their learning about the properties of magnets and reinforce their understanding of what will, and will not, be attracted to one. They will refine this knowledge by identifying that only some metals will be attracted to magnets and that these contain ferrous metal or iron. They will thus begin to reason that if a metal is attracted to a magnet, it must contain at least some iron.

WHAT YOU NEED
A collection of objects made from different materials, including a range of different metals and objects with hidden metal components, such as fabric-covered buttons; set rings; magnets; whiteboard and pen; large sheets of paper and pens.

WHAT TO DO
Sit the class group in a circle around your collection of objects so that they can all see. Ask them to look at the items in your collection and suggest how they can be sorted into groups. Let the children decide this for themselves and eventually lead them into sorting the items by the material from which they are made. Suggest that this is made more difficult as some objects are made from more than one material. Challenge the children to sort them into two groups – those they *think* will be attracted to a magnet, and those they *think* will not. Ask them to say why they put each object in the set they chose.

Most children will put all the metals in one set and all the other materials into another, because they have a limited understanding of the concept of magnetic attraction. Give them a magnet to check the items in the set that they think are magnetic, as well as those that are in the other set. Note with the children that not all metals are magnetic, as some of them are not attracted to a magnet. Any higher attaining children, or those who will know

immediately that some metals are not attracted to magnets, can start by sorting and classifying the metals into sets.

Work with the rest of the class to sort the two sets in different ways. Start by sorting the metals into two subsets: those that are attracted to a magnet, and those that are not. Explain that you have one set of metals, but two subsets, according to whether they are magnetic or not. Next sort the whole collection into sets of those that contain two or more materials and those that contain one. Ask the children to find out which ones contain metal. Ask them, *What do you notice about some of the objects? Why are the plastic paper clip and the fabric button attracted to the magnet?*

Look carefully at other fabric-covered buttons (some with plastic and others with metal inside) by passing them around and asking the children, *Is it made only from fabric? Could there be another material inside? What material could it be? How could we find out?* Listen to the children's suggestions before asking them how they could find out if it has a metal inside.

Suggest that if the button is attracted to the magnet, it must have some kind of metal inside. Ask, *What if the button had not been attracted to a magnet? Could we definitely say that it did not have metal inside?* Explain why not – that it could contain a metal that is not attracted to a magnet. Tell the children that the metals attracted to the magnet contain iron, and those that are not so attracted do not contain iron.

Show the children how to make a simple decision tree as another way to classify which materials and objects are magnetic and, therefore, contain iron. Use questions that will ensure that those which are attracted to magnets will be left in a set at the bottom.

Include:

- Is the material magnetic?
- Does it contain metal?
- Does it contain iron?

These questions will establish the children's understanding.

DIFFERENTIATION

Start higher attaining children on the second part of the activity as their introduction. Allow lower attaining children to investigate each material with the magnets to inform their sorting activity.

WHERE NEXT

Sort other collections of materials using the same classification process as an independent activity.

ASSESSMENT

Use the children's decision trees to note who understands how the sorting and classification processes can help to identify the properties of metals and magnets.

LEARNING OUTCOMES

Most children will understand how to use a decision tree as a classification scheme to find out about scientific processes. They will all establish their learning about sorting into (sub)sets.

FURTHER SCIENCE CHALLENGES

Steel or aluminium?

Find different ways of classifying whether empty food and drinks cans (checked to make sure there are no sharp edges) are made from steel or aluminium. The children can do this by sorting into sets, Carroll diagrams or decision trees. Can they use the classification system to draw conclusions about whether all food and drinks cans are magnetic, or do they need to include this in their classification criteria?

Question identification systems

Give the children a blank frame of a decision tree and a different set of objects made from a range of materials. Ask them to set up their own decision tree for the range of materials to find out which ones contain iron. They should identify questions that will conclusively identify particular materials or objects. Questions to check whether they have identified

suitable criteria for sorting include: *Which questions have you asked to identify that this object contains iron? How do you know? Show me how you sorted the objects by checking them against your questions.*

CHILDREN AT WAR

SUBJECT: HISTORY. QCA UNIT 9: WHAT WAS IT LIKE FOR CHILDREN IN THE SECOND WORLD WAR?

LEARNING OBJECTIVE

To empathise with how children in Great Britain felt during the Second World War.

THINKING OBJECTIVE

To locate areas.

THINKING SKILLS

The children will look at maps of Great Britain, Europe and the World to locate areas where the Second World War affected children. They will note where these are, and identify the ones where children's lives were most likely to have been affected, before doing a more detailed study of Great Britain. Through this research they will begin to link cause and effect in history. They will empathise with the way children felt about the war and how it affected their daily lives.

WHAT YOU NEED

Maps of Great Britain, Europe and the World that show the countries that were involved directly in the Second World War; a whiteboard and pen; colouring materials. *Yesterday's Britain* (Reader's Digest) is a really good source for updating your personal subject knowledge.

WHAT TO DO

Look first at a map of the World and locate countries with which the children are familiar. Ask them to say briefly what they know about them today. For each one, tell the children how it was involved in the Second World War and how this affected the lives of children living in that country. For example, those living in European countries were more affected by the war than those living in the USA, because they had the reality, or the threat, of enemy troops living amongst them. Note the wide spread of the areas where British troops were involved in the conflict, including Africa, the Far East and Europe. Explain that because so many countries were involved in the conflict, it was called the Second World War. Note how many children did not have fathers living at home because they were nearly all away fighting in another country.

Now look at the map of Europe. Name and locate the countries that were involved in the war. Note that they were nearly all involved, and how this must have affected the lives of children living at that time. Talk about why Germany invaded some of its neighbours and how this affected the safety and security of many children. Outline briefly what happened to many Jewish children.

Talk about how Germany did not manage to invade the mainland countries of Great Britain, but did send bombing missions. Look at the map of Great Britain and identify all the cities that were hit by the Blitz: London, Birmingham, Manchester and Coventry, and those around the coast where there were important docks, such as Liverpool, Hull and Southampton. Ask, *Why do you think the German forces targeted these places?* Note the importance of these cities – some had munitions factories; others were by the coast and brought goods into the country. Ask, *What were they hoping to do? Think about how children must have felt during these bombing raids. Where did they go for shelter? What do you think it would have been like, sleeping in the London Underground? Why did the people take shelter there? Do you think they would have felt safe?* Ask the children to make suggestions, and list all the likely feelings on the board.

Look also at other areas of Great Britain that were not subjected to bombing. Locate some of these. For example, rural Devon, Northern Ireland, Wales and Scotland, and discuss the nature of the landscape. Ask, *Which would be good places for city children to go to be safe from the bombing raids?* Locate these on the map, asking the children to give reasons for their choice of areas. Explain that many children were evacuated to places a long way from home, and that even those who did not have to go so far did not see their families for a long time because transport systems were much less accessible. Tell them that most families did not have cars and those who did could not get much petrol to run them.

Look back at the list of feelings that you made and cross out any feelings that the children now think are unlikely to be true. Ask, *Would the children feel safer once they were away from the main bombing target areas? Which feelings are left, and why?* Make a new list of the feelings that remain and add any new ones, such as loneliness, missing their parents or carers and so on.

DIFFERENTIATION

Look only at the map of Great Britain with lower attaining children, explaining to them the closeness of the bombing raids to their own location. Play a 'what if' game with them afterwards, such as *What if you lived in Coventry? How would you have been*

affected? Locate these places together to show the number of cities and areas that were affected.

Higher-attaining children might consider why children were evacuated from the south-east coast. Ask, *Why did they feel threatened in this area during the war?* Locate the area on the map and note how short a distance it is across the English Channel to the French coast, which was occupied by German forces during the war. Locate the Channel Islands and talk about how these were invaded, and what it must have been like for the children living there.

WHERE NEXT

Locate the major German cities that were targeted by Allied bombing raids, including Dresden, Berlin and Nuremberg, and think about how this must have affected the children living there. Consider whether they felt the same as threatened British children.

ASSESSMENT

As an assessment activity, give the children maps of Great Britain and ask them to locate all the areas that were affected directly and indirectly by the war. Shade the two areas in different colours so that the children can see how much of Britain was affected, and how. Ask them to locate and colour cities like Coventry, Birmingham, Hull, Manchester and London. They could also colour the south-east area that was not bombed but saw enemy bombers flying overhead and were first in line for any invasions, and rural areas that, although not directly bombed, were affected by the absence of fathers, brothers, nephews and uncles. Talk about the influx of children evacuated from large cities, and people who had to relocate because they were working for the war effort, like Land Army Girls. The children will find that all of Great Britain was affected in some way, and that this would have caused a range of feelings for children living at the time all around the country.

LEARNING OUTCOMES

Most children will locate the major cities of Great Britain that were bombed during the Second World War. Some may go further and locate those cities affected in this way abroad. They will process the information to form conclusions about why these places were targeted and note that this is because of their position, or because of activities important to the war effort.

FURTHER HISTORY CHALLENGES

Local war efforts

Look at a map of the local area, and ask the children to say how the Second World War would have affected them. Ask, *Would you have been evacuated, and where would you have been sent? Do you live in an area suitable for evacuees and, if so, where could they have stayed? What kind of activities would the people living at the time have taken part in to support the war effort?*

Legacies of war

Look at photographs of areas that were affected in some way by the war and locate things that remain as a constant reminder to people. This will include the war memorials located in nearly all cities, towns and villages across the country, the German hospital in Jersey, lookout points built around the coast, and Coventry's cathedral that was destroyed in the bombing raids.

SETTLE DOWN

SUBJECT: GEOGRAPHY. QCA UNIT 9: VILLAGE SETTLERS.

LEARNING OBJECTIVE

To learn that people settle in places because of their geographical features.

THINKING OBJECTIVE

To collect and analyse information.

THINKING SKILLS

The children will collect information about the features, land use and economic activities of a village settlement and note the changes that have occurred over the years. They will analyse the information to decide what attracts people to live in this type of area.

WHAT YOU NEED

Large maps of a rural and town locality (if your home area is not suitable then choose another, perhaps Lincolnshire, which is used in the QCA unit); Ordnance Survey or other large-scale maps of a number of small villages; large sheets of paper and pens; paper and writing materials.

WHAT TO DO

Look at the large maps of your chosen rural and town locations. Ask, *How do you know this is a town? How do you know this is a village? How is it different from the towns?* Analyse the information by noting similarities and differences between the village and the town. Similarities could include that they have some of the same features, such as rivers, roads, churches, post offices and pubs. Differences will be mainly the number, size and position of these features and additional services, such as railways in towns and farming land close to villages. Note how major roads tend to run through or close to towns, while villages are usually off the beaten track and have minor roads leading to, from and through them.

Look together at a larger scale map, probably an OS map, of your chosen village, which shows the buildings, farms and other physical features clearly. Talk about the features that would attract people to live in this place – the reasons they would choose to live in a village. Ask, *What are the good points? Are there any negative points?* (Travelling to work or school, getting snowed in, lack of local shops and amenities.) Talk about how these factors would affect our decisions today, but point out that this site may have been attractive to early settlers for different reasons. Ask, *What would they have liked about it? Is it close to a water source? Is there plenty of land for farming? How close is it to market towns or sea ports? Is it near a transport system such as a railway or canal?*

Look at the village together and use postcards, photographs, a large-scale map, and any first-hand knowledge to sort the information into four lists or sets: human features, physical features, economic activities and land use. Some things may be recorded more than once, for example a farm would be entered as a human feature, farming as an economic activity, and agriculture as a land use; an industrial estate as a human feature, economic activity and land use. Repeat the activity for a second village. Share and compare the information. Ask, *Are villages usually located close to rivers or other water sources? What human features do all villages have? How many roads are there? Do they always lead to a larger town?* Hypothesise with the children why this might be the case. Note the features that villages share, as well as the things that are different. Ask, *Are the similarities old features, such as farms or pubs, and the differences newer features, such as industrial units or changes in the way some buildings are used (such as manor houses that are now hotels)?*

Divide the class into groups and allocate each group a different village to research and analyse. Provide them with a larger map of their village. Encourage them to read the symbols, note the features and identify the land use. Tell them to count the number of farms that surround it. Ask, *Is there an industrial park close by? If so, is it in the middle of the village or on the outskirts?* Ask the children to think why this type of development might have moved to the outskirts of villages and towns rather than being built in the middle, linking the hypothesis to the transport systems now available. Note all the features that can be found in all the villages they have investigated, and other varied features that are new. Analyse this information by relating it to the way people used to travel, and talk about how a coaching inn was needed in most villages to rest horses and travellers. Railways came later, so while some villages have a railway station, others may not. In some there may be evidence of a railway system that used to be there but is now a tourist attraction. Are the similarities all old and the differences all new?

DIFFERENTIATION

Encourage higher attaining children to identify the pattern and processes in the changes of land use. They should be able to link their information to conclusions and hypotheses about change that has occurred because people no longer transport goods by water, or even rail, but usually by road. Let them locate the nearest motorway to their village and track how easy it is to reach the village from the motorway system.

Lower attaining children should answer direct questions that lead their collection of information in a certain direction.

WHERE NEXT

Compare the investigated rural area with another in a different part of the country. Identify whether the similarities and differences are the same and hypothesise why this may be the case. Ask, *Does it reflect the way people used to live and live now*?

ASSESSMENT

Make a note of the children who analyse the information in terms of the similarities and differences between the villages, how much the villages have stayed the same and how much they have changed. Note also those who are using this analysis to identify the changes in human activity and the reasons people chose this place to settle in the past and today.

LEARNING OUTCOMES

Most children will identify features and begin to analyse the information by noting similarities and differences between the villages. Some will begin to relate this analysis to the geographical patterns and processes in human activity and land use.

FURTHER GEOGRAPHY CHALLENGES

Village map

Give the children a photograph or aerial photograph of a village. Ask them to collect and analyse the information in the picture to draw a map to represent this village. Remind them to make a key in one corner to show what the symbols are.

Motorways

Use a map to locate a motorway system near you and ask the children to count how many exits there are. Analyse their position and the places they join. Tell the children that some businesses are located close to motorway exit points, especially distribution centres and shopping malls. Think about reasons for this. Track the route of a motorway and note where this goes. Ask, *Where does it lead? Does it always lead to big cities? Does it bypass villages? How easy is it to get to the motorway from your village? Is this good for businesses? List the types of people who might live in a village close to a motorway. Why would they want to live there?*

CHRISTMAS 3-D BOXES

SUBJECT: DESIGN AND TECHNOLOGY. QCA UNIT 3A: PACKAGING.

LEARNING OBJECTIVE
To learn how materials have been used and folded to make a package.

THINKING OBJECTIVE
To analyse packaging.

THINKING SKILLS
The children will look at a range of packaging and analyse how it has been put together. They will identify the different components, including nets and tabs, and will look at how these have been arranged.

WHAT YOU NEED
A large range (more than one per child) of packaging, in a range of shapes, sizes and colours, which can be analysed to identify the shape, the graphics, and the way they have been constructed (such as cylindrical, cuboid, cubic and pyramid-shaped sweet containers and gift boxes – Christmas is the best time to collect items for this activity); paper and pens.

WHAT TO DO
Look at the collection of packaging and talk about the variety of shapes and colours. Ask, *How is the shape of each box suitable for its contents? Is it made from a particular colour? Does it have a seasonal design? Does this catch the eye?*

Give each child a package to take apart. Ask them to look carefully at the net and how it folds to make the package. Ask, *What shapes does it have? How are they arranged or joined together? How is the net folded to make the box? How is the packet joined? Are the tabs glued or do the pieces interlock?*

Compare the different packaging and sort them into sets by the way they are joined, their graphics and the shape of the nets. Ask, *What is the most common net shape? Why do you think this is the case?*

Provide the children with lots of boxes and ask them to analyse each one according to the shape of the net, how it is joined and whether it is decorated in a seasonal way. Invite the children to complete a table, like the one below, to record their analysis.

DIFFERENTIATION
Initially, just give lower attaining children boxes that are the same shape, and help them to analyse each net, talking about how they are joined. Complete the table together, noting how they may be the same, apart from the way they are joined. Higher attaining children can analyse more complicated packaging that folds into shape and keeps its shape because of the design and the way it is folded, rather than being glued or stuck together. There are always particularly interesting examples of gift packaging around at Christmas. Look out for these, especially for bottles, scarves and perfumes.

WHERE NEXT
Find different styles of packaging in mail-order catalogues and let the children analyse how each one might be constructed.

ASSESSMENT
Note the children who identify the nets of boxes and use this analysis to work out how they are assembled and constructed. Note, too, those who understand how folds can help a box to take its shape and keep it together.

LEARNING OUTCOMES
Most children will analyse how a box is constructed, identifying its shape and whether it is glued or folded into shape.

FURTHER DESIGN AND TECHNOLOGY CHALLENGES
Sweet cartons
Use nets of pyramids, prisms and cones to make sweet cartons to hang on a Christmas tree. Encourage the children to analyse how to make these nets and construct them by joining tabs. They will also need

to decide how big these should be, and how they might be hung from a tree.

Table decorations

Use the children's analysis to make pyramids from nets as a base for making table decorations for the Christmas party. These might include Rudolph, angels, Santa, choir singers and Christmas trees. Let the children design each finished table decoration carefully, choosing materials and colours to decorate each one.

SWINGING SIXTIES

SUBJECT: ICT. QCA UNIT 4D: COLLECTING AND PRESENTING INFORMATION.

LEARNING OBJECTIVE

To use a database to sort and classify information and present findings.

THINKING OBJECTIVE

To collect, sort and analyse information.

THINKING SKILLS

The children will collect a range of information and put this into a database, then use the computer to sort the information according to the different fields. Finally, they will analyse the information by asking questions to find certain pieces of information about what life was like during the 1960s.

WHAT YOU NEED

Database software that allows you to enter data as a questionnaire and then to sort and present the data in different ways; paper and pens.

WHAT TO DO

As a class, produce a questionnaire to find out about different aspects of life in the 1960s. You might cover areas such as favourite pop stars, fashion, hobbies, TV programmes and toys. Include some multiple-choice questions, some that require a *Yes* or *No* answer and, some where a few items have to be put in order of preference.

The children should take the completed questionnaire home and ask an older relative to answer the questions. Back in class, let the children put the information they have collected into the computer. When they have all finished this, teach the class how to interrogate, sort and order the information by the different fields so that they can show the number of people who liked the Beatles best, and those who preferred a different group, such as the Hollies or he Swinging Blue Jeans. Show how

this information can be displayed as a graph. Ask, *What other information can be displayed as a graph?* Point out that the multiple-choice questions are best displayed in this way. Let the children repeat this with the other fields, working in pairs to explore and analyse the information to find out, for example, which was the most popular game, hobby, fashion and so on.

Gather together at the end of the lesson and let each pair report back what they found out. Who managed to analyse the information to find the most popular TV programme at the time? Who found a list of people who wore miniskirts? Who found out the number of people who played cricket?

DIFFERENTIATION

Challenge higher attainers to find out two things about one of the people who completed the questionnaire. For example, ask them to find a way of analysing and linking the information to find the person or people who liked the Beatles *and* wore a mini skirt. Work alongside lower attainers to show them how to ask the computer to sort the information and draw graphs about each of the fields.

WHERE NEXT

Carry out surveys of other things, such as minibeasts, plants and vehicles, asking the children to identify the fields they will need in order to organise the information, such as type, colour, size and habitat. Sort and analyse the information in different ways according to the capabilities of your software.

ASSESSMENT

Note which children successfully sort and analyse the data, and the different methods they use to find answers to particular questions.

LEARNING OUTCOMES

Most children will learn that computers help to sort and analyse information quickly.

FURTHER ICT CHALLENGES

Pop music challenge

Challenge the children to find out which type of music people enjoyed most in the 1960s – offer a range of styles, such as rock, country and western or Motown. Use questionnaires to find out people's favourite type of music and use the information to refine your database, which, when the information is sorted, will identify the most popular style, group and pop song in your survey.

Mini statement

Collect information about the make, model and colour of car people owned in the sixties. Enter the information into a database and sort it to find out the favourite car at the time. Was it a red mini?

SIGHTS FOR YOUR EYES

SUBJECT: ART AND DESIGN. QCA UNIT 4A: VIEWPOINTS.

LEARNING OBJECTIVE

To collect visual information to inform thoughts about how mood and effect in pictures are created.

THINKING OBJECTIVE

To collect and sort images.

THINKING SKILLS

The children will look at objects in the environment from different points of view and photograph them to make a collection of images. When developed, they will sort them into groups according to the feelings they evoke.

WHAT YOU NEED

A camera; viewfinders made from card; mirrors.

WHAT TO DO

Go outside with the mirrors and viewfinders when the ground is dry. Invite the children to lie down on their backs and look at the sky, taking care not to look at the sun. Ask, *What shapes can you see in the clouds? What do they remind you of? How do they make you feel?* Next, invite the children to look at some of the surrounding scenery, first without, and then through, their card viewfinder. Invite one or two to describe what they can see. Ask, *Does the view look different when you look through the viewfinder? Does it pick out the detail of what you are looking at more clearly? How does the view you have chosen look different? Would it make a good photograph?*

Finally, use the mirrors to look at things from different angles. Ask, *What do they look like now? How are they different? Do you feel differently about them?*

Select some of the views and take photographs of them from different angles. Develop these overnight, or load them onto the computer to print out the images.

Next day, look at the photographs together and discuss the mood and feelings each one creates. Ask, *Do some of the same views taken at different angles evoke different moods? Why do you think this is?* Ask the children to think about some of the feelings they experienced when collecting the images. Sort them into groups of nice, and not so nice, feelings and moods. Ask, *Why do you think some views evoked nicer feelings than others? Was it changes in colour, the effect of light, or the calm or busy appearance?*

DIFFERENTIATION

Work with lower attaining children, asking them what they can see and inviting them to express whether they do or do not like the view and why. Help them to photograph views they like and dislike. Invite higher attaining children to look for, and collect, views to reflect predetermined feelings or moods, perhaps with different shades of colour and reflections of light.

WHERE NEXT

Download some photographs onto the computer and use the effects tools (such as paint and colour effects, edge effects or touch-up) and any other special features within the software package to make changes to create different moods.

ASSESSMENT

Assess how well the children find and collect images from different viewpoints. Note how well they use their knowledge of artistic elements to sort the images into groups according to the feelings and moods they depict or evoke.

LEARNING OUTCOMES

Most children will be able to collect images from different viewpoints and sort them according to whether they evoke positive or negative feelings. Some will be able to give reasons for their sorting and relate these to the feelings and moods the pictures reminded them of through their use of colour, light and shadow.

FURTHER ART AND DESIGN CHALLENGES

Aborigine dreamtime

Read stories of the Aborigine dreamtime and look at the colours, shapes and symbols used by aboriginal artists to depict these. Make a collection of these and use them to design a class Dreamtime story. Make some of the symbols into print blocks, using paper or string, and create patterns with them, overprinting some with different colours.

Video sequence
Video some of the children's selected viewpoints that depict certain emotions, such as happiness, calm, peace and tranquillity, amusement and noise. Play them to the children and ask them to say why they collected these particular pictures. Ask, *Are they pretty, slow moving, have muted colours, quiet? Do they include vivid colours, wild shapes? Are they busy or noisy?* Talk about the colours, shading and effects and how these depict a particular mood and feeling.

OSTINATOS

SUBJECT: MUSIC. QCA UNIT 10: PLAY IT AGAIN.

30

LEARNING OBJECTIVE
To learn that a repeating rhythm is called an ostinato.

THINKING OBJECTIVE
To sequence notes and locate ostinatos.

THINKING SKILLS
In this activity the children will listen for and locate repeating rhythms in a familiar song before using the rhythmic phrase identified, and others, as an accompaniment. They will note the sequence of notes and play their repeating patterns together to make a rhythmic accompaniment. They will note the pattern and relationship within and between their own and other groups' patterns by identifying the sequence of notes that makes each one.

WHAT YOU NEED
A copy of the Christmas carol 'The Little Drummer Boy'; whiteboard and pen.

WHAT TO DO
Learn the carol together. Then divide the class in two and ask one half to perform the carol while the

other half listens for any rhythmic patterns that are repeated in the words. Agree that each line ends with the same rhythmic pattern, and then listen for the words that help identify the sequence of notes and write these down. Think about how the rhythm is put together. Ask, *What does the rhythm depict? How is it played?* Think about the first half of the rhythm (ru-pu-pom) and identify this as a drumming beat (two quavers and a crotchet). Sing the song through again, taking turns to play the rhythmic accompaniment that the children have identified. Explain that this is an ostinato because it is the same rhythmic phrase repeated over and over. Listen to the introduction to the carol and ask, *How does the introduction set out a repeating rhythm?* (Crotchet and two quavers.) Challenge them to identify the rhythmic pattern, another ostinato, that would fit together well with this one. They will need to consider the length of the bars and the number of notes which will fit.

Organise the children into groups and ask them to use percussion instruments to improvise and compose simple repeating rhythms to add to the carol as additional accompaniments. Invite each group to perform their rhythm and to say why it fits. Ask, *Is it an ostinato?* Invite the rest of the class to pick out and clap along to the ostinatos of the other groups as soon as they hear them. Ask, *How is this sequence of notes put together? Does it depict the words of the carol?* Write the sequence on the board and, if the children are able, talk about how they both have the same number of beats. If they do not, then make them the same by comparing the rhythms in the sequence.

DIFFERENTIATION
Lower attaining children should be invited to identify and play either an ostinato to the beat, if they can keep one, or one that fits with the phrase 'drummer boy'. Higher attaining children should think about how their rhythm fits in with the others in terms of the number and length of beats. Challenge them to identify and record the sequence of notes that make up their rhythm.

WHERE NEXT
Compose and add rhythmic

accompaniments to poems and rhymes with a regular beat. Read the children word phrases to spark ideas – for example, the phrase 'They went to sea in a sieve' from 'The Jumblies' by Edward Lear.

ASSESSMENT

As the children perform their repeating patterns to the rest of the class, assess how well they have understood the need to sequence the rhythms so that they repeat. Note the children who are able to locate ostinato patterns in pieces of music they listen to.

LEARNING OUTCOMES

Most children will identify a repeating pattern and note the similarities and differences between their own and others' rhythmic patterns. Some will use the information to sequence their own rhythms into repeating patterns to play with other songs and pieces of music.

FURTHER MUSIC CHALLENGES

Ostinato beat

Listen to other pieces of music with ostinatos, for example 'Bolero' by Ravel, or 'Tapestry of Nations' from Disney's The Millennium Music; and ostinato melodic phrases such as 'Mars' from Holst's Planets. Locate the rhythms in each one, and invite a group of children to identify the sequence of notes and play them as a repeating rhythm while other children play the tune.

Native North American chants

Locate and add different ostinatos to Native North American chants found on compilation CDs and songbooks. Examples include 'Indian Warrior' found in many recorder books, and the traditional canoeing song 'Land of the Silver Birch' published in *Flying a Round* (A and C Black). The ostinato can be composed by matching the rhythms to words from the songs, for example 'silver birch' or 'land of the', or phrases such as 'Land of the silver birch' clapped over and over to the end of the song while others sing the tune and words.

MEMORIES ARE MADE OF THIS

SUBJECT: RE. QCA UNIT 3A: WHAT DO SIGNS AND SYMBOLS MEAN IN RELIGION?

LEARNING OBJECTIVE

To learn that symbols remind us of things that have a special significance.

THINKING OBJECTIVE

To collect and sort signs and symbols.

THINKING SKILLS

The children will look at signs and symbols from their environment and identify what each one means. They will consider the difference between signs, which usually mean only one thing, and symbols, which give direction and are sometimes open to interpretation, before collecting, sorting and labelling how certain symbols remind us of special things.

WHAT YOU NEED

Representations of signs from the local environment that children have helped to collect (perhaps as a homework activity), such as the walking and standing figures on a pedestrian crossing, signs giving directions, names of shops or businesses; symbols from a range of products, such as cooking instructions, washing instruction labels and warning symbols on cleaning products; a number of pictures or actual artefacts that give religious messages, for example a menorah, a diva lamp or a rainbow; whiteboard and pen; large sheets of paper; writing and drawing materials.

WHAT TO DO

Look together at some of the signs you have collected and ask the children what they are for. Explain that signs like these usually give one specific message and ask the children to explain what significance they think these signs have. Ask them to work in groups to share, write down or draw as many signs as they can think of, and label each one with its own particular meaning. If necessary, give them a few ideas to start them off. For example, *This exit sign tells us that this is the way out. This sign tells us that this is a one-way street and there is no entry to traffic from this direction.*

After about ten minutes, share their ideas on signs before introducing the concept of a symbol. Tell the children that symbols can be the same as signs in some situations, as they do remind us of things, but that they are more open to interpretation. Look at one of the symbols on a product, such as the irritant symbol on the packaging of a cleaning product. Ask, *What is it telling us? Is it telling us something specific, or reminding us to do or not to do something? Is it representing something in particular? Is it as precise as the signs that you looked at?* Agree that, in this case, it is because it is giving us directions and reminding us to think about something. Repeat this with a few other symbols in your collection.

Explain to the children that religions often use symbols to give directions, or to remind us to think in a certain way or about something of significance. Ask the children to suggest possible religious symbols that remind us of something significant, such as a particular event, a prayer, or an inference on how we should behave. List all their suggestions, including any sacred texts or parts of religious buildings. Agree those that are religious artefacts and those that are also symbols, such as candles, the cross, diva lamps, and more obscure symbols such as water and light. Look together at a cross. Ask, *What does this symbol remind you of? What does it make you think about? Does it make you think about how you should behave?* Repeat this with a few other artefacts from different religions.

Let the children work in groups to sort the signs, symbols and pictures of religious artefacts into relevant groups. Encourage them to discuss why they have grouped them in the way that they have and to label each symbol with its special significance.

DIFFERENTIATION

To help lower attaining children understand the concept of symbols, start by looking at things that are very familiar to them – perhaps a birthday cake or a Christmas tree. Use these images to help the children understand that we associate certain things with significant events. This will help them to think of a collection of items or concepts that jog our memories before going on to collect symbols that do the same. Encourage higher attaining children to collect more obscure symbols and to talk about what these mean to them. They should include symbols from charities, such as the NSPCC logo of children holding hands, and Comic Relief red noses. Encourage discussion about what these symbols mean to them.

WHERE NEXT

Collect symbols and sort these according to the different religions. Ask, *Are some of these things common to several religions?* (Water to Christians, Moslems, Hindus and Sikhs; books to most religions.) Look at and discuss pictures of symbols from religious texts – perhaps a rainbow, a dove and an olive branch. Ask, *What do these remind you of? Why are they special? Are they there to remind us about something special?* Recall with the children the significance of any symbols they know.

ASSESSMENT

Assess the children's ability to collect and classify signs, symbols and other artefacts, objects and pictures, and their ability to talk about what each one means to them.

LEARNING OUTCOMES

Most children will learn that signs and many symbols are giving directions about what we should or

should not do. Some symbols, however, are open to interpretation because they will have a different significance to different people.

FURTHER RE CHALLENGES

My special memories

Ask the children to bring in things that hold special significance or memories for them. Display these alongside items that remind people of different religions, about God, or some religious event. Ask the children to say or write a few words to describe why their chosen items give them special memories.

Greetings

Collect a range of greetings cards and talk about how the pictures give a message or remind the receiver or giver of a particular memory. Include birthday, new job, congratulations, sympathy, wedding and anniversary cards. Some should have pictures and others symbols. Read the messages and talk about the memories these evoke.

FOOTBALL DANCE

SUBJECT: PE. QCA UNIT: INVASION GAMES – UNIT 2.

LEARNING OBJECTIVES

To develop the range and consistency of passing and receiving skills; to keep up an activity over a period of time.

THINKING OBJECTIVE

To match ball skills to a piece of music.

THINKING SKILLS

In this activity the children will listen to the beat of a piece of pop music and devise a sequence of moves to match the beat. They will then organise this sequence into a pattern to create a warm-up activity or a performance, working both individually and with a partner.

WHAT YOU NEED

A recent pop song or similar piece of lively, popular music on tape or CD; a CD or tape player; one football for each child; a large space in which to work.

WHAT TO DO

Listen to the song together and clap the beat. Before playing it a second time, give out the balls and invite the children to create lots of different moves to match the beat of the song. This could be bouncing the ball on the ground, kicking or throwing it to a partner, keeping the ball in the air with the head, knees or shoulders, or bouncing it to a partner.

When the piece has finished, play it through again, collecting the children's ideas by asking them to demonstrate, in pairs, one of their moves. As each pair finishes they should sit down so that the next two can demonstrate a different move. Continue until all the children's ideas have been demonstrated.

Choose four passes to perform over and over again to make a simple dance or warm-up sequence using the footballs. Practise the moves until the children can do each sequence with precision and match it closely to the beat of the music. Some may be able to bounce in double time to fit some of the rhythms.

Put the moves in a sequence, repeating them when the music repeats, as in the chorus. Perform the sequence to another class or use it as a warm-up activity for future games lessons.

DIFFERENTIATION

Encourage skilful footballers to pass the ball to a partner in time to the music, thinking about the speed and distance required for the ball to reach the partner in time. Lower attaining children should be

encouraged to work independently at first, patting the ball or bouncing it against a wall. The music will help them to concentrate on getting a flowing movement to their bouncing and catching skills.

WHERE NEXT

Repeat this activity with other pieces of music, concentrating on different passes, such as the chest and overarm pass. Find ways to make the moves more difficult, such as making the distance greater, or passing to a partner while moving rather than standing still.

ASSESSMENT

Watch the children and note those who improve as the music is repeated. Assess whether the passing and receiving skills become more fluent as they match the moves to the music.

LEARNING OUTCOMES

Most children will develop their passing and receiving skills within this fun context. The music will help them to concentrate and think about the length and strength of the pass and improve their control over the ball. They will be able to match the speed and direction of the pass to the beat in the music.

FURTHER PE CHALLENGES

Skipping beat

Make up a skipping warm-up sequence, perhaps to the 'Rodeo' track by the group Steps. This prompts the children to skip slowly and quickly at different times in the music.

What to do?

Photograph the children as they play small-group invasion games – any type of game will do. Ask them to look at each photograph and to say whether the person who has the ball should keep possession or pass the ball to a team member. Ask, *How did you make this decision? Was it because they were about to be tackled or because a team member was in a space and had a good shot at the goal?*

Display the photographs and ask the children to match appropriate 'pass' or 'keep' possession labels. Invite them to suggest other labels depending on the game, such as 'dribble', 'pass', 'bounce', 'throw', 'intercept', 'find a space', and match them to the different people in the photographs, suggesting what they should do next.

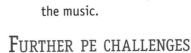

REASONING SKILLS

INTRODUCTION

Reasoning skills enable children to make considered decisions and give reasons for those decisions.

Asking children to explain what they are thinking, or to talk through how they reached a particular conclusion, will help to develop their reasoning skills. Seven-year-old children are usually just beginning to make links between different pieces of information and using these links to solve problems. This requires them to make judgements, interpret evidence and start to use inference and deduction skills to work out who carried out a particular action, and how something happened or why. Identifying links and predicting what may happen, and giving reasons for their opinions, are at the basis of the children's abilities to solve a problem. By the age of nine, with regular practice, many children will have started to use these skills independently to question what is happening, and why. Evidence of this provides another way of differentiating the work of higher attainers, whose learning is being extended.

One strategy for developing children's emerging reasoning skills is concept mapping, as it allows you to identify whether children are beginning to make, or are already making, links between different ideas. Many teachers use this to establish children's current knowledge and understanding of a concept or a new process before planning work matched at a suitable level for groups and individuals. A version of this strategy is used in the activities 'Buy me!' (page 53) and 'Religious symbols' (page 58) in this chapter. These activities ask the children to link ideas and give reasons for their choices.

Although concept mapping is used to particular effect in science, where new scientific concepts can be explored with the children and used as a basis for discussion, the same method can be used in other subjects to find out what the children already know and understand before you start to plan a unit of work. It can also be useful at the end of the unit to find out what they have learned. The children's ability to make links between ideas allows you to assess their understanding.

As well as concept mapping, children will need to use other strategies to develop their reasoning skills. For example, in English they are developing their reasoning skills when they are trying to find a solution for a character in a story, looking at pictures to try to predict the ending of a story, or explaining why something happened the way it did. In maths they will be solving word and number problems and explaining the strategies used to find an answer, while in PE they will need to think constantly about tactics and rules for games. Art and design, and design and technology, require the children to overcome problems of colour mixing or making moving parts work, while in music they must decide how particular effects are produced when listening, appraising and composing.

Whenever the skills listed below appear in the QCA schemes, you should be prepared to focus on reasoning skills. There are lots of examples in the history units of work, when the children are asked to infer, deduce and interpret different sources of evidence. The supplement of examples in the National Numeracy Strategy also provides many ideas on how to develop decision-making and reasoning skills when solving problems and reasoning about numbers, measures or shape. The following skills all form part of the reasoning process:

⦿ explaining
⦿ forming opinions
⦿ making judgements
⦿ making decisions
⦿ interpreting
⦿ inferring
⦿ deducing
⦿ giving reasons.

INTRODUCING REASONING SKILLS

Subject and QCA unit, NLS or NNS objective	Activity title	Thinking objective	Activity	Page
English. NLS objectives: To use the apostrophe to spell shortened forms of words; to distinguish the two forms its and it's, and to use these accurately in their own writing	It's mine	To deduce why an apostrophe is used and give reasons for this deduction	Deciding whether a possessive or contracted apostrophe is being used.	36
Maths. NNS objective: To solve a given problem by organising and interpreting numerical data in simple lists, tables and graphs	Clearly organised	To decide on, and give reasons to support the choice of, the most suitable format in which to record information to solve a given problem	Deciding which type of graph is best for presenting different pieces of information.	37
Science. QCA unit 3C: Characteristics of materials	Material world	To deduce; to give reasons	Constructing a decision tree to identify the material best suited to different purposes.	38
History. QCA unit 7: Why did Henry VIII marry six times?	Six wives	To interpret; to form opinions; to give reasons	To give reasons for Henry VIII's many marriages by interpreting different sources of historical evidence and linking problems with outcomes.	39
Geography. QCA unit 25: Geography and numbers	Getting from A to B	To deduce; to make decisions	Choosing the best option for getting from one place to another.	40
Design and technology: QCA unit 4B: Storybooks	Pop ups	To form opinions; to explain	Expressing opinions about which pop-up mechanisms they like best and why.	40
ICT. QCA unit 3D: Exploring simulations	Getting better	To make judgements	Judging whether to change decisions when playing a computer game for the second time.	41
Art and design. QCA unit 4A: Viewpoints	What can you see?	To deduce	Working out the objects in photographs that have been taken from an unusual angle.	42
Music. QCA unit 8: Ongoing skills	How many beats?	To deduce	Identifying how many beats there are in a bar in a range of songs.	42
RE. QCA unit 4B: Celebrations: Christmas journeys	Shepherds, angels and how many wise men?	To interpret evidence	The children will look closely at different sources and use this to interpret aspects of the Christmas story.	43
PE. QCA unit: Invasion games – unit 2	Piggy-in-the-middle	To deduce; to make decisions	Working out tactics for defending and attacking to keep or gain possession of the ball during a game.	44

IT'S MINE

SUBJECT: ENGLISH. NLS OBJECTIVES: TO USE THE APOSTROPHE TO SPELL SHORTENED FORMS OF WORDS; TO DISTINGUISH THE TWO FORMS ITS AND IT'S, AND TO USE THESE ACCURATELY IN THEIR OWN WRITING.

LEARNING OBJECTIVE
To learn that an apostrophe is used to indicate possession or a contracted word.

THINKING OBJECTIVE
To deduce why an apostrophe is used and give reasons for this deduction.

THINKING SKILLS
The children will look at a range of words that contain an apostrophe. They will read each word in context and decide whether the apostrophe is being used to show possession, or whether one contracted word is being used for two longer ones. They will give reasons for their deduction which will show whether they have understood the rule.

WHAT YOU NEED
A list of words (on a board or on paper) that contains possessive and contracted words. Include words that the children use often and sometimes get confused, such as *isn't*, *don't*, *there's*, *aren't*, *I'm*, *he's* and, for the more able, *they're*; possessives with a name, such as *Tom's* (you could use the name of your school or street), and some with other nouns, such as *mum's*, *dad's*, *friend's*, *dog's*, *cat's*, and so on, with which the children are familiar; sentences containing these words that show their meaning for the plenary session; yellow and red highlighter pens; whiteboard and pen.

WHAT TO DO
Look together at the list of words containing apostrophes and ask the children to say what all these words have in common. Note that they all have apostrophes and ask the children if they can tell you what job an apostrophe does in words. Accept that it sometimes tells a reader that someone possesses something, and sometimes that it is a shortened version of two words. Ask, *How can you tell the difference?* Remind the children that they should always read sentences carefully to understand the meaning before they make a decision. Sometimes it is easy if the possessor is a person. Sometimes you can tell because the possession is a noun.

Make up sentences orally to help the children make their decisions and deduce whether the word shows possession or not. Identify all the possessive nouns in the list and highlight them in yellow.

Look at the remaining words. Ask the children to think about what job the apostrophe is doing in these words. Agree that it shows that there is a letter or letters missing. Write a sentence to include one of the contracted words, for example, 'The weather isn't very sunny today'. Read this to the children and edit it by writing in the two words instead of the contracted word. For example, if the contracted word is *isn't*, prompt the children by writing *is* and challenging them to say what the other word should be. Find all the other contracted words on the list that end in *n't*, and think of a sentence for each, replacing the contraction with the two words that have been contracted.

Depending on the children's ability, let them work in groups, finding either the possessive apostrophes or those contracted words that end in *n't*; other words that have two letters missing (*we've*, *I've*, *you've*, *they've*, *he's* – he has); and finally those words with more than two letters missing (*won't* – there are not many others).

Talk about when to use there, their and they're with higher attaining children, if they are ready, and finish with a discussion about its and it's. Ask, *Can you tell which version is the possessive and which is the contracted word?* Invite them to give reasons for their deductions, as this will help them to remember which is which.

Show the children how *it is* is contracted to *it's*. Explain that the apostrophe is needed to show that the letter *i* is missing from *is*, and the possessive version does not have an apostrophe so that we do not get mixed up. It's the only possessive that does not have an apostrophe and is the exception to the rule.

During a plenary session, reinforce the learning. Read your pre-prepared sentences and identify the possessive and contacted words. Highlight the possessive words in yellow and the contracted ones in red. Challenge the children to find and deduce the use of the possessive in words they encounter when reading other texts, or as part of guided reading.

CLEARLY ORGANISED

SUBJECT: MATHS. NNS OBJECTIVE: TO SOLVE A GIVEN PROBLEM BY ORGANISING AND INTERPRETING NUMERICAL DATA IN SIMPLE LISTS, TABLES AND GRAPHS.

LEARNING OBJECTIVE
To learn to represent data in different forms.

THINKING OBJECTIVE
To decide on, and give reasons to support the choice of, the most suitable format in which to record information to solve a given problem.

THINKING SKILLS
The children will consider number problems and decide which is the most suitable method of recording or presentation to help solve each one. They will work in groups so that they can discuss ideas and the reasons for their decisions.

WHAT YOU NEED
Large sheets of paper and pens; whiteboard and pen; examples of tally charts, bar graphs and pictograms.

WHAT TO DO
Show the children examples of different ways of representing the same data to enable them to answer questions about this. If, for example, you have a tally chart that counts the number of children who travel to school by bus, by car and on foot, show them the same information represented as a pictogram, where each symbol represents more than one unit, and as a bar chart where the vertical axis is marked in twos, fives or tens. Agree with the children that these formats are good ways to display this type of information as it allows them to compare and calculate how many of each type there are.

Explain that you want to look at other ways to record numbers that will help them to find patterns and relationships quickly. You can then decide which is the most suitable method to show answers for the different problems you want to solve, and explain why.

Think together about other ways of presenting data with which the children may be familiar, such as tables or Venn and Carroll diagrams.

Give the class a number problem to solve in groups. Ask the children to find out which number between 2 and 30 has the most factors. Ask, *How can we solve this problem? How can we record and sort the information?* List all the numbers between two and thirty on the board. By the side of each one, identify all the factors for that number. For example, 2 has 1 and 2, while 24 has 1, 2, 3, 4, 6, 8, 12 and 24. Ask the children to find which number from the list has the most factors. Alternatively, provide groups with different numbers to analyse, giving lower attaining children smaller numbers and higher attaining children larger ones. Ask, *Does this organisation help us to identify quickly which number has the most factors?*

Next, organise the children into groups and ask them to sort the information into sets as Venn diagrams. For example, those with 2 as a factor in one set, 3 in another, and so on. Ask, *How can you interpret this organisation to find the number with the most factors?* Ask each group to note how many times 2 appears in their sets, then 3, and so on, to find out which number appears the most.

Relate factors to multiples by putting all the numbers to 30 that are multiples of 2 in one set, multiples of 3 in another, and so on, up to multiples of 10. Ask the children, *Which number appears in all the sets? What does this tell you about this number? Which number appears least? What does this tell you?* Together decide whether this is the best way of finding the answer to this problem. Can they suggest a different way, such as a frequency chart where the number is recorded on one axis and the number of factors on the other? Work with groups onm recording the information in frequency charts and Carroll diagrams, using labels such as 'has 2 as a factor/ does not have 2 as a factor' on the vertical and 'has 3/does not have 3' on the horizontal.

During the plenary session, look at the different ways of recording answers to the same investigation and decide which offers the clearest way of finding the answer to the problem.

Repeat the activity by finding the best way to solve the following problems:
◉ Which numbers are multiples of 5 and 10?
◉ Which numbers between 50 and 100 have the greatest number of factors?
◉ Which numbers between 25 and 60 are multiples of 3?

MATERIAL WORLD

SUBJECT: SCIENCE. QCA UNIT 3C: CHARACTERISTICS OF MATERIALS.

LEARNING OBJECTIVE

To learn that materials have different properties, some of which are suitable for making particular objects.

THINKING OBJECTIVES

To deduce; to give reasons.

THINKING SKILLS

The children will consider the properties of different materials and use a decision tree to classify objects according to these properties. They will use the information from the decision tree to deduce an object when given its material properties, and will extend their learning by considering the reason for a particular choice of material for each object. They will challenge other children in their group to identify a certain object or material using the tree.

WHAT YOU NEED

A collection of objects made from different materials, including the same objects made from different materials, for example, plastic and glass bottles, wooden and plastic chairs, and plastic and fabric buttons; several large sheets of paper and pens; card labels for questions; Blu-Tack.

WHAT TO DO

As a class, look at a small collection of objects and talk about what each one is used for. For example, look first at an empty plastic drink bottle. Ask, *What material is the bottle made from?* Discuss with the children why the bottle is made from this material. Consider the reasons they give for the properties of the material from which it is made. For example, it is made from plastic to make it lighter, so that you can see the drink inside, so that it can be made into the right shape, so that it does not break easily if it is dropped, so that it is strong enough to hold the amount of drink it does. Accept all the children's suggestions before moving on to another object in the same way. Continue with this discussion until the children have been introduced to at least

the concepts of hardness, flexibility, strength and transparency. You may also wish to introduce the opposites of these properties.

Now think of a set of questions to describe the properties of the material from which each object is made. Is it transparent? Is it flexible? Is it strong? Is it hard? Write each question on a card. Decide together the order in which you are going to ask these questions before setting them out. Attach the first one at the bottom of a large sheet of paper and draw two lines from this diagonally upwards labelled *yes* and *no*. Put down another question and draw two more lines from each line, so you now have two *yes* and *no* labels for this question about the already divided group of materials. Continue until the remaining questions are in a line from the bottom to the top of a large sheet of paper. Draw *yes/no* lines for each of the questions. Choose an object and place it on the first question on your sheet. Ask the children to answer this question for the object, then let them move the object up the *yes* or *no* line to the next question. Repeat the process until the object reaches the top branches of the decision tree. Repeat this for other items in your collection.

Now, tell the children that you are thinking about one of the objects in your collection. Describe its properties and ask them to deduce which one it is. For example, ask, *Which object is transparent, hard, rigid and fragile?* The children are likely to select something made of glass, and a glass bottle is more likely than a marble because of the fragility property. Make your descriptions more and more challenging so that the children really have to think hard and focus on the properties of the different materials. They could also track through the route of the questions to find the object to which your description relates.

Organise the children into groups and give each group a collection of materials to classify. When they have finished, ask each member of the group to take a turn at describing the properties of one object for the rest of the group to deduce, using the decision tree to track the route through the questions.

Try to find some good examples of the same object made from different materials and ask the children to consider how each one is suitable for its particular use. For example, a dining chair may be made of wood because it looks more attractive, but a child's chair may be made of plastic because it can be made in a bright colour and is easier to carry.

You may also wish to note the range of objects that are made from plastic and discuss why this is so. Explain that plastic is called a 'man-made' material because it is made from natural materials that have undergone a chemical process.

During the plenary session, tell the children that in the next lesson they will consider why certain objects have the properties they do. Prepare a list of questions about the properties of the materials from which different objects are made. For example, Why is the Coke bottle clear? Why is the Lilt bottle green? Why are they plastic? What else could they be made from? What are the disadvantages of glass and plastic? Why do supermarkets ask you to lay your bottles flat at the checkouts? Ask the children to consider answers to these questions to act as starting points for the subsequent lesson.

SIX WIVES

SUBJECT: HISTORY. QCA UNIT 7: WHY DID HENRY VIII MARRY SIX TIMES?

LEARNING OBJECTIVE
To understand that important people in the past often married for a range of different reasons.

THINKING OBJECTIVES
To interpret; to form opinions; to give reasons.

THINKING SKILLS
The children will work in groups to understand and define the problems experienced by the Tudor king, and to interpret evidence to decide whether he solved any of his problems by marrying each new wife. They will link problems with outcomes, deciding whether the problems were permanently or temporarily solved, giving reasons for their opinions.

WHAT YOU NEED
Large sheets of paper and pens; several sources of evidence detailing the life story of each of Henry VIII's wives; a list of problems and reasons (see the next section).

WHAT TO DO
In a previous lesson, define a list of problems and reasons why Henry VIII married six times. These include:
⊙ The importance of having a male heir.
⊙ The need for money.
⊙ The social standing of having a young and pretty wife.
⊙ Developing friendships with other countries.
⊙ Appeasing different religions.
⊙ Falling in love.

At the start of *this* lesson, give each group a large piece of paper and ask them to list the reasons or problems on the left-hand side. Divide the rest of the paper to the right of the list into six columns, one for each wife, headed with her name.

For each wife, talk about which of the reasons and problems were issues for Henry VIII when they married. For example, the reason Henry married Catherine of Aragon was to develop friendships with Spain. This caused a problem because he was not in love and she was not young and beautiful. The reason for marrying Anne Boleyn was because he wanted a male heir and a younger and more beautiful bride. This caused problems with foreign countries and the Roman Catholic church and, later, because she did not give him his male heir.

Reason for marriage	Catherine of Aragon	Anne Boleyn	Jane Seymour	Anne of Cleves	Catherine Howard	Katherine Parr
The importance of having a male heir	✗	✗	✓	✗	✗	✗
The need for money	✓	✗	✗	✓	✗	✗
The social standing of having a young and pretty wife	✗	✓	✓	✗	✓	✗
Developing friendships with other countries	✓	✗	✗	✓	✗	✗
Appeasing different religions	✓	✗	✗	✓	✗	✗
Falling in love	✗	✓	✓	✗	✓	✗

Let the children work for 15 to 20 minutes in their groups to discuss and agree which reasons were satisfied, or which problems solved, by each of the marriages, and which problems and reasons resurfaced when the marriage ended in death or divorce. Ask them to write 'solved' by each reason or problem that was solved by marrying that wife, and to place a cross beside those that were not. Underneath, ask them to tick those that reappeared when he divorced or beheaded her, or she died. The table shows one possible interpretation.

Gather the children together at the end of the group activity to talk about their decisions. Discuss any differences of opinion and emphasise that each group interpreted the evidence and formed individual opinions, for which they have reasons. Can anyone really say who has the right interpretation? Talk about any additional sources of evidence, such as CD-ROMs, Internet sites and reference books, that may be available to find the answer to any disagreements.

Finish by asking each group to research one of the wives, finding out as much as possible about the reasons for marrying her, the problems that were solved and those that were not. Use the information to revisit the children's decisions. Share the new data about each wife and see if this changes or clarifies the children's opinions. Were any problems solved permanently or did they always resurface? Did the reasons change for each wife and, if so, why?

GETTING FROM A TO B

SUBJECT: GEOGRAPHY. QCA UNIT 25: GEOGRAPHY AND NUMBERS.

LEARNING OBJECTIVE
To consider transport options for travelling from place to place.

THINKING OBJECTIVES
To deduce; to make decisions.

THINKING SKILLS
The children will look at a map and decide how far they must travel to get to a designated place from their present position. They will consider the transport options before making a detailed timetable of the journey. They will then use this information to decide which is the best option to take, and why.

WHAT YOU NEED
A map detailing the distance between the present position and the destination; access to local transport timetables, on paper or on the Internet; writing paper and pens; whiteboard and pen.

WHAT TO DO
Select a destination that the children might need to travel to by car, bus, train, boat or plane, and discuss how they might go about getting information on

how to make this journey. It could be a school trip, or an outing to the nearest seaside destination, to London or to Disneyland Paris. Show the children a map that shows both your local position and that of your planned destination. Note the distance between the two places. Ask, *What will you need to think about when planning a journey between the two places? Do you cross water? What does this involve?* Identify all the different travel options you could use to reach your chosen destination.

Next, consider the number of people going and the cost implications. Different transport options may be preferable depending on whether one person, four people or the whole class are travelling.

List the order of your enquiry on the board:
⊙   Where are we going?
⊙   How far away is that?
⊙   What transport options are there, and how long will each one take?
⊙   What times do trains and ferries leave and return?
⊙   What price are tickets?
⊙   What about petrol and parking costs for the car?
⊙   What about traffic jams and road works, which may slow down the journey?

Give groups of children a range of destinations, varying the difficulty and distance of the trips. Lower attaining children could work out the journey to the local town centre, while higher attaining children might be able to consider the trip to Paris.

When the children have collected the information, they should analyse it to deduce and decide on the best transport option for each journey, giving the reasons why. Extend the activity by deciding which is the best option for one, two, three or more people. Is it cheaper for one person to go to London by train, but for a group to go by coach?

POP UPS

SUBJECT: DESIGN AND TECHNOLOGY. QCA UNIT 4B: STORYBOOKS.

LEARNING OBJECTIVE
To use appropriate technical vocabulary to describe materials and mechanisms.

THINKING OBJECTIVE
To form opinions; to explain.

THINKING SKILLS
The children will look closely at a range of pop-up mechanisms and say which ones they like, and why. They will talk about this in terms of the context, but also in the way that the mechanisms work and the effects they create. They should be encouraged to talk to a partner about what they think, and why. Model this with lower attaining children or those new to English.

WHAT YOU NEED
A range of pop-up features in books and cards. Include things that work by levers and linkages, and things that are folded into place in different ways.

WHAT TO DO
Ask the children to sit in a circle and pass around the different books and cards with pop-up features. Let them examine these for a few minutes. Invite individuals to say which ones they like, and why.

Choose one feature and hold it up so all the children can see it. Draw their attention away from the pictures and encourage them to focus on the way it moves. Ask, *How does it work? Do the folds unfold in a certain way when you open the card or turn the page?* Ask them to express opinions about this.

Move on to the next card or book and repeat the process. If the children do not seem to be considering the effects of the linking, lever or folding technique when giving reasons for their opinions, then ask questions to direct their thinking towards these things. Ask, *Can you describe how this lever operates? When it is pulled, what happens to the feature in the picture? Why does it move in the opposite or the same direction as the lever?*

Organise the children into pairs and tell them that they have five minutes to tell their partner how one of the pop-up features works, and why. Monitor this activity closely so that you can add other information about how and why it works.

Finish by sharing some of the children's explanations with the rest of the class, encouraging them to say also which one they like and why.

GETTING BETTER

SUBJECT: ICT. QCA UNIT 3D: EXPLORING SIMULATIONS.

LEARNING OBJECTIVE
To explore options and discuss choices when using a computer simulation.

THINKING OBJECTIVE
To make judgements.

THINKING SKILLS
The children will work together in two pairs to talk about what they found when exploring the computer program *Crystal Rainforest*. They will agree what worked and what did not, and make judgements about the decisions they will make when they explore the game a second time.

WHAT YOU NEED
Computer; a copy of *Crystal Rainforest* or a similar computer adventure program, such as *Strawberry Magic*, *Granny's Garden* or *Max and the Secret Formula*; paper and pens.

WHAT TO DO
Let the children explore the first screen, which contains a problem (getting a drink from the machine), in pairs. Ask them to note down what they were asked to make decisions about, what they had to manoeuvre, and what they needed to collect. (For example, how to get a beaker, how to move it along the conveyor belt until it is under the drink machine, how and how full to fill the beaker, from where and how to put a lid on the beaker, and how to move it to the end of the belt.)

For each part of the task, ask them to identify the difficulties and mistakes that were made, and why. Ask, *What difficulties did you encounter? Did you make any mistakes? How did you get a beaker to put the drink in? How many beakers did you need? How many did you get? Why did the beakers keep coming out of the machine? What problems did you have? What were the consequences? How did you overcome these?* Repeat the questions for the other parts of the task.

Put two pairs together to talk about their experiences and judgements about the difficulties of the game. They should highlight and identify any problems both pairs met, or that one pair experienced, and exchange the strategies they used to overcome them.

Let both pairs repeat the screen, but this time basing judgements on their previous discussions. Continue until the children have successfully completed the first screen using the judgements they have made.

What can you see?

SUBJECT: ART AND DESIGN. QCA UNIT 4A: VIEWPOINTS.

Learning objective
To explore artistic effects in photography.

Thinking objective
To deduce.

Thinking skills
The children will look closely at pictures taken from unusual angles and deduce what these images are of. They will talk about how this creates certain effects and compare them with images taken by professional photographers. They will collect their own images of objects taken from unusual viewpoints and challenge the rest of the class to deduce the objects. They will download the photographs onto the computer and use photo software to add effects, and then ask other children to deduce the ones that they used to create certain effects.

What you need
A digital camera; photographs of objects found in the environment and taken from unusual viewpoints and angles, such as hinges of doors, drain covers, doorways or windows taken from a view between the legs; similar photographs taken by professional photographers (these can usually be found in clipart files or on the Internet); computer software that allows you to import photographs and create effects by zooming in and out or adding shadow features; paper and adhesive.

What to do
Show the children photographs of everyday objects, such as bushes, fence posts, gates or trees found in the school grounds that you have taken from unusual

angles – upside down, between the legs, or using reflections in mirrors and windows. It doesn't matter if there is glare, or the pictures are less than perfect, as this will make it even more challenging when the children are deducing where and what the images are. Ask them, *Can you say what these are?*

Now look at the photographs taken by professional photographers that use light to create certain effects. Talk about how these impressions have been achieved.

Let the children go outside into the school grounds in small groups, with adult support, selecting objects to photograph from unusual angles. Download these onto the computer and use software to add effects. Zoom in or out to make the object larger or smaller, select a small part of the object and enlarge it so that it loses its perspective, or add a shadow effect to blur the edges and outline. Your software may even allow you to change the photograph from colour to black and white, or to paint a different colour over certain parts by colour brushing.

When all the children have produced a photograph of a feature, set up a game where they deduce the object in each other's images and the effect that has been used. Give pairs of children two photographs stuck to a piece of paper, and ask them to identify first of all what and where the object is, and then the angle from which it was taken, and how it has been changed from its original look (for example, by being made smaller or larger, or by being given a shadow or a different colour effect). They may need to refer to the software to match the effect before making their deductions.

During a short plenary session, invite one or two pairs to share their thoughts with the rest of the class. Invite the other children to say whether they agree with the deductions or not. Display the photographs and the pairs' deductions so that other children in the class can agree or disagree with what the object is, and how it has been changed by an added effect.

How many beats?

SUBJECT: MUSIC. QCA UNIT 8: ONGOING SKILLS.

Learning objective
To learn that music has a pulse or beats.

THINKING OBJECTIVE
To deduce.

THINKING SKILLS
The children will listen to music with two, three and four beats in a bar, and deduce that different pieces have a different number of beats depending on their style and purpose. They will use this information to deduce how many beats there are in other songs they learn, thus understanding that most music is organised into bars with a certain number of beats.

WHAT YOU NEED
Music extracts that have two, three and four beats to a bar, for example marches, waltzes and lullabies (see suggestions in What to do).

WHAT TO DO
Listen to a march such as 'March of the Toys' from *Babes in Toyland* by Herbert or 'The Anvil Chorus' from Verdi's *Il Travatore* and let the children move around to it, if you have enough space. Alternatively, clap along to the beats. Ask, *How many beats are there in each bar? How many would you count to before starting from one again?* Relate this to the 'left, right' of marching feet. If necessary, give them an obvious clue that there are two beats by asking, *How many feet do we have? How many steps or beats in a bar? Do all the beats feel the same? Can you hear one stronger and one weaker beat?* Point this out to them, giving the first beat extra emphasis, for example as the blacksmith beats the anvil or the soldier puts forward the right foot, with the left step being less pronounced. Let them act out the action of one strong and one weaker beat as they listen to each time the anvil is struck, or march along to the march.

Listen next to a waltz, perhaps one by Strauss, such as 'The Blue Danube' or 'Tales from the Vienna Woods'. Work out together how many beats there are in this. Count to three and start again. Show the children how a conductor makes a triangle shape to show the orchestra which beat they are on. Conduct a waltz together to internalise the three beats in the bars of this music.

Finally, listen to your piece of music that has four beats. 'The Dance of the Sugar Plum Fairy' from Tchaikovsky's *Nutcracker Suite* is a good example, because you can hear the strong beat very clearly. Ask, *How many beats does this piece of music have? Are there four or two? Could you march to this piece of music? How can we tell the difference between two and four beats?* Suggest listening carefully for the first or stronger beat, then finding how many you can count in your head before you hear the strong beat again.

Encourage the children to think more about beats in music by singing songs which have rests, or beats missing, and which require the singers to count the rests before they begin. Caribbean calypsos have good syncopated rhythms, and songs such as 'Head and Shoulders' leave out words in subsequent verses. Experience of this type of music will help the children to internalise the beats or pulse.

SHEPHERDS, ANGELS AND HOW MANY WISE MEN?

SUBJECT: RE. QCA UNIT 4B: CELEBRATIONS: CHRISTMAS JOURNEYS.

LEARNING OBJECTIVE
To understand the facts about the Christmas journey.

THINKING OBJECTIVE
To interpret evidence.

THINKING SKILLS
The children will look at the Christmas story told in the Gospels of the New Testament of the Bible and list the facts given there. They will link this with the story told in carols and decide whether the writer of the carol has interpreted any aspects of the story differently. They will then work in groups so that they can discuss their own thinking and consider other people's interpretations of the evidence.

WHAT YOU NEED
Copies of favourite modern and traditional carols that tell all or part of the Christmas story, such as 'While shepherds watched', 'O Little Town of Bethlehem' or 'Little Donkey'; the story of Christmas from the New Testament Gospels of Matthew and Luke; modern versions of the Christmas story, including play scripts and musical adaptations; whiteboard and pen; two large sheets of paper (one divided into six equal rows and six equal columns); paper and pens.

WHAT TO DO
Remind the children of the Christmas story and the events that led to the journeys undertaken by the various groups who went to Bethlehem, including those who went to see Jesus. Think together who these are and list them in the first column of the large piece of paper. For each character group, think of all the information that the children can fill in:
- the **number** of shepherds, angels and wise men
- the **place** where they started their journeys
- the **reasons** for the journey
- **what they took** with them

⊙ **what they did** when they got there

⊙ whether any **names** are mentioned.

Write these as a list on the board. Then read together Matthew's version of the Christmas story and identify the relevant information. Now give pairs or groups of children a different source of evidence, and ask them to find and note down information in answer to the questions.

	Mary and Joseph	Angels	Shepherds	Wise Men
Number	2	A host		3
Starting point	Nazareth		Fields around Bethlehem	The East
Reason for journey	Population census	To tell the shepherds about the birth of Jesus		
What they brought				Gold, frankincense and myrrh
What they did	Had a baby	Visited the shepherds		
Names	Mary and Joseph	Gabriel		

Discuss the different interpretations of the story. Ask, *What do you notice about the information? Which source is most reliable? Can you say for sure? Have different people interpreted the information differently? Why are the three wise men sometimes called kings in carols? What are they called in the Bible? Why are there three? How many does the Bible say there are? Does the Bible give them names?* Identify all the differences that the children have noticed between the information you found as a class in the Bible, and the way it is presented in other stories and carols, and collate this on a large sheet of paper. For example, in the Bible the three kings are always referred to as wise men, but in many carols they are referred to as kings.

Extend the activity by looking at Christmas card designs, paintings and musicals, and discussing the different interpretations of the Christmas story. Look in a traditional carol book for those that have some of the details as they are told in the Bible.

PIGGY-IN-THE-MIDDLE

SUBJECT: PE. QCA UNIT: INVASION GAMES – UNIT 2.

LEARNING OBJECTIVE
To improve the children's ability to choose, use and adapt simple tactics and strategies.

THINKING OBJECTIVES
To deduce; to make decisions.

THINKING SKILLS
The children will consider their positions in the game Piggy-in-the-middle and will deduce where they need to be to pass and receive the ball to keep possession, and where to position themselves when they are trying to intercept and gain possession.

WHAT YOU NEED
A large ball for each group of three; a large space in which to work, such as the playground, field or hall.

WHAT TO DO
Follow your usual warm-up and skills practice to prepare the class for the group activity. Let the children play Piggy-in-the-middle for a few minutes. Then gather them together and ask who was successful in keeping possession. Ask, *How did you do this? Did you move into a space so that your partner could pass the ball?*

Help the children to deduce the strategies they need to use to keep possession of the ball. Ask, *If the defender is looking at your partner, can you choose to go either way? How will you let your partner know which way you will move?* Agree that they *can* move either way, and should indicate the direction by putting up their left or right hand. Now ask, *What if the defender is looking at you? What should you do?* Agree with the children that they should watch to see which way their partner is moving, and then move in the same direction to receive the ball.

Play the game again, then ask, *Did you manage to keep possession more effectively? How did you decide which way to move? Did you base your decision on the defender's position and the direction in which he or she was looking?*

Next, help the children to deduce how the person in the middle can gain possession. Ask, *Where should you stand? Should you stand next to the sender or mark the receiver? Why should you stand next to the person receiving the ball?* Talk about all the reasons why it is a good idea to mark the receiver rather than the sender, for example:

⊙ the ball may fall short

⊙ the person receiving may find it difficult to move into a space

⊙ the defender will have time to watch and follow the ball, making interception easier.

Play the game again, and note the children who deduce where they need to move in order to intercept the ball. Did they position themselves by the sender or the receiver? Develop the game to two on two and three on two, and discuss the changes in tactics.

EXTENDING REASONING SKILLS

Subject and QCA unit, NLS or NNS objective	Activity title	Thinking objective	Activity	Page
English. NLS objective: To identify the main characteristics of the key characters, drawing on the text to justify their views, and using the information to predict actions	A school trip	To ask inferential and non-literal questions to aid deeper understanding of a text	Identifying characters and predicting actions by inferring from the text.	46
Maths. NNS objective: To develop and refine written methods	Exchanging tens	To make decisions	Exchanging units and tens to gain an understanding of place value.	47
Science. QCA unit 4D: Solids, liquids and how they can be separated	Separating soup	To give reasons	Separating solids using different sieves and nets and giving reasons for the way they have carried out the investigation.	48
History. QCA unit 18: What was it like to live here in the past?	Every picture tells a story	To interpret evidence	Looking at a photograph and creating different stories that it could tell about the way people used to live.	50
Geography. QCA unit 6: Investigating our local area	Let's go shopping	To deduce; to make decisions	Conducting a shopping survey of the local and a contrasting place to see what shopping facilities are on offer in each.	51
Design and technology. QCA unit 3A: Packaging	Buy me!	To deduce; to give reasons	Using clues to link packaging to its product.	53
ICT. QCA unit 4A: Writing for different audiences	No smoking	To make judgements and decisions	Planning, designing and producing a leaflet to inform of the dangers of smoking.	54
Art and design. QCA unit 4B: Take a seat	Settle down	To form opinions	Designing a seat for a favourite storybook character.	56
Music. QCA unit 8: Ongoing skills	Hand jive	To interpret music	Interpreting the number of beats in a bar and phrase and composing a hand jive to fit.	57
RE. QCA unit 3A: What do signs and symbols mean in religion?	Religious symbols	To infer	Inferring the meaning behind the religious symbol of water.	58
PE. QCA unit: Outdoor and adventurous activities – unit 2	Letter orienteering	To deduce	Finding letters in the school grounds using orienteering techniques.	59

A SCHOOL TRIP

SUBJECT: ENGLISH. NLS OBJECTIVE: TO IDENTIFY THE MAIN CHARACTERISTICS OF THE KEY CHARACTERS, DRAWING ON THE TEXT TO JUSTIFY THEIR VIEWS, AND USING THE INFORMATION TO PREDICT ACTIONS.

LEARNING OBJECTIVE
To infer from the text what characters are present in the story.

THINKING OBJECTIVE
To ask inferential and non-literal questions to aid deeper understanding of a text.

THINKING SKILLS
The children will listen to the start of a story and get to know the characters and initial events. They will predict what they think will happen at intervals while the story is being read, which should be done in ten-minute sessions each day. This lesson is based on the part of the story where the school bus arrives at the farm and the farmer and his wife come to the door. They will listen to the descriptions of the farmer and his wife and ask inferential questions to identify that the pair are, in fact, the bank robbers.

WHAT YOU NEED
A copy of *Follow that Bus!* by Pat Hutchins (Red Fox); a large sheet of paper and coloured pens.

WHAT TO DO
A few days before the lesson, read the opening of the story until you get to the part where the school bus arrives at the farm for the school visit. During text-level work, read the part of the story where the farmer and his wife come to the door to welcome the children. Read the description of the couple and think about what the children in Class 6 are thinking when they see the farmer's wife. Ask, *What might they be thinking about the way the farmer's wife looks? What would you ask? What do you think about her looks? Why has she got flour spread over her face? Is she trying to hide something? What could she be trying to hide?* Listen to the children's suggestions and answers to your questions and ask further questions to encourage them to infer that the farmer's wife may be one of the bank robbers. Ask, *In that case, who is the farmer? Where is the real farmer's wife? What are they doing at the farm?*

Discuss the story so far and ask the children to think about other questions about the likelihood of certain things happening. For example, *What will happen when the children open the bag to eat their lunch? What will they find inside? How do you know?*

Use the pictures in the book to ask inferential questions together to work out what may happen next.

DIFFERENTIATION
Draw a simple picture of the farmer's wife from the description. Use this to help lower attaining pupils think of questions about the way she looks. Challenge higher attaining children to think of other inferential questions about the earlier part of the book. For example, *What sort of bag do the bank robbers have? What is significant about this?*

WHERE NEXT
Make a list of questions to answer as you read the rest of the story. Think of more questions as you work your way through the book. Ten minutes a day will soon finish the story.

ASSESSMENT
Listen carefully to the children's questions and note those who need support to ask inferential questions.

LEARNING OUTCOMES
Most children will ask questions to help them predict what they think will happen next in the story. Some will ask questions to help them deduce who certain characters are, what will happen in the story, and why.

FURTHER ENGLISH CHALLENGES
Inferential questions
Plan work where the children can ask direct and inferential questions about a picture and text, such as a family making breakfast. Explain that direct or literal questions are those where the answer can be found in the text or picture, such as:
- What can you see?
- What is happening?
- What are the people doing?

Inferential or non-literal questions are those where the answer cannot be found directly in the text or picture, but can be inferred from information contained in it:
- The clock says 9.30. What do you think the characters are thinking if it is a school day?

○ Will they be thinking something different if it is Saturday? How do you know?

○ What could you smell in the picture (if the toaster has just popped up)?

Note the objects in the picture that will help the children infer or deduce smells and sounds, and what people may be thinking.

What happens next?

Read the poem 'Dad on the line' by Allan Ahlberg in *Friendly Matches* (Puffin). Talk about what is happening before asking inferential questions about what the boy is feeling. Ask, *How do we know? Where in the text can we find that he is resigned to his dad coming to watch him play football every week?* Ask the children to think of other inferential questions that give a clue to the context of the poem. Ask, *How do we know it could be a dream before we start to read it? What is the subtitle of the poem? Why is it called 'or a boy's nightmare'?*

EXCHANGING TENS

SUBJECT: MATHEMATICS. NNS OBJECTIVE: TO DEVELOP AND REFINE WRITTEN METHODS FOR COLUMN ADDITION AND SUBTRACTION OF TWO WHOLE NUMBERS LESS THAN 1000, AND ADDITION OF MORE THAN TWO SUCH NUMBERS.

LEARNING OBJECTIVE

To learn how to solve vertical addition and subtraction.

THINKING OBJECTIVE

To make decisions.

THINKING SKILLS

The children will be asked to think about the number of units that make ten, and then the number of tens that make one hundred. This ability to exchange units for the correct number of tens and hundreds will help the children to gain a deeper understanding of place value. In deciding for themselves when and how many to exchange, they will be thinking through the process of what they are doing.

WHAT YOU NEED

A large dice; a large number of units, tens, and hundreds; a large sheet of paper and several smaller ones all divided into three columns and labelled units, tens, and hundreds; writing materials.

WHAT TO DO

Sit the children in a semicircle in front of the large sheet of paper, so that they can all see the paper the right way up. Show them the units and explain the rules of the game, saying *Each dot on a dice is worth one unit.* Ask, *How many units will you get if a 4 is thrown? How many if a 6 is thrown?* Continue with this line of questioning until most of the children understand.

Play the game as a class, initially. Throw the dice and invite a child to take the number of units thrown. Place these in the units column on your sheet of paper. Explain that they must be placed here because of their value. This column is the right place for units. Throw the dice again and add the corresponding number of units. Continue until you get ten or more units in this column and space becomes a problem.

Ask the children if there is anything they can think of that you can do to reduce this number. Encourage someone to suggest that you can exchange ten units for a ten, as ten units have the same value as one ten. The ten must be put in the tens column because this is the place for its value. Continue with the game, exchanging units for tens, until you have ten tens. Ask, *What can we exchange this number for? What has the same value as ten tens? Which column does this have to be placed in?*

When the children understand the rules and process of the game, organise them into mixed-ability groups to play the game again. Monitor two groups at a time to make sure they are playing the game correctly. When they are able to play the game as a group activity, set it up as a competition so that they take it in turns and exchange their units, tens and hundreds individually. The first to get a hundred is the winner.

DIFFERENTIATION

Let lower attaining children stop at 20 and play the game again with an adult until they understand the idea of exchanging, and can see that tens and units are put in different places because of their value. With more able children, start with 99 and take units away until you get down to less than six on the paper. They will need to exchange a ten for ten units and put these into the correct place to take, for example, 5 away from 42.

WHERE NEXT

Let the children play the game independently in groups when they have understood the rules and the process.

Relate the game to money and other units of measurement to reinforce their knowledge of how many pence in £1, and how many millimetres and centimetres in a metre. Extend the exchanging labels to include 1000.

ASSESSMENT

Observe which children make decisions independently and use them to understand place value. Note those who can relate this to solving other place-value problems.

LEARNING OUTCOMES

Most children will learn to decide for themselves when to exchange ten units for a ten, and ten tens for a hundred.

FURTHER MATHS CHALLENGES

Adding beyond 100

Use the same sheets to add two three-digit numbers vertically. Solve a few sums together in small groups, before giving the children some examples to solve independently. Start with one where the numbers do not require exchanging, to reinforce how to add the totals. Then add together 356 and 178. Put out three hundreds, five tens and six units in the correct places for their value. Underneath these, put out one hundred, seven tens and eight units, also in the correct places. Put the units together, exchanging ten units for a ten, then the tens and finally the hundreds. Work out how many you have in each column. Extend this to solving money problems and adding three numbers.

Take away numbers

Start with 567 – 135. Move on to 341 – 128, in which the children will need to exchange a ten for ten units. Provide similar problems for them to solve.

Equivalent fractions

Make each unit a fraction, for example 1/4, and exchange these to make 1/2, 3/4 and one whole. Develop the idea of equivalence by changing the value of units to 1/8 and making the other columns 1/4, 1/2 and 3/4. Do the children notice that they need two eighths to make a quarter, four eighths to make a half, and six eighths to make three quarters?

Long sums

Ask the children to give you numbers between 10 and 20, and list these as a long sum. Together, look at the list and count the tens that can be made with pairs of numbers: 7 and 3, 5 and 5, 6 and 4, and so on. Add these to the tens in the tens column to find the total.

SEPARATING SOUP

SUBJECT: SCIENCE. QCA UNIT 4D: SOLIDS, LIQUIDS AND HOW THEY CAN BE SEPARATED.

LEARNING OBJECTIVE

To separate solids by sieving.

THINKING OBJECTIVE

To give reasons.

THINKING SKILLS

The children will find a way to separate solids of different sizes that are found in a familiar product.

This activity is set within a realistic problem-solving situation to add meaning to the task. They will give reasons about why they have chosen a particular method to separate the pasta or croutons from some instant soup, and why they have used much finer sieves for other parts of the separation exercise. They will talk about the size of the solids they have separated, and relate this to the equipment they have used. They will extend their thinking by considering how they can do this when the soup has had liquid added.

WHAT YOU NEED

A packet of soup that contains ingredients of different sizes, such as croutons, pasta, dried vegetables and powder; or pasta, salt, powder soup, dried vegetables and croutons to make your own; equipment for the children to choose from, such as sieves of different fineness, colanders, filter paper and spoons; paper and pens.

WHAT TO DO

Open the packet of soup and look at the contents together. Identify as many solids as you can, such as pasta, croutons, dried vegetables and powder. Talk about how hot water can be added to these ingredients to make the soup.

Set the children this problem: Imagine that your family is planning to have soup, but Dad does not like pasta, your brother hates croutons, and your sister will not eat vegetables. Ask the children if they can think of ways to remove these solids from the dry soup mixture before the water is added so that everyone in the family can enjoy the soup, and will not need to pick out those things they do not like. Ask, *How can you separate each of the solids from each other?*

Let the children suggest the resources they need to separate the different components. Divide them into groups and ask them to prepare a group plan of how they will do this. They should identify the necessary equipment and label it to show how it will be used and why.

When they have completed and discussed the plan, ask them to separate the solids to make up suitable soup mixtures for each member of the family. During the plenary discussion, share the methods they used to separate the solids and talk about the difficulties they met. Ask, *Which was the most difficult solid to separate? Why? How did you overcome the problems? Did you find a different method or use a different piece of equipment? Did some of ingredients you didn't want in the finished soup fall through the holes?*

Encourage the children to suggest improved methods of separating the solids.

DIFFERENTIATION

Give higher attaining children the soup already made up, with hot water added and then allowed to cool, to give them an additional substance to separate. Ask them to separate this out as far as they can before probing to see if they can suggest a way to separate the water from the ingredients that are left (by using evaporation). Monitor the involvement of lower attaining children in their groups to make sure they are involved in the planning, or talk to this group separately to help them understand the process of sieving, and offer them the opportunity to give reasons why this method of separation works.

WHERE NEXT

Separate other mixtures including metal by using magnets, or salt and sand by using water to dissolve the salt. Challenge higher attaining children to think of a way to separate sugar and salt. Why can't you use dissolving as a method? Why is sieving the best way? How fine does the equipment need to be?

ASSESSMENT

Record some of the children's reasoning on how they can separate the components. Encourage them to use scientific vocabulary and terms during their explanations, especially the higher attaining children who are trying to separate solids from liquids.

LEARNING OUTCOMES

Most children will be able to separate solids and give reasons why their methods work. Higher attaining children will begin to understand how to separate solids from liquids.

FURTHER SCIENCE CHALLENGES

Has it disappeared?

Dissolve salt and sugar separately in water and talk about what has happened. Ask, *Has the salt or sugar disappeared? How can you find out whether it is still there? Why is it not a good idea to taste it?* Remind the children that they know this solution contains salt or sugar and that it will not harm them, but that it is not a good idea to find out what a liquid is by tasting it. Talk to the children about evaporation and show them how, when you boil a small amount of the water in the solution away, crystals of salt and sugar remain. Note the similarities and differences between the two crystals.

Soil and sand

Give the children a mixture of sand, soil and stones and ask them to separate these components as far as possible. They should give reasons for the way they chose to separate the materials.

EVERY PICTURE TELLS A STORY

SUBJECT: HISTORY. QCA UNIT 18: WHAT WAS IT LIKE TO LIVE HERE IN THE PAST?

LEARNING OBJECTIVE

To learn that we find out about the past from sources of evidence that have survived.

THINKING OBJECTIVE

To interpret evidence.

THINKING SKILLS

The children will all look at the same type of evidence and interpret it in their own way. They will work together in groups inferring what the evidence tells them about life in the local area in the past. They will then write an account and share and compare this with other groups to learn that when they look at evidence they are usually getting one person's interpretation or point of view.

WHAT YOU NEED

Old photographs of the local area that show people, buildings and transport from different historical periods – the immediate past to 100 years or so ago, or at a time of specific interest to your particular area. You should be able to get these from older residents, the local council office, or newspapers.

WHAT TO DO

Look at one of the photographs and locate where it was taken, before identifying all the features, people, buildings and types of transport. Choose one feature and describe this as fully as possible. For example, identify the name and purpose of a building, the materials used to build it, and its style and position. Ask the children, *Is this still in the area or has it been demolished? In what ways is it the same? In what ways is it different? What words can you think of to describe this building's historical past? Can you see any clues to tell you when it was built? Perhaps a date stone, a name, or the materials and style?* If possible, show the children a photograph of the same building taken twenty years later, and again today. Note the changes and consider how you know which photograph is the oldest and which the newest. Ask, *What information is in the photograph apart from the colour, black and white or other photographic features?*

Show the children another photograph, which contains images of people, and ask them to imagine what it was like to live here in the past. Ask them, *What does the photo tell you about this? What does it tell you about the way people got around? How do you know people did not use cars as much? What clues are in the picture? Where do you think the people in the photo are going? Where would they work? Would they work locally or at a distance? How do you know?* Imagine who took the photograph and the reason for this. Ask, *Why did they choose this particular subject?* If possible, relate this to a specific aspect of life in the past, such as working at a local shop, factory or mine (which may have since closed down), or working on the land or in service for wealthy families. Note the different ways that the information on the photograph can be interpreted. Ask, *Does it really tell us about the past?* Encourage the children to disagree, if they wish, and to put forward different interpretations of what the photograph is showing.

Now give each group a photograph and ask them to interpret what they see. Remind them to look for clues that tell them about the way people used to live, how they got about, what they wore, where they were going and the jobs they did. Ask them to write a short account of this to share with the rest of the class at the end of the lesson. If possible, provide two groups with photographs of the same place taken at different times.

Discuss all the different things that the children noticed in the photographs and ask them what they think they learned about the past. Ask, *How has your interpretation of what is in the photograph helped you to build up this picture?* Look at two photographs taken of the area at different times, and think again about how the area has changed over time. Were the two groups' interpretations the same or different? Talk about why they need to compare what they think against other sources of evidence. Explain that they have given *their* interpretation of how the photograph gives information about the past.

DIFFERENTIATION

Organise the class into mixed-ability groups so that low and high attainers can work together to extend their ideas. Encourage the higher attaining children to act as scribes for the others' ideas before contributing some ideas of their own. Brief them with questions to ask the other children in the class to prompt ideas and focus attention on certain aspects of the photographs.

WHERE NEXT

Invite an older local resident to come into school to tell the children what life was like in the past. Afterwards, choose a relevant photograph and interpret how it supports or disproves the story told by the visitor.

ASSESSMENT

Assess how well the children look at the evidence and then carry out their own interpretation of the way people used to live.

LEARNING OUTCOMES

Most children will understand that historical evidence can be interpreted in different ways and that we need more than one source to give us a balanced point of view.

FURTHER HISTORY CHALLENGES

Historical objects

Look at artefacts from the past and try to think of how, and by whom, they were used. Start with easy ones, such as a flat iron, and build up to more obscure ones, such as boot hooks and hatpins. Challenge the children to interpret the artefacts to think about how people would use them, and for what.

Army uniforms

Look at clothing and equipment from the armed forces (either real or in pictures) and compare the materials and styles. Interpret this evidence and talk about how each item was used, and how it helps or helped soldiers. Think about how easy it was to wear or use. This activity can be related to a range of clothing and accessories linked to particular jobs.

LET'S GO SHOPPING

SUBJECT: GEOGRAPHY. QCA UNIT 6: INVESTIGATING OUR LOCAL AREA.

LEARNING OBJECTIVE

To find out about shopping facilities in the local area.

THINKING OBJECTIVES

To deduce; to make decisions.

THINKING SKILLS

The children will carry out a shopping survey locally, and in a contrasting area. They will use the information they gather to deduce where they can buy certain items and the distance they need to travel to purchase them. They will also identify alternatives, such as mail order and Internet shopping, and decide which is the best way for people living in different types of places to shop.

WHAT YOU NEED

Visit, or use a detailed map of, the local area; visit, or use a map of, the nearest shopping centre (maps are usually found at the entrances to these centres); a collection of mail-order catalogues; whiteboard and pen; paper and pens.

WHAT TO DO

Use a map which details the information, or visit the local area, to carry out a shopping survey of your local facilities. Note the number of different shops that sell food, clothing, furniture, stationery, and so on, as well as speciality shops. Decide in advance how to record the information, perhaps by listing the different types of shop you expect to find in your town or village and tallying each time you find one. Note the size of the shops and whether they hold a wide or a limited range of goods.

Back in the classroom, analyse the information and, with the children working in groups, give them five minutes to list as many items as they can think of that can be bought from this first shopping area. Then give them five minutes to think of as many items as they can that *cannot* be bought here, and the reasons why. Make a list of all suggestions, and identify the nearest shopping centre, town or city where it might be possible to buy them. Using a detailed map or a visit to the area, carry out a second survey to see if the items on the list can indeed be bought from here.

Refine the list further by adding yet more items to the list of things, which cannot be bought from either place. Move on to ask, *Can you think of alternative ways of buying things* (from the Internet and mail order)*?* Look at your collection of mail-order catalogues and note those things on the list that can be bought in this way. Go back to the original list and decide whether to buy each item locally, from another shopping centre close by, or via mail order (perhaps through the Internet).

Think about different types of places where people live, such as the Highlands of Scotland, remote islands or large cities, and decide which methods of shopping would be most suitable for the people who live in these areas. Consider everyday items such as groceries, stationery and cleaning materials; those that are bought less frequently such as clothes, shoes, and car accessories; and those that are bought occasionally such as furniture, carpets and cars.

Ask the children to consider whether people who live in remote areas need to shop in a different way to those who live close to large shopping centres for everyday items, things that are bought less frequently, and specialist items that are bought occasionally.

DIFFERENTIATION
Take lower attaining children through the process step by step to make sure they are drawing conclusions or making deductions about the range of shopping facilities in each area, and the reasons why this is so. Higher attaining children should be encouraged to write reasons why shopping centres are more and more frequently found on the outskirts of towns, and relate this to the different groups of people who have a connection with these shops, including workers, customers, delivery people and inhabitants.

WHERE NEXT
Identify reasons why shopping centres and malls are more and more frequently located on the outskirts of towns and cities. Discuss the transport options to these places and make links between public transport and the location of shops. Think, too, about deliveries of goods – how they are easier to deliver if they are close to major roads and motorways and do not need to be taken through the centre of towns. Discuss the implications of this for those encouraging people to travel into town and city centres to shop.

Investigate selected Internet sites where people can order shopping. Abacus (www.abacus.com), Sainsburys (www.sainsburys.co.uk) and Tesco (www.tesco.co.uk) all have useful sites.

Investigate the range of goods it is possible to purchase by mail order and discuss the implications of this on traffic and transport arrangements in getting the goods from warehouses, to distribution centres in different areas around the country, and then to individual households. You might be able to track a parcel from the country of origin, to the warehouse, to the distribution centre, to the school.

ASSESSMENT
Assess how well the children interpret the information to draw conclusions about why certain shops are found in certain types of places. Note those

who are able to use the information to deduce and identify other possible ways of shopping for certain items, and to decide which is the best method for people who live in different types of places.

LEARNING OUTCOMES
Most children will begin to deduce why particular types of shops are found in certain areas, and why. They will make decisions about the best place to buy certain items, and why, depending on where you live.

FURTHER GEOGRAPHY CHALLENGES
Shopping in remote areas
Choose a remote area in Britain, such as the Welsh mountain areas, Scottish Highlands or a small island. Choose an area for which you can get suitable information from the Internet, or the local tourist or information centre. Look at the available facilities on a map of the area and identify the types of things that can be bought from any nearby shops, such as groceries. Perhaps the shop doubles as a post office? Note the nearest large towns where people are likely to buy specialist food, clothing, furniture and other items. Ask the children, *What would be the best places or methods for people who live here to buy these things? How often do you think these people would go shopping or place an order? Would a delivery service make a daily delivery to these outlying areas? What do you think their minimum order would be?*
Tourist areas
Compare the types of shops in your home area with a contrasting tourist or seaside area or, if you live in this type of area, a town or city-centre location. Compare the number and types of shops and deduce why the range of shops is different. This will lead the children towards considering what the area needs

to provide for both visitors and inhabitants. Deduce which types of shops are likely to be found on the outskirts of towns (usually for local residents) and those found in the centre (often specialist or gift shops for visitors). Give the children a list of things to buy and ask them to decide where to buy them.

Buy me!

SUBJECT: DESIGN AND TECHNOLOGY.
QCA UNIT 3A: PACKAGING.

LEARNING OBJECTIVE
To look at the different designs used on packaging to attract buyers.

THINKING OBJECTIVES
To deduce; to give reasons.

THINKING SKILLS
The children will work in groups to look at a range of packaging and use the information to deduce which products belong to which package. They will give reasons for their choices, which could include knowing the product from adverts, or other clues on the packaging. This activity involves concept mapping.

WHAT YOU NEED
A range of packaging for different types of products with the name cut out and saved separately, such as boxes of chocolates, sweets, ice lollies, gateaux, washing powder, Chinese takeaway boxes, and so on; writing and drawing materials; whiteboard and pen.

WHAT TO DO
Look at some food packaging that is not heavily advertised, and with which the children are unlikely to be familiar – perhaps a supermarket Chinese takeaway meal. Ask, *What sort of product would you expect to find inside this packaging?* Identify the clues together – they may find pictures, names and descriptions to help with their deductions. Look at five more items of empty packaging from your collection and, using the same clues, identify what product each one could have contained. List the six products the children have deduced and link each one to the packaging they think it belongs to. Ask them, *How do you know this?*

For each decision, write the children's reasons for linking the packaging to the product. For example, *It shows a picture of the product. It has a catchy slogan that describes what is inside. The description makes you think of something sweet* and so on. Produce the names of the products, one by one, and show them

which item goes with which packaging. Ask, *How well was the product advertised by the packaging? How did the pictures and contents list help? Did it make you want to buy the item? Why?*

Now give groups of children a different range of boxes and packaging with the title removed. Ask them to draw pictures of the packaging on one side of a piece of paper and what they think the product is on the other. The children should draw lines from the packaging to the product and write their reasons for linking them together.

Once the groups have completed this exercise, look at the reasons the children have given and identify the main features of good packaging. Ask, *Did the picture provide a good clue? What about the text, the ingredients, the slogan?*

Form opinions about the packaging the class like, and the reasons why. Ask, *How well does each one 'sell' the product? How much do you want to buy the product as a result of the packaging? Did the colour of the packaging catch your eye? How well does it attract you and invite you to buy?*

Make a list of the features that the children have identified as making the packaging attractive (it has a bright and busy pattern), giving information about the product that entices us to buy it (it washes white clothes whiter), showing the product invitingly as a picture (it looks good enough to eat), and so on.

DIFFERENTIATION
Give the lower attaining children the packaging and a list of suggested products to link. Higher attaining children could be given only the trade names and use this information to deduce what the products are and which packaging matches to them. Ask them, *How does the name give us a clue to the product? Is it inviting and enticing?* Tell them to decide which is the most enticing, and why.

WHERE NEXT
Use the work done in the main activity to design packaging for an imaginary product of their own, such as a new type of cake or biscuit. Children could work individually, in pairs or in groups. Some of these designs should be produced on the computer. Can other children deduce what the product is from the packaging?

ASSESSMENT
Note the children who give good reasons for their choices and base these on the clues on the packaging. Let as many children as possible design their own packaging, encouraging them to use the deductions and reasons they have heard in class as starting points for their ideas.

LEARNING OUTCOMES

Most children will look for clues on the packaging and use these to deduce which product each one contains. They will base the reasons for their decisions on these clues.

FURTHER DESIGN AND TECHNOLOGY CHALLENGES

Advertising chaos

Put a number of advertisements for products on a table. Remove all product names and ask the children to deduce which type of product belongs with each by finding clues in the advertisements.

Unusual shaped packaging

Look at a range of packaging in unusual shapes and talk about how these catch the eye. Deduce what may be found inside and give reasons for thinking this. Christmas is a good time to collect unusual packaging that may not have the name of the product printed on the outside. Items should include pyramid-shaped chocolate boxes, spherical soap packaging, and cylindrical sweet containers.

NO SMOKING

SUBJECT: ICT. QCA UNIT 4A: WRITING FOR DIFFERENT AUDIENCES.

LEARNING OBJECTIVE

To use ICT to organise, reorganise and analyse ideas and information.

THINKING OBJECTIVE

To make judgements and decisions.

THINKING SKILLS

The children will consider the layout and content of a range of leaflets and use this analysis to make judgements and decisions about how effective they are at getting their message across. They will then take these things into consideration when designing and making brochures to warn people about the dangers of smoking. They will consider the needs of their audience before putting together leaflets, choosing the graphics, text and style of presentation.

WHAT YOU NEED

A collection of leaflets (on any topic) containing different graphics, text and layouts to present information; computers; a word-processing package that allows text and graphics to be combined; access to the Internet; clipart CD-ROMs; an interactive whiteboard or a large sheet of paper and a pen.

WHAT TO DO

Seat the children in a circle and pass the leaflets around for them to analyse. Draw their attention to the pictures, the style, size and colour of the text, and the way the information is presented (the layout). Put the children into pairs and ask them to analyse one leaflet in terms of the impact that the different graphics, text and layout has on the reader. Ask them, *Does the leaflet get the message across to the intended audience quickly and effectively? How?* Ask the pairs to report back to the class, expressing opinions about the things they like, those they don't, and why.

Tell the children that they will be designing and making a leaflet to warn people about the dangers of smoking. Together, agree the audience at whom the leaflet should be targeted. Take a large sheet of paper to list the process and the things the children will need to consider in their designs. Start a numbered 'process list', putting the audience at number one. Point out to the children how important it is to keep in mind the people for whom they are producing the leaflet. This could be adults who already smoke (but being sensitive to children whose parents smoke), teenagers who may be tempted into trying smoking for the first time, or younger children who should not be smoking but who nevertheless often try it out.

Next, consider the components that will be needed in the leaflet and list these on the 'process list' too. For example, title, caption or slogan could be number two, graphics number three, main text message number four, and so on, depending on what the children suggest. Then use the interactive whiteboard and follow the 'process list' to produce a sample of the type of work you expect. Start by agreeing the audience, then show them how to produce and make the slogan, title or caption eye-catching by exploring the range of graphics that are available on CD-ROMs or the Internet. Let the children select a few, adjust their sizes, and place them on the screen. Decide on the words you want to use, and explore the size, style and colours of these. Spell a few words incorrectly to show or remind the children how to use the spell check. Revise or teach the children how to insert, resize and rotate graphics, and how to insert text using a text box to wrap around the graphics, if appropriate.

Finally, consider the layout. Show the children how to use the cut and paste facility to move things around the screen. List 'layout' as the final item on your 'process list' to remind the children to consider it. Invite the children to work in pairs to agree their audience, which can be the same as or different to the class one, and then to follow the 'process list' to design and make a leaflet in a style of their choosing. Encourage them to think carefully about the layout, and refer them to the process list to remind them of the things they need to consider.

Talk to the children as they work about the impact they want their leaflet to have. Ask, *Will it reach your intended audience? Why? How effectively have your graphics been presented? How well do they support the text? Does the text stand out – is it eye-catching?*

Share all the leaflets as a class, asking children to outline why they decided on the contents, colours, style, and layout they chose. Display the leaflets, with labels of the decisions and judgements the children needed to make during the process.

DIFFERENTIATION
Talk to higher attaining children about how to use text boxes, frames and borders to improve the layout of the information and to make certain words and messages stand out. Evaluate these together to see how well these devices catch the reader's attention. Pair lower attaining children with a more able partner so that ideas can be extended. Monitor these partnerships carefully to make sure one is not impeding the progress of the other.

WHERE NEXT
Make leaflets for other topics that are being studied in PSHE.

ASSESSMENT
Note those who use the information from their analysis to help them make decisions and judgements about what to include in their leaflets. Note, too, the effectiveness of the finished leaflets.

LEARNING OUTCOMES
Most children will make decisions and judgements about what to include in their leaflets, and how the information will be presented. They will demonstrate a clear understanding of why these features are important to getting the message across to the audience.

FURTHER ICT CHALLENGES
Bookmarks
Explain to the children that you want them to make a bookmark. Show them how to change the background on screen and to explore the impact of the text in different styles, sizes and colours on different coloured screens. Ask them to write a name and title for their bookmark, insert a picture and explore different colour combinations of the text and background until they have decided on the two combinations they like best. Invite the children to show their bookmarks to a friend who can judge which one they prefer, giving reasons why. Ask the children, *Which bookmarks do you like? Why? Is it the colour, style, components or layout?*
Copy cat
Draw a picture of a cat and colour it in using the flood or fill colour tool. Give the cat a name, then use copy and paste to repeat the cat and name a number of times. Change the colour of the titles and the cat. Ask, *How many different versions can you find?* Choose the combination the children like best, encouraging them to base their decisions and judgements on the impact and layout of the two. Explore further changes to the style, size and position of the picture and text until the children are happy with the finished design. Wonder at the infinite number of ways that the picture can be presented. Other pictures can obviously be substituted for the cat.

SETTLE DOWN

SUBJECT: ART AND DESIGN. QCA UNIT 4B: TAKE A SEAT.

LEARNING OBJECTIVE
To combine visual effects to create a design.

THINKING OBJECTIVE
To form opinions.

THINKING SKILLS
The children will consider what they like and dislike in order to plan and design a seat for a favourite storybook character. They will think about the character's personality and try to capture something of this through colour, texture and shape.

WHAT YOU NEED
Paper and paints; adhesive; colour charts, wallpaper and fabric swatches in a range of textures and colours; your own favourite chair; pictures of chairs and seats in a range of styles and materials (IKEA catalogues will provide suitable interesting and modern designs).

WHAT TO DO
Seat the children where they can all see your favourite chair. Talk about why you like it. Model the language you want the children to consider, mentioning features such as colour shades, contrasting and complementary colours, and textures – are they interesting to touch?
Look at any patterns in the chair's upholstery or design and talk about how these make you feel. Model the language of mood and feeling, such as 'busy', 'quiet', 'colourful', 'calming', 'happy' and 'stress-free'. Relate this language to the colours used in the design and pattern.

Look at the style of the chair. Ask the children, *How big is it? What is it made from? Is the seat comfortable or hard? Does the chair have arms? Does it have a tall back? A footstool?* Invite the children to express their opinions of your favourite chair and what they would do if it belonged to them. Ask, *Would you want to change the colour or the style? Can you tell me about your favourite chair?*

Think of a favourite storybook character together and identify the character's personality – Harry Potter or Frodo Baggins would be topical examples. Ask, *What colours do you think he would like? Why? What sort of chair would suit this character?*

Ask the children to work in pairs and choose a favourite storybook character for whom to design a chair. They should draw the design and choose and label the materials from which it will be made. Encourage them to draw the chair from different viewpoints, and let them mix colour tones and add a suitable colour chart in one quarter of their paper to show the shades they intend to use in the soft furnishings. They should then explore the range of fabrics and textures and add colour swatches next to, or under, the colour chart. When they have finished, ask the children to express their opinions on the colours and textures of their design and to link this with the personality of the character for whom they have designed the chair.

DIFFERENTIATION
Let the lower attaining children design a chair for

someone they know or, if they prefer, for themselves. They should think carefully about what they want the chair for – a particular room or activity – before they start choosing the style and materials. Higher attaining children should write a description of their character and link the different parts to the design features of the chair.

WHERE NEXT
Make a small prototype of some of the chairs before making a full-scale version of one or two for the book corner area of the classroom.

ASSESSMENT
Assess how well the children link the personality traits of their chosen character to the design features of the chair. Note how well they express their opinions, whether they link these with likes and dislikes of colour and texture, and how these relate to the purpose of the design.

LEARNING OUTCOMES
Most children will be able to talk about their preferences of colour and shade and begin to relate these to the personality of the character for whom they are designing the chair.

FURTHER ART AND DESIGN CHALLENGES
One-piece chair
Look at pictures of chairs made from one piece of wood, bent and shaped into a chair. These can be found in furniture catalogues, such as IKEA's, and other mail-order catalogues. Talk about how this works, and why. Ask, *Do you like this style of chair? Why? What is it about the design that you like? Do you think it is comfortable? Do any of you know this from personal experience?* Bring one into school for them to try out, if possible, and ask them to express their opinion. Ask, *Where do you think you might use a chair like this? Is it comfortable enough to relax in? To snuggle down with a good book? Will you need a cushion? What colours would you choose to finish off furnishing this chair? Why?*
Beanbags
Try out a range of beanbags and form opinions about their suitability for book corners and the library. Ask, *How comfortable are they? Are they big enough for the oldest children? Are they small enough for the youngest children? Is there room for two children so that they can share a book? How can we shape them into a sofa or chair?* Recall with the children how and where they have sat on beanbags, and form opinions about their suitability as seats. Ask them, *Where would they not be appropriate?*

HAND JIVE

SUBJECT: MUSIC. QCA UNIT 8: ONGOING SKILLS.

LEARNING OBJECTIVE
To practise keeping a pulse.

THINKING OBJECTIVE
To interpret music.

THINKING SKILLS
The children will listen to a piece of music and interpret the beats and rhythms in order to develop a hand jive to fit the number of beats in a bar and phrase. They will then anticipate what will happen if they change the number of movements in each phrase.

WHAT YOU NEED
A suitable piece of music for a hand-jive sequence. 'Poetry in Motion' by Johnny Tillotson works well because it has 16 beats and is not too fast. Once the children have got the idea, try using a song with a faster beat. Most pop songs from the 1950s or 60s with a steady beat are suitable. Check the words first!

WHAT TO DO
Listen to the song and talk about the pulse or beat. How many beats can you hear in each phrase? (This will be 16 beats, ending after 'walking by my side'.) Develop a hand jive that fits this by using two claps, two knee slaps, two right hands over left, two left hands over right, two hot potato right on left and two left on right, and finish with finger spins in each hand over the corresponding shoulder for two beats each.

This forms the basic four-beat phrase, which makes a hand jive. Practise the sequence until the children can, or can almost, perform this from memory. Put on the song and hand jive along to it, interpreting the phrases and beats as you go. Evaluate how well you did afterwards and agree how well the children interpreted the song.

Play another piece of music with 16 beats and invite the children to work in pairs to make up their own hand-jive sequence to fit the number of beats. They will need to interpret the beats and phrasing of this to make their sequence fit.

DIFFERENTIATION
Prepare a simple hand jive (such as clap to four, slap to four, click to four and tap to four) for pupils who have difficulty keeping a pulse. Children who find it easy to keep the pulse could change the order of

the sequence and work in groups performing the same jives, but in a different order, to make the performance appear more complicated.

WHERE NEXT
Perform the same hand jive to other songs that have eight or sixteen beats, such as 'Greased Lightning' from *Grease*.

ASSESSMENT
Watch the children as they perform to identify those who interpret the correct number of beats to match their hand-jive composition.

LEARNING OUTCOMES
Most children will be able to sustain a simple hand jive to regular beats. They will all have the opportunity to interpret the music to make up hand jives of their own which will fit the pulse.

FURTHER MUSIC CHALLENGES
Ten-beat hand jive
Compose hand jives to different songs that have a different number of beats in bars and phrases. Interpret the music to decide which number of beats is most effective, and work out how to make the hand jives fit. Vary the number of claps and slaps, perhaps making these in sequences of four and using them to make a 32-beat hand jive. You may find the children want to introduce other hand-jive movements, such as finger snaps or thigh slaps.

Disco beat
Learn a dance sequence that fits into a 16-beat phrase. You may wish to start with a familiar one that the children know. Alternatively, make up your own by interpreting the words and music of 'The Locomotion' (versions by Little Eva or Kylie Minogue).

RELIGIOUS SYMBOLS

SUBJECT: RE. QCA UNIT 3A: WHAT DO SIGNS AND SYMBOLS MEAN IN RELIGION?

LEARNING OBJECTIVE
To learn about and from the use of symbols in different religions.

THINKING OBJECTIVE
To infer.

THINKING SKILLS
The children will think beyond the literal and note the inferential meaning of the less obvious religious symbol of water.

WHAT YOU NEED
Pictures of different religious festivals that use light and/or water as symbols to remember God, Jesus or the significance of different religious ceremonies; labels; pens; large sheets of paper and somewhere to display these; Blu-Tack.

WHAT TO DO
Ask the children for their ideas about how water is used. Write their suggestions on labels and stick them under relevant headings, such as *washing*, *cooking*, *cleaning*, and *drinking*.

If the children have not already thought of how water is used in religious ceremonies and services, move on to this now. Use the pictures as prompts, and think about different religions so that the children can understand the importance of water to many religions in the world. For example, talk about the meaning of baptism to Christians, the importance of cleanliness before prayer to Moslems and the significance of the River Ganges to Hindus and Sikhs.

Tell the children that Holy Water is provided at the entrance of some Christian churches and ask them to infer what the term 'Holy Water' means. Ask, *Do you think it means that it has been blessed by the priest?* Relate this to how the vicar blesses the water before baptising someone, and how some Christian worshippers cross themselves before entering a holy place. Ask, *Do you think there is increased significance in this because they know the water has been blessed?*

If possible, ask children to talk from personal experience about visiting a mosque to pray, the purpose of washing their hands before handling the Qu'ran, or the significance of bathing in the River Ganges to Hindus and Sikhs.

Set up a simple concept map for the children to work in small groups to record their ideas. Ask them to list the different religions down one side of a large sheet of paper and record the different ways water is used in religious services and practices for each one. Ask them to link the religion with the practice and to write the significance of the act to each religion. Ask, *What can be inferred from the way water is used in each religion?* Display these concept maps.

DIFFERENTIATION
Work with lower attaining children on one religion at a time in order not to confuse their thinking. They should note the different ways water is used in Hindu or Christian worship and practices, and why, before moving on to different religions.

WHERE NEXT
Discuss how water is considered important in Aboriginal beliefs, and talk about how this is portrayed in their Dreamtime stories. Repeat the activity for the symbol of light and how this is used in many religions.

ASSESSMENT
Look at the children's ideas and note whether they have inferred the significance of water to different religions.

LEARNING OUTCOMES
Most children will understand that water is important to different religions. Some will infer why this is the case and record the significance of its inclusion in religious services and practices.

FURTHER RE CHALLENGES
Sayings and proverbs
Look at different sayings and proverbs and draw cartoon pictures for each one. Next to this, ask the children to write what they infer or think the saying means. For example, 'wear your heart on your sleeve' means to be open about your feelings; 'God is my rock' means that believing in God gives me strength. The children's interpretations will depend on their personal views and thoughts.

Which practice?
Look at a range of artefacts from different religions and ask the children to select any which are used in a service that uses water as a symbol of faith. Ask the children to draw the artefact and record the name of the service or ceremony, writing a reason why the water is significant to this particular practice. They may give a fact, or something they have inferred from the information gained during the lesson.

LETTER ORIENTEERING

SUBJECT: PE. QCA UNIT: OUTDOOR AND ADVENTUROUS ACTIVITIES – UNIT 2.

LEARNING OBJECTIVE
To develop and refine orienteering skills when working in groups and on their own.

THINKING OBJECTIVE
To deduce.

THINKING SKILLS
The children will follow a map and trail to identify positions. They will deduce where the positions, or stations, marked on the map are actually located, and collect letters to spell out words, or clues – for example, 'Behind the PE shed' to indicate the position of a treasure trove. This activity could be adapted for an Easter egg hunt at the end of the Spring term.

WHAT YOU NEED
A detailed map of the school grounds, with the positions you want the children to find numbered from one to ten, or whatever system you decide to use; letters positioned at different places around the school grounds at the positions marked on the map; cards divided into squares with the numbers 1–10 across the top and empty space to write the letters collected underneath; pens.

WHAT TO DO
Set up the positions and prepare the numbers and letter markers in advance.

Before you go outside, look at the map together and identify some of the places that are marked. Ask, *Can you see the PE shed (or similar temporary building)? Can you see the posts of the fence around the perimeter? How can you tell which part of the fence the number corresponds to? Where on the building will marker number (3) be? Is it on a wall, a window or a door? How do you know?* Talk about the positions of a few of the markers in terms of the distance between the two ends of the building or fence. If you have a fence with posts, the children will be able to count along to find the corresponding post on the map. Explain to the children that at each of the ten positions marked on the map they will find letters. When they have collected all these letters correctly, and have had their card checked, they will be given a final letter.

Name									
1	2	3	4	5	6	7	8	9	10

When they put these letters in the right order, they will spell out the name of the place where the treasure (say, Easter eggs) can be found. Divide the children into groups of three or four and go over the rules: Stay together. No running ahead. Keep safe. Return promptly. Explain that if a group does not return together, they will not be given the final letter.

Go outside as a class and find one of the positions together. Make sure the children are using the clues on the map to locate the position and deduce exactly where this is. For example, the number may be between the third and fourth fence post on the right-hand side of the perimeter. Ask a group to take you there. As you approach, stop the children and ask, *Have you led me to the correct place? How do you know?*

Stand in the middle of the school grounds so that you can see where all the groups are at any time. Whisper a number to each group and let them go off a few seconds apart to find the position and locate the corresponding letter. Remind them to use the map to assist their search.

Continue sending groups to different places on the map until they have collected all the letters, checking after each one that they have the correct letter in the correct number square on their card. When they have collected all ten letters, give them any additional letters they need to work out where the treasure can be found.

On return to the classroom, enjoy the treasure together and talk about how the children managed to find each of the markers. Ask, *Did you use the map to go directly to the marker or did you go in the general direction and look around the area when you got there until you found what you were looking for?* You will know because you will have watched them closely during the practical task.

DIFFERENTIATION

Ask an additional adult to work with a group of lower attaining children. This will provide them with help to read the map and will allow them full participation, reducing the possibility of the activity being monopolised by higher attaining children.

Set up additional numbers in more obscure places for higher attaining children to locate.

WHERE NEXT

Set up other numbers and letters to solve coded messages in a different area.

ASSESSMENT

Watch the children carefully to check that they are using the maps to deduce where the number positions are located. Remind them if they do not seem to be doing this. If they are simply wandering around the grounds hoping to find the numbers, they will not be deducing the positions.

LEARNING OUTCOMES

Most children will begin to develop early orienteering skills in a safe environment and learn to use a map to deduce where items are located. Some will do this with help while others will manage independently.

FURTHER PE CHALLENGES

Word search

Set up a word search around the school grounds. Work with the children to give different features in the school grounds imaginary names. Hide letters in these places and, armed with a plan of the school grounds, give each group of children the imaginary names of the places where the hidden letters are. They will need to deduce where the places are from the position on the map, as they will be unfamiliar with the imaginary name. The letters will spell out words you want the children to learn. Organise several words for the children to find and differentiate the activity by asking them to find different words, according to their abilities.

Number search

Reorganise the numbered positions to set up a trail for the children to follow. Challenge them to deduce where each number is and to locate its position on the map. As they move from one position to another, ask them to draw the trail they are following on the map. They should start from 1 and follow the numbered positions until they get to 10. Reorganise the numbers and reposition them to make the trails different each time. You could set up the activity in a safe local park and, with additional adults to supervise, provide more challenge for the children.

ENQUIRY SKILLS

INTRODUCTION

The enquiry process is a means through which children can be fully involved in their own learning. This process gives them the opportunity to identify why they are learning something, as well as how and what. The ability to ask questions is fundamental to the development of children's independent enquiry skills. Once they are able to ask questions, the next step is to identify the right questions to suit the needs of their research requirements. These questions can only be identified if the children can note what the problem is and what they need to find out in order to solve it. Only then can they begin to plan research into a topic or area.

Too often children are presented with a ready-made set of questions and, therefore, play no part in developing the skill of asking questions themselves. The process undertaken with scientific enquiry can be applied to other subjects and is a good starting point through which to develop children's enquiry skills. Teachers of young children often start with a question in science, yet rarely do so for other subjects. By identifying questions for each unit of work in all subjects, you will be setting up the enquiry process, allowing the children to find things out for themselves and to develop their enquiry skills.

This is the start of planning their own research, which will involve them asking their own questions to start off an independent enquiry. While teachers generally model the asking of questions clearly in science to help identify a problem, enquiry or investigation (which gives the children the opportunity to plan their investigation and carry out a test), they tend not to revisit the investigation to improve ideas or refine the hypothesis, which may lead to a redefinition of the problem to make it more precise. This is the point at which children may begin to construct and ask their own questions to lead them into investigations and to conduct research, which takes their achievement beyond the average. Thinking becomes visible from this point forward.

The enquiry process is generally addressed as a whole, and the links between the skills are established easily. The activities in this chapter are planned to focus on particular aspects of the enquiry process, but at the same time recognising that these are probably set within a whole research project. It will, therefore, be difficult to see the skills on their own in all activities and the overlap between them.

The enquiry process and skills are:
⊙ asking questions
⊙ defining a problem
⊙ planning research
⊙ predicting outcomes
⊙ anticipating consequences
⊙ testing conclusions
⊙ improving ideas.

INTRODUCING ENQUIRY SKILLS

Subject and QCA unit, NLS or NNS objective	Activity title	Thinking objective	Activity	Page
English. NLS objective: To identify misspelt words in their own writing	Check your spelling	To define a problem	Identifying misspelt words independently.	63
Maths. NNS objective: To understand division as grouping or sharing	Understanding division	To define a problem and anticipate consequences	Sharing biscuits between a group of people whose number keeps changing.	63
Science. QCA unit 3B: Helping plants grow well	Green potatoes	To define a problem and find a solution	Deciding what happens when a potato is left in the light for a few days.	64
History. QCA unit 9: What was it like for children in the Second World War?	Then and now, here and there	To ask and answer questions	Noting differences between the past and present and identifying questions to find out what it was like to live through the Second World War.	65
Geography. QCA unit 7: Weather around the world	School events	To predict outcomes and anticipate consequences	Looking at weather forecasts and using the information to decide when and where to hold the school fete.	65
Design and technology. QCA unit 3C: Moving monsters	Model monsters	To plan research	Planning research into how they can make their model monsters move in the way they want.	66
ICT. QCA unit 4B: Developing images using repeating patterns	Am I symmetrical?	To anticipate consequences	Scanning and flipping images and predicting whether they are likely to look the same.	67
Art and design. QCA unit 3A: Portraying relationships	Family portrait	To define a problem	Organising family groups into different poses to fit the size of space available in a camera lens, ensuring that interest is added for the observer of the resulting photograph.	67
Music. QCA unit 8: Ongoing skills	Ghost train	To test conclusions	Deciding what effects to add to a song to make it sound scary.	68
RE. QCA unit 3E: What is faith, and what difference does it make?	I believe	To ask questions; to plan research	Planning research to identify questions in order to find out about a religious figure.	69
PE. QCA unit: Any	Sports personality	To ask questions	Asking questions to find out about a sports personality.	70

CHECK YOUR SPELLING

SUBJECT: ENGLISH. NLS OBJECTIVE: TO IDENTIFY MISSPELT WORDS IN THEIR OWN WRITING.

LEARNING OBJECTIVE
To identify misspelt words and use the information to check their own spelling.

THINKING OBJECTIVE
To define a problem.

THINKING SKILLS
In this activity, the children will look closely at words and decide whether they are spelled correctly, using previous knowledge of spelling patterns and strategies. They will define the problem of needing to find out for themselves whether words have been spelled correctly or not, and will use and ask questions about spelling rules to help them work this out and remember the correct spellings.

WHAT YOU NEED
The list of words from *Literacy Strategy* page 62 for Year 4 pupils in Term 1, 2 and 3; a list of words that the children should know, but regularly spell incorrectly (use your assessment information to identify these); words written on word cards (see What to do); whiteboard and pen.

WHAT TO DO
Write *latch* on the board and ask the children to read it. Ask, *Is it spelled correctly? How do you know? Do you know another word that sounds and looks the same?* Identify the letter string and think of other words that fit this group of spellings, such as *match, catch* and *snatch*. There are many more. Agree that identifying the letter string is one way of learning spellings – using a word that you already know how to spell to help with unknown or new words.

Write *mother* on the board and identify the onset and rhyme, (m-other). Identify other words with this rhyme, such as *other, another, brother* and *smother*. Agree that this is another way to learn spellings.

Write the word *something*, but misspell it, for example, *sumthink*. Ask, *Is this spelled correctly? What is the problem?* Define the problem further by asking, *Which bit of the word is wrong?* What can the children tell you about the way this word is structured? Ask, *Can you think of smaller words to help you with this spelling?* Revisit learning about compound words from Year 2, if necessary. Ask, *Does this knowledge help us to remember this spelling?*

Help the children to learn other compound words from the Year 4 list, using the same rules.

Give the children words written on word cards, some spelled correctly and others that are not. Words to include are *walked, jumpt, walk, tork, sometiems, today* (which cover all the strategies above) and any others from the list. Ask the children to look at each one, decide whether it is spelled correctly, and then sort them into piles according to whether they are spelled correctly or not. They should be able to give reasons for their decisions.

Challenge them to define the problem with the words that are spelled incorrectly and to ask questions to put them right.

⊙ *What is the problem?* The word is not spelled correctly.

⊙ *What must we do?* Correct the spelling.

⊙ *How can we correct the spelling?* Identify which bit is wrong.

⊙ *How can we find out how to put it right?* Decide on a suitable strategy.

Encourage them to ask questions like, *Does it have a familiar letter pattern I know? Does it have an onset and rhyme? Is it a compound word?* In addition, ask other questions to encourage them to think about the strategies they already have to spell words correctly. *Does the word sound like another word you know how to spell? Is the letter sound pattern familiar? Can you hear a smaller word inside, at the beginning or at the end? Can you see the same word inside, at the beginning or at the end of your spelling? What is the vowel sound? Does your letter string make this vowel sound?*

Finish by reinforcing the final important question, *How can we be sure that it is right?* Check the spelling in a dictionary or ask an adult.

UNDERSTANDING DIVISION

SUBJECT: MATHS. NNS OBJECTIVE: TO UNDERSTAND DIVISION AS GROUPING OR SHARING.

LEARNING OBJECTIVE
Understand that division is sharing.

THINKING OBJECTIVE
To define a problem and anticipate consequences.

THINKING SKILLS
The children will learn to share biscuits between a growing number of people who come to the door. They will solve this through sharing, and anticipating what will happen once they have more visitors than biscuits.

WHAT YOU NEED

A copy of *The Doorbell Rang* by Pat Hutchins (Econo-clad books); a large packet of biscuits and a plate.

WHAT TO DO

Read the story and talk about what is happening. Ask, *How many biscuits does the hostess start with?* (The first time you do this, you could use the number 24, as this will make the division easier.) *If she expects one visitor, how many biscuits can they each have?* As each new visitor arrives and rings the bell, anticipate what happens to the number of biscuits each person can have. Define the problem by asking, *If we have 24 biscuits and we need to share them between two visitors, how many biscuits will they have each?*

Encourage the children to break down the problem to identify the information they already have, and what they still need to find out. Say, *This will help you to decide what you need to do with the numbers to help you solve the problem.*

⦿ *What do we know?* We have 24 biscuits, two visitors and the hostess.

⦿ *What do we still need to find out?* How many biscuits they can have each.

⦿ *How will we solve the problem?* Share the biscuits between the total number of people. $24 \div 3 = 8$.

⦿ *What have we found out?* They can have eight biscuits each.

Each time a new visitor arrives, define the problem in the same way. After a few more arrivals, children will be able to define the problem themselves to identify the calculation they need to make.

Note what happens when the number of biscuits will not divide exactly – for example, by five. Change the number of visitors, if necessary, or let two visitors arrive to make the next division after four, six; and after six, eight. Ask, *What will happen when you have more visitors than biscuits? What will they need to do with the biscuits then?*

Choose different numbers of biscuits each time you listen to the story. Ask the children to work in groups to solve the problem, giving them different starting numbers of biscuits. You can adapt the number of biscuits so that lower attaining children do not have to work with numbers less than one whole. Middle and higher attaining children can divide to make fractions, while others can decide whether there will be any biscuits left over.

GREEN POTATOES

SUBJECT: SCIENCE. QCA UNIT 3B:
HELPING PLANTS GROW WELL.

LEARNING OBJECTIVE

To find a way to stop potatoes going green.

THINKING OBJECTIVE

To define a problem and find a solution.

THINKING SKILLS

The children will notice how a potato goes green if it is left in the light and define the problem to find the most suitable storage place to keep it in the best condition.

WHAT YOU NEED

Several potatoes; whiteboard, paper and pens.

WHAT TO DO

Leave a potato in the light for about two weeks, explaining to the children that you want to find out what happens to it. Some may already know that it will go green, and that, in this state, it is not wise to eat it. This is because it contains chlorophyll, which is dangerous for humans to consume in large quantities. The day before the lesson, peel a second potato and leave it open to the air to go red and starchy.

Show the children the green potato and remind them that it is no longer a good idea to eat it because it has gone green. Ask them what they think made the potato go green and list all their suggestions. Discuss the options, and decide that sunlight made this happen.

Now look at the starch that has appeared on the peeled potato. Talk about the fact that potatoes contain starch and explain how this, plus the sunlight and carbon dioxide from the air, makes a chemical called chlorophyll. This is what makes the potato go green.

Ask the children what the problem is. Discuss this until you have defined the problem to be that potatoes go green if they are left in the sunlight. Ask, *What can you do about this? How could you choose a suitable new place to store the potato? How can you find out the best place to store the potato?* Collect the children's suggestions and plan an investigation to find out.

Give groups of children a potato to leave in the place they think is best to stop it going green. Address the definition by checking with each group that their chosen place is protected from sunlight. Encourage the groups to find different places and leave potatoes there for a few days. Check them to note whether they are going green, and draw conclusions about whether each chosen storage place has been suitable. Note whether there are any other changes to the potato – perhaps it has gone soft or started to grow. Use these observations of changes to define any other problems with storing potatoes in the different places.

THEN AND NOW, HERE AND THERE

SUBJECT: HISTORY. QCA UNIT 9: WHAT WAS IT LIKE FOR CHILDREN IN THE SECOND WORLD WAR?

LEARNING OBJECTIVE
To learn what life was like for children during the Second World War.

THINKING OBJECTIVE
To ask and answer questions.

THINKING SKILLS
The children will consider what their life is like today, and will use this information to agree a set of questions that will help them to find out what life was like for children during the Second World War. They will conclude from the answers how life has changed and whether this is for the better.

WHAT YOU NEED
Large sheets of paper, whiteboards and pens; reference materials and sources to spark children's ideas and help them find answers to the questions they identify – include photos, children's accounts from the time, magazines, reference books, CD-ROMs and newspaper articles.

WHAT TO DO
Talk to the class about the things they like to do, food they like to eat, places they like to go. If you have already done a series of 'favourite things' graphs you can use this information to focus the discussion.

List the favourite things that the children do today under the following headings on the board so they can be referred to during the group work: food, toys, games, hobbies, TV programmes, music, clothes, holidays, and any others the children think of.

Ask the class to think about things that children would have done during the Second World War. Ask, *Would they have watched TV? Why not? What would their hobbies have been? How many clothes would they have had? What would these have been like? What fabrics would they have been made from? Would they have been bought from a shop or made at home? What would they have to eat? What toys would they play with? Would they be the same as today?* Wonder with the children whether there was the same range of foods available then as today.

Give each group of children one of the headings on the board and ask them to think of a set of questions on this topic to find out more about what life was like for children during the Second World War. Give them a context for the questions by telling them that it may be possible to ask an older person who was a child at this time. Let the children organise themselves to record the questions. Tell the groups that they can use any of the resources to help them think of suitable and relevant questions. They can also use their own favourite things as starting points to consider whether children liked these during the Second World War. Ask, *How can we phrase this as a question?* Monitor each group, asking questions to focus their thinking and reflecting with them on certain things.

Use some of the questions to make up a questionnaire for the children to ask older relatives or neighbours about what life was like during the Second World War. If this is not possible, find the answers in reference materials.

Draw conclusions from the answers about the effects of rationing, and other ways in which children's lives during the Second World War were different. Ask, *Would you have liked to be a child at this time, or do you prefer your life today. Why?*

SCHOOL EVENTS

SUBJECT: GEOGRAPHY. QCA UNIT 7: WEATHER AROUND THE WORLD.

LEARNING OBJECTIVE
To learn that weather predictions can be located from a range of sources.

THINKING OBJECTIVE
To predict outcomes and anticipate consequences.

THINKING SKILLS
The children will use weather forecasts from a range of sources to predict what impact the weather is likely to have on a school event, and the

consequences of this in terms of where the event will be held and what they are likely to sell.

WHAT YOU NEED
Access to weather forecast information; whiteboard and pen; paper and pens.

WHAT TO DO
A few days before a school fair or similar event, ask the children to check the weather forecast to find out what the weather is likely to be.

List all the places where the children think they could find this out, for example, Teletext, weather telephone lines, newspapers, the Internet, and TV and radio weather forecasts.

Ask different groups of children to research the weather from these different sources. Then share the information they have gathered. Ask, *What does this information tell us? Can we predict what the weather will be like from this? What sort of weather is it likely to be? Will it be wet or sunny?* If there is a reasonable chance of rain, ask the children what impact this will have on planning for the event. Agree that it may have to be moved indoors, or under some kind of shelter.

Now ask, *What if the weather is going to be extremely hot? What are the implications of this?* The children may decide that more cold drinks will be needed than hot, more ice creams may be sold and more shade will be needed. Agree all the consequences arising from the weather outlook and predict outcomes for the event.

MODEL MONSTERS

SUBJECT: DESIGN AND TECHNOLOGY. QCA UNIT 3C: MOVING MONSTERS.

LEARNING OBJECTIVE
To identify how mechanisms work, and evaluate and decide which one is best for making models move in the way they want.

THINKING OBJECTIVE
To plan research.

THINKING SKILLS
The children will consider their own designs of monsters and think about the way they want their model monster to move and look. They will then consider how to plan research to find out the best mechanism for it to do what they want.

WHAT YOU NEED
Children's designs of their moving monsters developed in a previous lesson; various kits or actual models, which move in different ways; a board or a large sheet of paper.

WHAT TO DO
Ask one of the children to show and talk about their model design. Ask questions to identify how it moves and the mechanism needed to make it work. Ask, *How do you want it to move? Does it move in a circle, up and down, or in some other way? How do you want it to look? What mechanisms will you need to make it work and look the way you want?* Record these as key questions on the board or on a large sheet of paper.

Think together how they might go about finding a solution to these questions, and talk about how they can plan their research. Share each other's ideas about what they need to find out. Ask, *Where could you look? What will you do with the information? How will you know when you have found a suitable solution?* List these ideas after the key questions above.

How do you want it to move?	A head that goes round and a neck that goes up and down.
Does it move in a circle, up and down or in some other way?	In a straight line on wheels so that it can be used as a pull-along toy.
How do you want it to look?	A large head with scary eyes and big teeth.
What mechanisms will you need to make it work and look the way you want?	Wheels and axles, a cam mechanism and an electric motor.
Where could she look?	Analyse other toys that work in the same way, experiment with commercial kits looking at their diagrams to see if there is one which will help.
What will she do with the information?	Plan how to put together the different parts of the model.
How will she dknow when she has found a suitable solution?	Trial and error.

Organise the children into groups and ask them to share their thoughts about what they need to decide about their moving monster before they can begin to make the mechanism. Ask them to list their questions, such as, *What does the monster have to do? How does it have to look? What materials can you use? Where can you find out how to make it move in the way you want? How will you make it? What could you use? What will you need to do first?* Explain that they should answer these questions to identify the materials and making process, and record these as a research plan.

Allow the children to follow their plans to explore different mechanisms and materials, then make the models using the mechanisms and materials they have identified.

Am I symmetrical?

SUBJECT: ICT. QCA UNIT 4B: DEVELOPING IMAGES USING REPEATING PATTERNS.

LEARNING OBJECTIVE
To use visual effects such as symmetry, and the 'save as' facility.

THINKING OBJECTIVE
To anticipate consequences.

THINKING SKILLS
The children will scan or download their own image into the computer and anticipate what will happen when one half is copied and flipped over to make a new image. They will predict whether this will look the same, or different. They will then carry out the task to find out whether they were right. The task can be extended by anticipating whether a third image will be produced by copying and flipping the side that was deleted in the first task. This activity also uses reasoning skills (covered in Chapter 2).

WHAT YOU NEED
Suitable software to scan and flip images, such as *Paint Shop Pro* by Jasc Software (www.jasc.com); a digital camera and photographs taken with it of the children in the class; whiteboard and pen.

WHAT TO DO
Show the children how to scan or download images of their faces from digital photographs which were taken earlier that day or the day before. Save these for later comparisons. Look at the faces and discuss whether they think these are symmetrical.

Ask, *How could you find out?* Collect children's ideas for this. Some may suggest using a mirror, which will work. Ask, *Does anyone know a way we could use a computer to find out?* Show or remind the children how to create a mirror image on a computer screen using software tools.

Ask them to predict or anticipate what they would look like if one half of their image were copied, flipped over and put together with its reflection. Ask, *Do you think you will look different?* Show them how they can cut their pictures in half, delete one half, copy the half that is left and flip the image over, putting the two halves together. Ask, *Did you anticipate correctly what you would look like? Is your face symmetrical? How different do you look?* Bring up the original photograph and compare the two. Show the children how to use the 'save as' facility so that they can keep both images for future reference.

Now ask the children to say whether the images would look the same if they deleted the other half, then copied the remaining side and flipped it over. Ask, *Who thinks it will create a third image? Who thinks it will look like the second one? Do you think the end result will look the same as the starting photo?* Carry out the task and compare the images made with the original photo and the second image. Once the idea has been established, have some more fun with the children's photos. Make some reflective copies of the top and bottom halves of photos, or combine two faces. Display these images as a 'Rogue's Gallery' for the children to guess who each one represents.

Work with other pictures and anticipate whether these will be symmetrical if one half is deleted and flipped over. Sort the pictures into two sets according to whether or not they are symmetrical when one half is flipped over.

FAMILY PORTRAIT

SUBJECT: ART AND DESIGN. QCA UNIT 3A: PORTRAYING RELATIONSHIPS.

LEARNING OBJECTIVE
To understand how to organise different groups of people to get different forms and effects.

THINKING OBJECTIVE
To define a problem.

THINKING SKILLS
The children will define the problem a photographer has when fitting an entire family group inside the camera viewfinder. They will consider the form, presentation and overall look of the photograph, and decide how successful the photographer has been in overcoming the problem. They will then take it in turns to look through a camera at a group of people and follow the definition to create different poses to show off the group to best effect, fitting them all into the available space and providing interest for the observer.

WHAT YOU NEED
A camera; various family photographs (wedding photographs are suitable for this); prints of paintings

of family portraits; school, team and class photos; cut out pictures of people; scissors; paper and pens; whiteboard and pens; adhesive.

WHAT TO DO

Look together at family wedding photographs and note the different groups represented. Discuss how these people are positioned in different poses to make sure they all are shown to advantage. Note how the bride and groom take the central pose in many photographs. Ask, *Are all the people standing? What about the photograph of the whole family? How did the photographer fit everyone in? Who are the most important people in the photograph? How do we know from the place where they are positioned?*

Define the problems that the photographer had in taking this photograph of a large group.

⊙ *How many people do I have?* Count them.

⊙ *How can I fit everyone in?* Organise people into rows.

⊙ *How can I make sure that they will all be seen?* Arrange them according to height.

⊙ *How can I keep the focus on the most important people?* Position the bride and groom centrally.

⊙ *How can I keep the photograph interesting?* Put the people into some kind of order to give the photograph form.

Agree on how successful the photographer was, relating this to how well he defined the problems he was likely to encounter before he started, and had formulated a plan to overcome the difficulties identified.

Now look at a class or school photograph. Remind the children how they were put in height order before being placed in their positions by the photographer. Ask, *Why did the photographer do this? Did they want to make the photograph balanced? Where did the teacher sit? Why did they sit in the middle?* If there is more than one adult, they are likely to be at either side of the standing group. Discuss the way the photograph has been composed and the difficulties the photographer may have had in fitting everyone in. Follow the definition and identify how the photographer overcame the problems of fitting everyone into the picture.

At this point, let the children take turns to look through the camera at a group of ten children to see how difficult it is to fit everyone inside the viewfinder. Ask, *How can you rearrange the group to make sure they all fit in?* Swap the groups around until they have all seen how difficult this can be.

Divide the children into groups and allocate each group one of the following tasks. Give one group the task of arranging a photograph of, for example, the school football team. Ask them to take photographs of different arrangements so that they can evaluate these and choose the one they like best. If possible, ask another adult to supervise this activity, questioning them whether they can fit the group into the picture, whether they need to stand farther back or ask the children in the picture to get closer together.

Work with another group to look at some prints of painted family portraits. Talk about how the artist has portrayed these, and note the different poses of the different family members. Ask, *What are they doing? Where are they standing? Are any sitting?* Express ideas about how the artist could have organised the portrait. Ask, *Are all family members included? Who is the most important or central character? Is this clear?*

Ask another group to look at pictures such as team, class and school photographs, and define the problems the photographer faced in each case.

Give a further group of children cut-out pictures of people and a piece of paper, and ask them to arrange the cut-outs into a posed photograph. Below the finished pose, ask them to list the problems they had fitting all the people into the space, and how they overcame them.

Bring the groups back together to share their different experiences. Allow them to try out each other's activities, if time permits.

GHOST TRAIN

SUBJECT: MUSIC. QCA UNIT 8: ONGOING SKILLS.

LEARNING OBJECTIVE

To learn how to perform songs that use musical elements to create certain moods and effects.

Thinking objective
To test conclusions.

Thinking skills
The children will learn a song and decide how the musical elements are used to create a frightening effect. They will suggest changes to these, anticipating beforehand whether this will make the song more or less frightening. They will then test their ideas.

What you need
A copy of the song 'The Ghost Train' by Peter Canwell from *The Multi-Coloured Music Bus* (Collins).

What to do

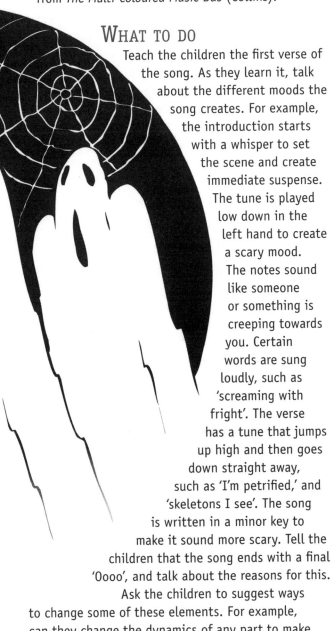

Teach the children the first verse of the song. As they learn it, talk about the different moods the song creates. For example, the introduction starts with a whisper to set the scene and create immediate suspense. The tune is played low down in the left hand to create a scary mood. The notes sound like someone or something is creeping towards you. Certain words are sung loudly, such as 'screaming with fright'. The verse has a tune that jumps up high and then goes down straight away, such as 'I'm petrified,' and 'skeletons I see'. The song is written in a minor key to make it sound more scary. Tell the children that the song ends with a final 'Oooo', and talk about the reasons for this.

Ask the children to suggest ways to change some of these elements. For example, can they change the dynamics of any part to make it more dramatic, such as a quieter part for 'he sits upon my knee'? Ask, *Will this make the song more or less scary? Can we change the tempo of some parts of the song, such as slowing down the piano creeping accompaniment between the chorus and verse, or*

adding sound effects with musical instruments? Would a repeating, creeping rhythm make the song sound scarier? Would it be more effective if we added it all the way through the chorus and verse, or just during the chorus? *Try these out to test the children's ideas. Agree whether or not each suggested change makes the song more or less scary.

Divide the children into eight groups and give four groups verse two and the others verse three. Let them explore changing the dynamics to add atmosphere and effects to the song. After about ten minutes, ask each group to perform their verse to the rest of the class and note how effective their changes are. Choose to keep all the suggested changes that make the song more frightening, and discard those that the children agree do not.

I BELIEVE

SUBJECT: RE. QCA UNIT 3E: WHAT IS FAITH, AND WHAT DIFFERENCE DOES IT MAKE?

69

Learning objective
To research a famous religious figure.

Thinking objective
To ask questions; to plan research.

Thinking skills
The children will identify questions to reflect the kind of information they want to find out about a famous religious figure. You can choose anyone, from any faith that fits the needs of your school population.

What you need
A range of books and newspaper articles that include pictures, stories and accounts of the person being researched; CD-ROMs and access to the Internet; whiteboard or large sheet of paper and pens.

What to do
Introduce the religious figure to the children. Tell them his or her name. Ask, *Has anyone heard of this person?* If they have, ask them to say what they know. If not, ask the children why they think this person is thought to be particularly religious. Tell them the religion the person is associated with. Ask the children to identify key areas they could research about this character, such as their religion, when and where they were born, what they are noted for, and why they are remembered today. List key words (such as name, place of birth, religion, and so on) that the children should use for their research.

Divide the children into groups, and give them ten minutes to identify a list of questions that will help them focus on the information they want to collect about the famous person. Share the questions and note those that are useful for the research. Collate a list of these on the board or a large sheet of paper for all the children to refer to. These will vary depending on the children's ideas and the individual involved, but are likely to include questions like, *What did this person become famous for? How do we know? Did they have anything named after them? Why was this? Where did they live while carrying out their work? Did they write anything famous?*

Still working in groups, ask the children to locate relevant information in the range of resources by scanning for answers to the research questions. If individual children research answers for different questions, this will make the task shorter. They can then share what they have found out.

Ask the children to write a short biographical paragraph about the person to share with the rest of the class. Ask, *What have you found out about the person? What can we learn from them? Does their life and behaviour help us to think about the way we should lead our lives? How does this make us better people?*

In groups, use the questions to research another figure and share the information with the rest of the class. Note all the things that these people have in common with each other that we can learn from, such as learning to live in harmony together, or believing in one God. Note any differences and discuss why these occur.

Sports personality

Subject: PE. QCA unit: Any.

Learning objective
To find out about a famous sports personality and think about their contribution to their sport.

Thinking objective
To ask questions.

Thinking skills
This activity links to ICT, and the children are expected to identify the questions for their own research. They will then use a range of evidence to find out what they can about the chosen person.

What you need
Access to the Internet; video extracts of sporting events; reference books, sporting magazines and accounts from newspapers; paper and pens.

What to do
Brainstorm the names of all the famous sports personalities that the children can think of. Prompt them by showing video extracts and/or reading simple articles from newspapers and magazines about recent sporting events, if necessary. For each one they name, ask them to say what their sport is and how they think they keep fit.

As a class, choose one personality and identify all the things that the children already know. For example, if you are thinking about David Beckham, the children may say he is a footballer who began his career with Manchester United and has captained England. Ask them to identify what they would like to find out about this person.

Turn their ideas into questions (for example, *Does he play any other sports in his spare time?*) and record them on the board or a large sheet of paper. Talk about key words in the questions (such as the person's name and the sport they take part in) that may be useful when they are looking things up in books or on the Internet.

Organise the children into friendship or interest groups to identify questions about their favourite sports personality – this should not be the person considered by the class group. Encourage them to follow the same process: to identify what they already know, then what they would like to know, and finally phrase these thoughts as questions. Ask them to underline the key words that might help them find the information they are looking for and list the range of information sources they intend to use.

Carry out the activity and let the groups share what they have found out. Ask them to present their information in the following format:

The person we have chosen to find out about plays... We chose this person because... We wanted to know... The questions we have identified are... We are going to look...

EXTENDING ENQUIRY SKILLS

Subject and QCA unit, NLS or NNS objective	Activity title	Thinking objective	Activity	Page
English. NLS objective: To prepare for factual research by reviewing what is known, what is needed, what is available and where one might search	What can I find out?	To ask questions to inform and structure research	Identifying questions to plan research.	72
Maths. NNS objective: To suggest suitable units and measuring equipment to measure mass and capacity.	How much?	To define a problem	Suggesting and finding suitable equipment to measure with.	73
Science. QCA unit 4E: Friction	Sticking power	To test conclusions; to improve ideas	Testing various surfaces for sticking power and using the information to improve ideas.	75
History. QCA unit 6: Why have people invaded and settled in Britain in the past?	Anglo-Saxon fashions	To define a problem	Thinking about how and from what Anglo-Saxons made their clothes.	76
Geography. QCA unit 10: A village in India	A different place to live	To ask questions	Making a list of questions to direct enquiries about a different place.	78
Design and technology. QCA unit 4A: Money containers	Purses	To identify and ask questions to plan research	Planning research into designs and materials used for making different purses.	80
ICT. QCA unit 3E: E-mail	Location, location	To ask appropriate questions	Sending e-mails to find out where someone is on holiday.	81
Art and design. QCA unit 3B: Investigating pattern	Dishy leaves	To anticipate consequences	Making leaf dishes from clay, anticipating and overcoming problems.	82
Music. QCA unit 12: Dragon scales	Pentatonic scales	To ask questions to identify songs which use the pentatonic scale	Identifying songs that use five notes.	83
RE. QCA unit 4D: What religions are represented in our neighbourhood?	Religious importance	To ask questions	To identify questions to ask to help them learn about different religions in their own community and further afield.	85
PE. QCA unit: Dance activities – unit 4	Delhi dancing	To improve ideas	Moving to the beat and rhythm of Indian music after watching Indian dances to learn moves.	86

What can I find out?

Subject: English. NLS objective: To prepare for factual research by reviewing what is known, what is needed, what is available and where one might search.

Learning objective

To develop skills of scanning and skimming for information, using questions to inform searches.

Thinking objective

To ask questions to inform and structure research.

Thinking skills

The children will use a sequence of questions to help them structure the research process. They will follow this process to locate information from different sources. They will begin to use skimming and scanning techniques to find certain key words and read around these carefully to gain the information they need. This activity investigates an historical topic, but would be equally effective for any other topic you are studying in school.

What you need

A collection of books for your chosen subject, including a Big Book version for the class text-level work (this can be linked to any current class topic); CD-ROMs and access to the Internet; paper and pens.

What to do

Show the class the front cover of your Big Book. Ask the children, *What is it about? How do you know? How else can you find out what sort of information the book contains? What do you know about this topic already? What else would you like to find out?* For one or two questions the children raise, look in the Contents and/or Index to locate the information in the book. Skim and scan the writing and illustrations to find the key words in their question. For example, if the children say they would like to know what weapons the Roman soldiers carried, identify and scan for possible key words such as weapons, sword or shield.

Tell the class that you want to find out about Roman soldiers. Ask, *Where should we start our research? Should we look in books, on the Internet, or ask someone? How can we go about finding out about Roman soldiers?* Collect the children's ideas and give a positive response to each one before asking how this particular information source will help. How do you know it will help? Relate the children's suggestions to the questions they must be asking in their heads: *David said that this book will help because it has a picture of a Roman soldier on the front, so he must have asked himself a question like 'Does the book have a relevant picture on the cover?'*

Explain to the children how important it is to structure research so that you are not wasting time reading everything about a subject, but can focus on exactly what you are looking for. Ask, *Are we happy with general information or do we want to find out something in particular?* Tell them that one way to make research more focused and specific is to follow a list of questions.

The first question should always be:
◉ *What do we already know?* This will help to identify key words. Write this question on the board.
◉ *What do we still want to know or find out?* List these things as phrases.
◉ *What questions will help us find out these things?* Identify one or two questions to help focus the research.
◉ *What are the key words that will guide our research?* List some of these from the questions you previously identified.
◉ *Where can we find references to these key words?* Relate this to the Index and Contents pages in books, to CD-ROMs and the Internet.
◉ *When we have found the page, how will we find the key words quickly?* Relate this to the skills of scanning and skimming.
◉ *If we find the key word, what should we do next?* This will depend on the research context, but will usually mean either printing off the page from the Internet or CD-ROM, or making notes from a book.
◉ *How can we present what we have found out?* Describe the different ways that information can be presented.

Explain to the children that you have just identified a list of questions which will provide a structure for the research. Follow the sequence to show the children how this will work. For example, for *We want to find out what Roman soldiers wear*, start by rephrasing this as a question:
◉ *What do Roman soldiers wear?*
◉ *What are the key words?*
◉ *Can they be found in the Index or Contents page?*
◉ *Can you scan and skim the text to find the relevant words?*
◉ *What have you found out?*
◉ *How can you present this?*

Organise the children into small groups or pairs, giving each group or pair a different question to research. Ask them to follow the research plan to find answers to their question. Suggest that they identify the key words, then locate these and scan for information. Ask them to find at least three facts in response to their question by looking in different sources of information. This will allow them to practise and develop the skills. Share the facts at the end of the lesson and evaluate how useful the children found the plan in directing their research.

DIFFERENTIATION

Work with the less able children in a group with CD-ROMs to show them the similarities with book Index and Contents pages. Explain how these are organised and how they would look like a book if the information were printed off.

Ask more able children to use encyclopedias, CD-ROMs and the Internet to locate the information they need, using questions, general headings and key words to help structure their research.

WHERE NEXT

Extend the research to collect information about other aspects of Roman Britain. Let the children organise this for themselves, following the structure of the research plan. Allocate different questions to different groups of children.

ASSESSMENT

Assess how well the children identify the questions they need to help them sequence their research. Note those who need help during the activity to help them structure this more precisely.

LEARNING OUTCOMES

Most children will learn how to structure research through asking questions to guide the process. Some will require help, while others will be sufficiently confident to apply this learning to other research projects as well.

FURTHER ENGLISH CHALLENGES

Key word questions

Give the children a theme to research and ask them to think of a series of questions to help direct and structure their research. They will need to decide what they already know to help them consider what they would like to find out. Ask them to underline the key words in their questions, which will help them focus and locate the information they need.

Index and contents

Give the children a set of questions about different aspects of a theme. Ask them to organise these into a contents page of general information that could be used as chapter headings. Identify the key words within the questions and organise these into an index in alphabetical order.

HOW MUCH?

SUBJECT: MATHS. NNS OBJECTIVE: TO SUGGEST SUITABLE UNITS AND MEASURING EQUIPMENT TO MEASURE MASS AND CAPACITY.

LEARNING OBJECTIVE

To learn how to read scales accurately.

THINKING OBJECTIVE

To define a problem.

THINKING SKILLS

The children will think about the problem they face and, by defining this, will identify the relevant unit of measure, and the measuring equipment they need to use to solve the problem.

WHAT YOU NEED

Measuring equipment to measure mass and capacity to the nearest 10g (such as electronic scales), 25g (such as kitchen scales) and 50ml (such as measuring spoons); a recipe for a cake or biscuits like this one:

Viennese Cherry Cakes
225g plain flour
3 tbsp custard powder
60g sugar
175g butter
150ml double cream
Glacé cherries for decoration

WHAT TO DO

Revisit the children's knowledge and understanding of the relationship between litres and millilitres, grams and kilograms as a class discussion. Revise these, and their abbreviations, as necessary so that the children have a secure understanding of these measures before continuing with the activity.

Explain to the children that you want to make some small cakes. Read the recipe for Viennese cherry cakes (or the one you have chosen) and interpret the numbers. Ask, *What does the recipe say you need to make these cakes?*

Look at each of the listed quantities and ask the children whether these indicate mass or capacity. Identify each measure like this where you can. Note any measures that are not precise, such as 3 tablespoons of custard powder. Define the problem with the children:

◉ *How much does this mean precisely?*
◉ *What problem do we have with this particular measure?*
◉ *What if we do not have a tablespoon?*
◉ *What do we need to do to find out how much a tablespoon holds exactly?*

Show the children the possible measuring equipment they could use to resolve this problem. Repeat this with other spoonful measurements if you wish. Agree that by using a measuring spoon, the measurements will be more precise.

Together, identify the measuring equipment you need to measure each of the quantities in your recipe precisely. Gather these together and look at the scale on each one. Ask, for example, *If we want to measure out 225 grams of flour, would the kitchen scales be all right for this? How does this scale help us to measure the quantities?* Measure out 225 grams of flour and show the children how the kitchen scales are suitable for this measurement because the scale is graduated in 25-gram intervals. Next, consider a quantity that cannot be measured so easily on the kitchen scales – for example, 60 grams of sugar. Try to find 60 grams on the kitchen scales. Recognise that it will be difficult to weigh 60 grams precisely on these scales, and discuss the need to find measuring equipment that will deal with all the required measurements before starting to prepare the recipe. Show the children the electronic scales and note how these are graduated in 10-gram intervals. They are therefore better for weighing out amounts in 10-gram multiples.

What about equipment for measuring capacity? How are these graduated? Are they all the same, or are the units at different intervals? For example, some pieces of equipment may be marked off in 50-millilitre intervals, while others may be in 250-millilitre intervals. Look carefully at these.

Set up different group activities for the children to do during the week where they measure different quantities, using a variety of scales to read the units. Organise a different group at a time to prepare and cook a recipe, identifying for themselves the equipment they need for the different quantities.

DIFFERENTIATION

Lower attaining children should measure quantities in grams to the nearest half or quarter of a kilogram and relate this to 250 and 500 grams respectively. They should also measure liquid in half or quarter litres.

Higher attaining children should be asked to convert grams to kilograms, and so on. They must define the problem they have when the quantities in the recipe are presented in kilograms and the scales on the weighing equipment are in grams.

WHERE NEXT

Repeat the activities for other recipes. Expect the children to identify the measuring equipment they will need to measure the given quantities.

Organise activities where the children need to measure how much different containers hold in grams and millilitres. Ask them to define the problem by asking, *What do you know? What do you need to know? What do you need to find out? How will you do this?*

ASSESSMENT

Assess how well the children define the problem of reading the different types of scales and use this knowledge to read the measures accurately.

LEARNING OUTCOMES

Most children will define the problems associated with the different types of measuring equipment and the way the measures are graduated on the scales of different equipment.

FURTHER MATHS CHALLENGES

Drinks for all

Set the children a problem to find out how much water they need to give everyone in the class a certain size of drink. Ask them to define the problem by identifying what they already know, what they need to find out, what they need to use, how they will use this and how they will set about finding out.

50-gram puzzle

Set the children the following problem:

You only have weighing scales that balance gram weights with the ingredients. You need to measure 200 grams, but you only have one 50-gram weight and one 250-gram weight. What is the problem and how are you going to solve it?

STICKING POWER

SUBJECT: SCIENCE. QCA UNIT 4E: FRICTION.

LEARNING OBJECTIVE

To learn that friction is a rubbing force that creates heat.

THINKING OBJECTIVES

To test conclusions; to improve ideas.

THINKING SKILLS

The children will hold a tug-of-war competition to form ideas about what to wear to win the competition. They will test out their conclusions and improve their ideas by changing what they wear on their hands and feet. More able children will find the best place to hold the contest to provide more sticking power so that they do not slide forward.

WHAT YOU NEED

A strong rope or ropes; gloves; non-slip footwear; a suitable place, such as the playground, field or hall, large enough for the children to carry out the activity; whiteboard and pen; paper and pens.

WHAT TO DO

Monitor the activity very closely and make sure the children know the rules before they start. Organise them into pairs that are fairly well matched in strength.

Tell the children that you want to hold a tug-of-war to find out who has the greatest pulling power. Help them to decide the rules together. These may include:

◉ No more than four in each team.
◉ Do not wrap the rope around your hands or any other parts of your body.
◉ No sudden pulls on the rope to drag the opposing team over.
◉ Only pull when an adult is holding the centre of the rope and says it is safe to pull.
◉ Do not let go of the rope.

Demonstrate how you want the children to carry out the competition. Choose two sensible children and ask them to hold the ends of the rope. Remind them of the agreed rules and check these are followed. Hold the centre of the rope yourself so that you can hold the tension, control the pull and prevent anyone from falling over if one child lets go of the rope.

Tell the tuggers to take the strain and pull. Ask the other children in the class to watch. Ask, *What is happening to the tuggers' feet? Are they sliding forward?* After about half a minute, ask the two children to stop and look at their hands. Ask, *What do they feel like? Are they warm?* Ask the children to predict what will happen if they continue to pull the rope. Ask them, *Will your hands get sore? Why?*

Talk about friction at this point and identify where it has an effect in the tug-of-war. Ask, *What would happen if you did the tug of war in your socks? Why would you slide forward? Does this increase or decrease the friction? Can you think of ways to increase the friction between the rope and your hands, but to decrease the friction to stop your hands getting sore? Can you think of a way to increase the friction between the floor and your feet, to stop yourselves sliding forward?*

Organise the children into groups of four and ask them to list their suggestions on how they can reduce and increase friction in each case. Let them plan an investigation to find either the best shoes or gloves and then carry this out. Go round the groups questioning their ideas. Ask, *What types of shoes have you chosen to test? Will they increase the friction and stop you sliding forward? How do you know? Which shoes do you think will be the most effective? What will you do to find out? How many times will you test out each type of shoe? Will one team always wear the same type of shoe and one team change theirs? Which gloves will be best to wear to increase friction with the rope, but reduce friction on the hands? What types can you test out? How will you do this? How will you measure this? Do you think the thickest gloves will reduce the friction between the rope and hands but increase the friction between the rope and gloves?*

Let the children work in groups of eight to follow their plan and test out their conclusions. Ask one or two groups to test out the effectiveness of the shoes, while two other groups test the gloves. You will need additional adult rope-holders to monitor the practical test carefully and control the safety.

At the end of the activity, look at the results and draw conclusions about which shoes and gloves are best for stopping the team sliding forward and preventing hands from becoming sore. Ask, *What evidence is there to support this? What is special about these shoes? Whose hands are least sore? Is it because of the gloves you are wearing?*

Encourage the children to clarify the conclusions they have reached: 'The trainers have most grip because they beat the school shoes, and the school shoes beat all the other types.' 'The leather gloves are best because our hands did not get hot and the rope did not slip through them.'

Differentiation
Work with the lower attaining children as they plan the investigation in their groups, and prompt them with ideas about the types of shoes and/or gloves they could try out. Ask them to say which they think will be most effective, and why. They can then join mixed ability groups to carry out the tests and make any improvements. Higher attaining children should be encouraged to think about the surface on which the tug-of-war is best carried out. Ask, *Which surface has the greatest friction? How do you know?*

Where next
Set up an investigation where the children try to pick up a range of objects made from different materials, some of which are very slippery. Encourage them to test out conclusions and improve their ideas about friction.

Assessment
Observe the children as they test out their conclusions, and watch how they use the information they have gained to make improvements to their footwear and gloves to increase the friction and prevent them slipping. These children will have developed a good understanding of friction.

Learning outcomes
Most children will understand how to test out their ideas and make improvements to stop themselves slipping forward.

Further science challenges
Cotton reel challenge
Make cotton reel tanks with cotton reels and rubber band winders. Challenge the children to make them climb up a ramp.

Drinks bottle climbers
Make other tanks with bottles. These will have a greater surface area touching the slope and, therefore, reduced friction. Challenge the children to improve their ideas by getting these to climb up a slippery slope.

Anglo-Saxon fashions

Subject: History. QCA unit 6: Why have people invaded and settled in Britain in the past?

Learning objective
To learn that clothing was produced very differently in Anglo-Saxon times.

Thinking objective
To define a problem.

Thinking skills
This activity covers a series of lessons in which the children will define the problems that Anglo-Saxons met at each part of the process of making their clothes. They will begin by considering how, and from what materials, clothes are made today. They will determine which fabrics are made from natural, and which from man-made materials, before relating this to those available in Anglo-Saxon times. They will think about how colours are produced in modern clothing, and how clothes are stitched and embroidered. Finally, they will consider all these processes to define the problems Anglo-Saxons met when making their clothes, before trying to make things themselves following the same processes.

What you need
Pictures or examples of modern and Saxon clothing; untreated and washed sheep's wool; simple equipment for carding, spinning and weaving as outlined in the activity (you may need to borrow this from an educational museum); large sheets of paper and pens.

WHAT TO DO

Start the first session by looking at modern clothing to identify:

- ⊙ the materials from which the fabrics are made
- ⊙ the way they have been woven, knitted, stitched and joined
- ⊙ the likely machinery that has been used in this process.

Organise the children into four groups to each examine one of the different items of clothing. Ask them to answer questions about the type of fabric, whether it is made from natural materials or is man-made, how the fabric has been made, how the pieces have been stitched together, how the colours have been printed and the range of machinery and tools that could have been used in the process. Go round the groups as they discuss their item and talk about the manufacture, the type of material and how the finished item is decorated, and whether it is embroidered. Ask each group to share the materials, ways of production, the stitching and machinery used with the rest of the class.

Now look at pictures or reproduced items of clothing from Saxon times. Compare these with modern clothes. Ask the children, *How are the styles different? How are the materials different? Are the colours the same? What about fastenings? Are they the same or different? Do the Saxon clothes all look the same? How are they different from modern styles?* Think about why modern clothes are more varied. Complete a chart to note the similarities and differences between Saxon and modern clothes.

Begin a second session by telling the children that they are going to imagine they are Saxons and try to make some fabric for clothes, just as the Saxons would have done. Use the information gained from analysing the modern clothing to define the problems that people who lived in Saxon times would encounter when they made their clothes. Think about the difficulties they would have faced finding materials from which to make the clothes, how they would have woven, stitched and joined the materials, and the tools they would have used in their production. For each part of the process, define the problems the Saxons would have faced.

Hypothesise what the raw materials would look like. Ask, *How would they go about preparing the material to make it suitable for making fabric?* Show

the children the untreated wool and ask them what problems they would anticipate with this. Allow them to make suggestions, but make sure that they note the smell, the oily texture and the fact that the wool sticks together. This makes it difficult to work into thread or fabric, as well as having too much dirt and oil and an unpleasant smell. Once you have identified the negative things about the wool, define the problems:

- ⊙ the wool is dirty and smelly, and therefore needs washing
- ⊙ it sticks together and needs untangling.

Compare the untreated wool with some that has been washed. Then, define the problems that Saxons would have faced separating the fibres. Show the children how to separate the fibres of the washed wool by carding. Once the wool is soft and fluffy, demonstrate how it is much easier to spin into threads. Tell them how the Saxons would have done this by suspending a spindle from the wool to stretch out the fibres, and spinning the spindle round. Throughout the demonstration, consider the amount of work that went into the process of preparation and why this had to be followed. Record the problems they would have encountered for each part of the process on a large sheet of paper.

Organise the children into groups for the next part of the lesson. Ask them to consider the difficulties and define the problems Saxons would have faced when spinning and weaving the wool. Move around the groups, ensuring they consider the colour of the thread. Ask, *Is it always off-white? What is the problem with this?* Agree that the clothes would always be a dirty white colour and would show dirt easily. Explain that the wool would have been dyed. Continue to define the problem by thinking about how the thread would have been coloured, as there would have been no commercial dyes at that time. Ask, *What could the Saxons have used instead?* Collect the children's ideas and then tell them how they used natural materials like berries, vegetable skins and nettles to dye the wool different colours. Explain the limited number of colours that could be produced in this way, mainly reds, greens, browns, yellows and oranges. Compare these with how we make dyes today. *Ask, Do we use other things?*

When considering how the wool was woven into cloth, talk about how machinery is used today to weave cloth. Ask, *How would Saxons have carried out this process, and what problems would they have encountered?*

In a final session, use some wool to weave fabrics on a card loom and use simple stitches to join pieces together to make small items of clothing. Review the children's simple designs and think about all the problems they have met. Consider the problems the Saxons would have faced stitching the material into shape. Ask, *Did they have needles? What would they have been made from? How easy would it have been to stitch the fabrics? Did they stitch the fabric?* Think about the machinery we have today and how this helps us in the manufacture of clothes. Ask, *Would this have been available then? What would the people have used instead, if anything?* What conclusions can the children draw from this information in terms of the style and variety of Saxon clothing?

Conclude with the children why Saxon clothing used simple styles and was joined in simple ways. Ask, *Why did many clothes look the same?*

DIFFERENTIATION

With lower attaining children, use just two items of clothing for your initial comparison – perhaps a Saxon tunic and a modern dress. Talk to them about whether boys and girls wore the same, or different, types of clothing. Note similarities and differences between them before defining how each item was made, detailing the materials, stitching, machinery and tools as above. Define together the problems that the Saxons would encounter in their manufacture.

Invite higher attaining children to research the range of fabrics available today and those at the time of the Saxons. Challenge them to define the problem of making clothing with other types of substances, such as hemp and other plant materials.

WHERE NEXT

This activity could be set within a Viking and Roman clothing context. Compare the differences in the styles and materials of the clothing and think about the processes that each race would have followed. List the problems they would have encountered that we have now overcome.

Look at how clothes are manufactured today, and think about the problems that the children would face if they had to make these for themselves.

ASSESSMENT

Assess how well the children understand the problems that people in the past would encounter in carrying out a simple task such as making a dress or tunic to wear. Note those who can define the problems at each stage of manufacture, and relate this to the types of materials and the tools and machinery available today that were not then, and the different colours that can be used today to decorate the fabrics. Note those who draw conclusions about the styles of clothing worn in the past, in terms of the facilities that were available at that time.

LEARNING OUTCOMES

Most children will understand the problems Saxon people faced in the manufacture of their clothing and why the styles had to be so simple.

FURTHER HISTORY CHALLENGES
Saxon jewellery

Look at the range of jewellery worn today and think about its purpose. Think about how each piece is made and the equipment available today to do this. Then look at pictures of Saxon jewellery and think about how it was made. Ask, *What problems would the jewellers have had to overcome? How did they make the different pieces of jewellery? For what purpose were they made?* Define the problems that the Saxons would have met and use this thinking to find out how they overcame these problems.

Homes and houses

Look at pictures of Saxon buildings and houses. Discuss the materials used and the way they have been constructed. Ask the children to work in groups to define the problems that Saxons would have faced in their construction. List these on a sheet of paper. Compare the children's ideas.

A DIFFERENT PLACE TO LIVE

SUBJECT: GEOGRAPHY. QCA UNIT 10: A VILLAGE IN INDIA.

LEARNING OBJECTIVE

To collect information about a place from pictures and maps.

THINKING OBJECTIVE

To ask questions.

THINKING SKILLS

The children will look closely at pictures and maps of a contrasting area to their own locality and make a list of questions to direct their enquiry about the features, land use and economic activities. They will pair these statements with those about their own location, and note the similarities and differences between the two areas to identify geographical pattern and processes.

WHAT YOU NEED

Pictures, photographs, maps, books and Internet access to sites that have information about your chosen area (The QCA document uses the example of Chembakolli, but you can use a village in any developing country or area. ActionAid has packs, and you may find alternative information from organisations such as Plan International.); large sheets of paper and pens.

WHAT TO DO

Look at one picture of your chosen contrasting area together and ask the children to say what they can see. Make two lists on a large sheet of paper of the physical and human features. Depending on your chosen area, these might be fields, hills, mountains, rivers, lakes, houses, factories, churches, parks, and so on. The list of possibilities is endless. Take one feature at a time and break this down into precise descriptions about the size, shape, location and material from which it is made. Rephrase the descriptions as questions and list them on a sheet of paper. For example, for the buildings ask, *What buildings can you see? Are there lots of houses? What material has been used to build them? Do they have windows? What else do you notice about them?* Encourage some children to take this further by asking whether there are any clues about the type of fuel used, for example chimneys or exhaust pipes. Ask, *How are the houses heated? How many rooms do you think there are in each one? What is the decoration likely to be like? How would food be cooked?*

Look at a map or plan of your contrasting area and note whether the same features are included. Ask, *Are there any features on the map that are not in the photograph?* Explain that this may be the case, because the photograph is a small snapshot, while the map shows the features of the whole area.

Organise the children into groups, give them a map and picture of the area, and ask them to think of a series of similar questions about one of the other features. They should consider what they can see and what this tells them before phrasing their thoughts as questions. Challenge them to think of non-literal questions that can be answered through the picture, such as, *What do you think you will hear, or smell?*

Share the questions with the rest of the class at the end of the lesson, letting them give you the answers by looking at the map or the pictures. Ask,

How do the questions help us to find out about the way people live in this place, for example, whether there are shops in the vicinity, what religion they belong to, whether the children go to school, the jobs people do? What facts have we found out about the area so far from the questions we have raised?

DIFFERENTIATION

Encourage higher attaining children to ask precise and focused questions about a particular aspect, including non-literal questions, which start to relate the information they want to the way people live. For example, *Are there any cars? Is there a bus stop?* This will lead the children to infer that the people do not travel to work by road. Give lower attaining children a set of questions to focus their observations of the pictures and map.

WHERE NEXT

Use similar questions to find out about any other contrasting location of the children's own choice, as an independent activity.

Compare the new area with one in another part of the world. Identify the similarities, too.

ASSESSMENT

Assess how well the children refine their questions to inform their research. Which children ask precise and focused questions, and which ask questions of a more general nature?

LEARNING OUTCOMES

Most children will be able to ask questions about a locality using pictures for evidence. Some will define these more precisely and begin to relate them to the way people live their lives.

FURTHER GEOGRAPHY CHALLENGES

City life

Ask the children to compose questions that will help them to find out about a large city in India. They can evaluate the questions to identify any that are similar to those used in the main activity, and any which will help them to research and compare this with a large city in England (possibly the place where the children live, or a large city nearby). This will provide them with a greater challenge, as some of the differences will not be so great.

Indian summer

Consider the climate in India and identify a series of questions that will help the children find out how it differs from the weather in England. Identify questions that will note the significance of this in terms of the impact of climate on growing crops, getting from one place to another and keeping cool.

PURSES

SUBJECT: DESIGN AND TECHNOLOGY. QCA UNIT 4A: MONEY CONTAINERS.

LEARNING OBJECTIVE
To understand the importance of designing a product before beginning to make it.

THINKING OBJECTIVE
To identify and ask questions to plan research.

THINKING SKILLS
The children will think about how they can research the full range of purse designs and manufacture. They will learn how important this research is in designing their own purses, and in helping them to think about the materials they will use and how they will join the materials. They will also consider the importance of a high standard of finishing off.

WHAT YOU NEED
A large sheet of paper and pens; access to the Internet; mail-order catalogues and brochures.

WHAT TO DO
Explain to the children that you want to find out all you can about purses to help them to design one of their own. Ask, *How can we start our research? What do we need to know and where can we look?*

Identify the stages of good research with the children and make a list of this sequence. Ask questions until you have a list similar to this one.

- *What are we trying to find out?*
- *What questions can we ask?*
- *Where can we look? Where would we find purses?*
- *Will there be ideas on the Internet? What key word would we use to set up a search? How would this help?*
- *How can we locate what we need in the books and web pages we have found?*
- *Can we use pictures and photographs?*
- *Can we send a letter to parents asking for the loan of purses and money containers? What will we say?*
- *How will we know when we have found what we are looking for?*
- *What will we do when we have collected our purses? What do we need to find out? What questions will we ask?*

Help the children follow the research plan in smaller groups to find pictures and actual purses to analyse. Ask one group to write a letter to parents asking them to lend their unwanted purses to the school, reminding them to put their name on a label inside their purse first. Ask another group to look for purses on the Internet, while a third can look in mail-order catalogues and brochures.

Once you have collected a range of purses of different types, themes and materials, help the children to identify a second set of questions to help them consider the size, the number of compartments, the fastenings and the material from which the purses are made. Ask, *Do any have a theme? Do they have a handle or chain? How are wallets different to purses? How do they close? Are there any parts that are three-dimensional?*

Help the children to use the questions to design their own purses. Label the designs as appropriate.

DIFFERENTIATION
Challenge higher attainers to design a themed purse by finding a suitable picture to copy from the Internet – a ladybird or a bumblebee, for example. Plan research into how they can create the three main body parts and attach different pieces as wings or antennae. Give less able children one type of purse around which to plan their research – perhaps a purse decorated with stickers rather than themed in shape or style. Set up a series of questions about the size, colour, material and shape, and how the purse closes.

WHERE NEXT
Design and make the purses, taking care to complete them to a good quality finish.

ASSESSMENT
Question children as they plan and design purses to assess whether they understand the research process.

LEARNING OUTCOMES
Most children will understand how to plan research and the steps that this involves. They will understand the importance of this planning in the designing stage of the design and technology process.

FURTHER DESIGN AND TECHNOLOGY CHALLENGES
Pyjama case
Plan research on the range of pyjama cases in shops. Use it to design pyjama cases to sell at a school fair.

Money boxes

Plan research for designing and making money boxes. Ask, *What designs have we found? How can we use these to help our ideas? What materials are they made from? Where is the slot for the coin? How can we make round ones?* (Use papier mâché balloons.)

Telephone holder

Plan research to make a holder for a mobile telephone. Think about the person for whom it will be made – perhaps a favourite TV character or a family member. Plan research into different ways to close the phone holder to make it easy to get the telephone in and out.

LOCATION, LOCATION

SUBJECT: ICT. QCA UNIT 3E: E-MAIL.

LEARNING OBJECTIVE

To gather, exchange and develop information using e-mail.

THINKING OBJECTIVE

To ask appropriate questions.

THINKING SKILLS

The children will use e-mail to send questions to a person who is pretending to be on holiday at a particular location (in this country or anywhere else in the world). They will use their geographical knowledge and understanding to help them find where this person is by sending e-mail questions. The children will need to consider their questions carefully, thinking about how they can build on the answers to previous questions to narrow down their field of enquiry quickly, while using a world map, CD-ROM and the Internet for reference. They should work in pairs to write their e-mails and send them off. When they receive answers, they will ask other questions until the destination is revealed.

WHAT YOU NEED

Access to the Internet and CD-ROMs, as well as the facility to send e-mail; atlases and reference books; a co-operative adult or older children with prepared e-mails to send to pairs of children in the class with information about their holiday.

WHAT TO DO

Ask an adult, or older children in another class, to pretend to be on holiday somewhere in the world. If you ask older children, you can give each child in your class a different place to locate by asking questions about the features, the weather and what

the journey was like. Alternatively, use the class computer and do it as a class lesson.

Tell the children that someone they know is on holiday. Their challenge is to find out where in the world this person is by asking questions. They should send their questions by e-mail and use atlases, CD-ROMs and the Internet to research likely places.

Go into the mailbox and locate the e-mail from the friend, which tells them that they are on holiday and the way that they got there. Ask, *What does this tell us about where they may be? For example, if it says that they travelled by car, could they be in the USA? Why not?* This will also allow you to limit lower attaining children's area of search to Great Britain.

Suggest that the children work in their pairs to research the likely countries that the holidaymaker can get to by this method of transport. When they have narrowed down the search area, they will be able to send their first question via e-mail to their holidaying friend, who will answer this to give them more information about their destination. Prompt the children to relate this question to particular features of the place, rather than guessing where it may be straight away. For example, ask *What is the weather like at this time of the year? Are these normal conditions for this place?* The children can then narrow down their search to relevant countries, matching the information they have to particular parts of the world, and ask their next question. So, for example, if it is very wet, and it is summer, the children might ask if they are in a rainforest environment. They may need prompts for this. They can then set up a search of likely areas, using 'rainforest' as the key word. Other possible questions include, *Are you in a beach setting? Are you on an island? Are you close to a large city? Does the place have historical interest? What is your accommodation like? What can you see from your hotel window?* Prompt your holidaymakers to reply as quickly as they can. They should elaborate as much as they like as long as they do not give away the name of their destination.

Check for responses later in the day. The amount of time it takes to receive replies will depend on your system. Encourage the children to use the answers to research likely places and send another question by e-mail to narrow the search further. Continue until all the children have discovered their friend's location.

Share the e-mails and answers with other pairs to let them guess where each holidaymaker is.

DIFFERENTIATION

Higher attaining children should be encouraged to refine their questions by finding a more precise location, such as a city, town, village or street. With lower attaining children, limit the area of research to familiar countries in Europe initially, or an area they have already studied.

WHERE NEXT

Repeat the task as often as you like, extending it by opening and sending attachments, such as photographs or other documents that ask for and give information about the particular location. These will prompt more precise questions from the children.

ASSESSMENT

Assess how well the children ask questions to find where the person is on holiday. Note how careful and precise they are in considering how their next question will build on the answer to the previous question to eliminate certain parts of the country or world.

LEARNING OUTCOMES

Most children will learn how to question someone about their whereabouts, building their next question on the answers of the previous ones.

FURTHER ICT CHALLENGES

Hunt the treasure

Tell the children that you have hidden some treasure somewhere in the school. Use several locations so that the children can be given different places to find. Number each place so that you know which position the different pairs are looking for, and record the number you have given each pair by the side of their names each time. Challenge the children to send e-mails asking questions (which require a *yes* or *no* answer) to guess the position of the treasure in the school. To speed up the process, you can pretend to receive the question yourself and give each pair or group their reply, ready to ask the next question. Continue until the children have guessed the position of the treasure. Repeat the challenge as many times as you like. This activity could be extended by hiding the treasure somewhere in the local area, Great Britain or even the world.

Holiday questionnaire

Set the questions as a questionnaire which, when the questions are answered, will give the location of the holidaymaker. Ask the children to put together a series of questions to send to their holidaying friend. Develop multiple-choice and direct questions and others that require a *yes* or *no* answer. Analyse the answers and use them to locate where the person is. Ask, *What difficulties did you have? Are the questions precise enough? What additional questions do you need to ask?* Refine the questionnaire and try again. This activity develops enquiry and reasoning, information processing and evaluation skills.

DISHY LEAVES

SUBJECT: ART AND DESIGN. QCA UNIT 3B: INVESTIGATING PATTERN.

LEARNING OBJECTIVE

To use tools with control.

THINKING OBJECTIVE

To anticipate consequences.

THINKING SKILLS

The children will learn to anticipate and overcome problems of size and shape when designing and making a dish. They will explore a range of natural materials before deciding which to use in their designs.

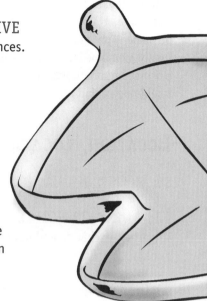

WHAT YOU NEED

A selection of large leaves and other things from nature with interesting shapes; a paper leaf template; a range of materials for the children to explore dish shapes, such as plastic sheets, wood, card and foil; clay; slip; rolling pins; cutting tools; paint; glaze; a way of firing the clay.

WHAT TO DO

In a previous lesson, look at and collect things from nature that have interesting shapes and forms. Include a variety of leaves, preferably large ones, and talk about their colours, shapes and sizes.

Produce this collection at the start of the lesson and explain that the children are going to design and make a small decorative fruit dish, using shapes from nature as starting points for the designs. Discuss things that would make suitable and interesting shapes, such as leaves and flowers. The children may think of other things, so do not limit them. Discuss why leaves would make interesting shapes and which would be most suitable. Ask, *Which leaf design would you like to use? Is it big enough to make a dish? Is it a suitable shape?* Ask the children what material they could use to make the dish. Ask them, *Would paper be a good choice?* Show the children how the paper template you have prepared collapses and doesn't keep its shape. Ask the children what other materials would be suitable to make a dish shape. Explain that these should bend to give a lip to stop things from falling out, but keep their shape. Give them ten or fifteen minutes to explore the range of materials that they suggest and which you have in your collection.

Question the children about the materials they have considered, and guide them towards using clay to make their dishes. Talk about the processes needed to make the dish. Then demonstrate, before allowing the children to make their own.

Ask them, *What will you need to do first?* As you roll out the clay, talk about how thin this needs to be. Ask, *What will happen if the clay is rolled too thinly?* When you made the clay about 5mm thick, place your chosen leaf on top and cut around its outline very carefully. Remove the excess clay and mark the veins and possible blemishes, making the leaf as realistic as possible. Talk about how you can make the dish shape and how you need to curl up the edges. Do this now. Finish the leaf by firing, painting, glazing and firing again. Use a range of tones, tints and blemishes.

Let the children choose a leaf or flower shape to create their own dishes.

If they decide on a flower, make the middle of the flower by sticking a circle of clay to the centre with slip and making small indentations all over it. Curl the petals to make the sides of the dish.

DIFFERENTIATION

Work alongside lower attaining children and ask them questions individually to give them the chance to consider their own answers. If necessary, roll some leaves out too thinly or leave them too thick to show how this would affect the dish. Higher attaining children can research what happens when clay is not fired (or fired incorrectly) by researching in books or on the Internet. They can then be asked to anticipate what will happen if this is not carried out correctly.

WHERE NEXT

Use the same method to make flat pictures of other natural objects and build up a clay mural. Combine the leaf designs to make stencils and prints.

ASSESSMENT

Listen to the children's answers to your questions as they make their leaves and note those who can anticipate what will happen if they roll the clay too thinly or fire the dish for the wrong length of time.

LEARNING OUTCOMES

The children will learn to talk about the visual qualities of their work, explain how they created

certain effects, and comment on the differences in the designs. They will anticipate what may happen if they forget to carry out any part of the process or roll out their clay too thinly or thickly.

FURTHER ART AND DESIGN CHALLENGES

Fossil tiles

Make clay 'fossil' tiles containing prints of natural objects set into the clay. Paint these in a variety of bright colours and attach them to wooden posts in an outdoor area. Plastic insects can be used to create fossil animal lookalikes. Anticipate the difficulties of attaching the tiles to the posts. Ask, *What do you need to add to the tile before it is fired to make sure you will be able to hang it from a nail?*

Nature display

Give small groups of children a collection of objects that have designs from nature, such as crockery, wallpaper, brooches, models and fabrics. Challenge them to make an attractive and original display of these objects. Give them cards and ask them to write questions which will encourage the rest of the class to work out the reasoning behind their display. For example, *Which objects have we grouped together and why? Why have we put this crockery together? Does it have the same design? How will you get these to stand?* Talk about the heights that they want to create and the problems they will encounter when trying to get round objects to stand upright.

PENTATONIC SCALES

SUBJECT: MUSIC. QCA UNIT 12: DRAGON SCALES.

LEARNING OBJECTIVE

To learn that some music uses a five-note scale.

THINKING OBJECTIVE

To ask questions to identify songs that use the pentatonic scale.

THINKING SKILLS

The children will listen to a range of music and answer questions to identify whether the tune uses a pentatonic or tonic sol-fa scale.

WHAT YOU NEED

A xylophone or similar instrument that shows the notes of an octave; a piece of Chinese music (usually found on world music compilation CDs).

WHAT TO DO

Play an octave scale from middle C to top C. Establish that it is called an octave because it has eight notes.

Agree that the first and last notes are the same, but eight notes apart. Relate the root *oct-*, meaning eight, to other words that the children know, such as *octopus* and *octagon*. Play the octave from top to bottom and ask the children what it reminds them of. Some may say church bells and others may say it just makes them feel happy. Both responses are fine.

Remove three notes from the scale to make the pentatonic scale – this will be notes F and B, and top C as well. Ask the children to suggest why this is called the pentatonic scale. Give them hints and clues, such as, *Octave meant eight notes – what do you think* penta- *might mean?* Let them work out that a pentatonic scale has five notes. For higher attaining children, you may wish to explain that the missing ones are the half notes or semitones, and the ones that are left are the whole tones. Together, compose some questions that will help the children to identify whether a tune uses five or eight notes. For example, *How many notes can I hear? Does the tune jump up and down? Does it sound full or in a different style? Are there five notes in the tune, or eight?* Play a simple tune on the pentatonic scale and ask the children to say what this reminds them of. Agree that it sounds like Chinese music.

Play your piece of Chinese music and ask the children whether this has five or eight notes. Ask, *How do you know that it has five notes? Is it because it sounds different to the tunes you are used to hearing and singing? How is it different? Did the tune use five or eight notes? How do you know? Can you hear the difference?*

Play a game, asking the children to identify whether a tune is written with eight or five notes. Use songs from Native North America such as 'Land of the Silver Birch' and 'I'm an Indian Warrior' as examples of pentatonic, and contrast these with any familiar song written in a major key. Use the children's questions to help them make their judgements.

DIFFERENTIATION

Introduce higher attaining children to songs written in minor keys and ask them to say whether a minor key or a pentatonic scale is being used. This is more difficult to identify by listening. Explain that the music written in the minor key sounds more sombre, while the pentatonic scale sounds bright and cheerful. Seat lower attaining children where they can see the xylophone (or other instrument), and encourage them to judge by watching and counting the number of notes used, as well as listening to the tune being played.

WHERE NEXT

When you learn a new song, ask the children whether it uses a conventional major scale or a pentatonic scale.

Compose a beat and tune for a dragon-boat race. The song should have a regular beat for the oars that the rowers can keep in time to, and a simple tune for them to sing. Keep the words simple and repetitive, such as, *Dragon boats keep moving, Dragon boats don't stop.* Challenge the children to think of a series of questions which, when answered, will correctly indicate that their tune is composed using five notes, has a regular rhythm and evokes the pictures of dragon boats racing.

ASSESSMENT

Assess which children can identify pentatonic scales in tunes by the way that they sound. Question them to see if they are asking questions to reach their judgements.

LEARNING OUTCOMES

Most children will learn to ask questions which will help them to identify, by listening to the tone of a tune, whether it is written in a pentatonic scale.

FURTHER MUSIC CHALLENGES
Pentatonic melodies
In pairs, compose simple tunes which use the pentatonic scale. Encourage the children to ask questions that will help them deduce what each tune is. For example, *Does the tune start on a C? Is the next note higher? Does it go up in a step or a jump?* The questions should ensure that the tunes are written as notes or letters. Encourage the children to think about where the notes go in relation to the others in the tune, to show the fall and rise. The pairs should use the questions to work out each other's tunes.
Musical structures
Consider a set of questions which will help the children compose music with a structure. For example, *Will the music repeat itself? Does the first phrase also finish the tune? Will the tune go up in steps? Will it start and finish on the same note?*

Religious importance

SUBJECT: RE. QCA UNIT 4D: WHAT RELIGIONS ARE REPRESENTED IN OUR NEIGHBOURHOOD?

LEARNING OBJECTIVE
To learn about, and from, the main religious beliefs, practices and buildings of people who live in the neighbourhood.

THINKING OBJECTIVE
To ask questions.

THINKING SKILLS
The children will think about their own religion and so identify questions to ask a range of visitors from different religions represented in the immediate neighbourhood, and others from farther afield.

WHAT YOU NEED
Paper and pens; whiteboard and pen.

WHAT TO DO
Depending on your context, talk about the main religions represented by children in the class. If there is no predominant religion, pretend that you have visitors coming into the class and you want the children to identify a series of questions to ask them. Consider their main beliefs, practices and places of worship. Write these on a sheet of paper under columns for each religion, and note the similarities.

Organise the children into small groups and encourage children from one faith to ask others questions about their religion.

Invite a small group of one faith to come to the front of the class to take questions. Ask an adult or higher attaining children to record the questions asked. When they have finished, swap over groups and ask the same questions of a second group. Afterwards compare the sets of answers and think about what the children have learned. Ask, *How much more do you know now about these two different religions? What have you learned from these answers? Have you learned that the two religions have very similar beliefs? Have you learned that both religions pray to a God?*

Use the questions to research particular aspects of other religions.

DIFFERENTIATION
Ask higher attaining children to list the questions for display where the rest of the class can add additional questions over the next few days. Work with less able children to revisit the questions asked in the main activity and identify others that they could ask.

WHERE NEXT
Use the questions as an interview sheet to ask other groups of pupils and visiting speakers from different religions represented in the neighbourhood. After you have interviewed all the visitors, list all the things that the religions have in common – all the similarities. Note the philosophy held by each one, and how they teach people to behave in similar ways and hold similar moral values.

Organise visits to different places of worship and note further similarities.

ASSESSMENT
Note the names of children who asked a particular question and encourage them to refine this further. Target particular children who have not asked a question by working with them in a smaller group.

LEARNING OUTCOMES
All the children will learn to ask questions to find out facts about different religions, either independently or in a smaller targeted group.

FURTHER RE CHALLENGES
Musical worship
Listen to traditional Christian hymns and note the features of this music. List the values and morals expressed in the words. Ask, *How does the music reflect the mood of the service or celebration?* Think about questions to ask people from other religions about how music supports their worship, particularly weddings. Compare music used in Christian weddings to that used in Hindu and Sikh weddings, and answer the questions raised beforehand.

Religious art
Look at Islamic patterns used to decorate mosques and prayer mats. Ask questions to learn about the purpose and meaning of these, and relate these questions to other religions, asking how and when pattern is used, and how the colours are chosen. For example, questions that will enquire about the purpose, meaning, and religious significance of Mendhi patterns and Rangoli patterns.

DELHI DANCING

SUBJECT: PE. QCA UNIT: DANCE ACTIVITIES – UNIT 4.

LEARNING OBJECTIVE
To develop Indian dance motifs.

THINKING OBJECTIVE
To improve ideas.

THINKING SKILLS

The children will watch different Indian dances and use the information to develop their own dance motifs. They will listen to a range of Indian music and decide which is most suitable for their dance. They will then practise the routines, making improvements as they build motifs into phrases, and phrases into sequences. They may wish to think about telling a story, as this is often the basis for dance in India. This lesson can be adapted to develop dances of different cultures.

WHAT YOU NEED

A video of Indian dancers, or a visiting artist; Indian music which has clear musical phrases – the music from *Bombay Dreams* is suitable.

WHAT TO DO

A few days before the lesson, watch the video and discuss the varied dance motifs. Pick out those motifs that are similar. Look closely at the hand movements and the way the head moves. Discuss the circular movements and the shape of the hands during these. Look how the eyes often follow the hand movements.

Think of adjectives to describe the motifs, such as *smooth, sharp, precise, stamp* and *flowing*. List the different types of movement with the feet, such as hop, jump, step, spin and skip. Watch how the toe and heel move as they touch the ground. Over the next few days, listen to different Indian music and select some extracts that the children like and which they wish to use for their dance composition.

At the beginning of the lesson, listen to your chosen extract and start to warm up by copying the hand, head and feet movements. Develop some stretches into the warm-up routines, focusing on the Indian style of circulating hands, pointing upwards and to the side, twisting high and low and spinning around.

Play the music for about three minutes and let the children move freely, developing and trying out their ideas. Evaluate the moves and select some of those you like. Continue until you have chosen four to six motifs for the children to refine. Take each one and perform them one after another to build them into a phrase. Let the children, working in groups of four, five or six, decide on the order of the motifs so that they develop different phrases.

Focus on improving the hand and head movements. Ask the children to suggest how they can develop their motifs by extending and improving the way the hands and head movements add quality to their dance phrases.

Perform the dance in assembly, perhaps as a celebration of a festival, or to reflect the studies completed in a topic about India.

DIFFERENTIATION

Focus on two motifs with less able children and talk them through how they can improve their hand movements to add quality to their work. Let them perform these motifs standing still, moving around in a circle, and in a straight line, to add interest and extend the ideas. Higher attaining children should be encouraged to develop their motifs and phrases into a paired dance, to contrast and complement their movements. They should also think about how to change the levels and dynamics of their dance.

WHERE NEXT

Develop the phrases into a sequence, perhaps adding additional ones as a middle section, or a coda at the end.

ASSESSMENT

Assess how well the children develop a basic idea, and note the dance elements they use to make improvements to their phrases. Note those who enhance their ideas by changing the order, or the way in which they repeat their phrases and sequences.

LEARNING OUTCOMES

Most children will develop simple motifs and improve these by thinking about the way their hands and heads support their dance sequences. A few will go beyond this and think about using different levels and dynamics to enrich their ideas.

FURTHER PE CHALLENGES

Animal cameo

Listen to Indian animal stories, such as *The Just So Stories* by Rudyard Kipling, and use the motifs to create a dance that tells the story of different animal movements. Discuss the way the animals move and use the children's ideas to choose a suitable piece of Indian music. When the children are familiar with the music, challenge them to refine their ideas to fit it, and create more drama in their movements.

Mendhi patterns

Look at the patterns created on hands with henna dye. Look at the curves and how they meet and go away from each other in curls and curves. Put together a group dance which draws these patterns. Each group of four can decide where to start, but together in a central group would work well. They can then compose a mirror-image dance in two sets of pairs who go away from the centre in a curl and curved pattern, finishing at four points of a square.

CREATIVE THINKING SKILLS

INTRODUCTION

Creative thinking is not just about creating poems, pieces of art, music, dance or gymnastic sequences, although these do provide good opportunities for children to think creatively. It is also about identifying possible solutions to problems or difficulties when, for example, trying to depict a special moment in their lives. By thinking creatively, children can learn to identify why an author has chosen a particular theme, or used a particular style of writing in their work. This will allow them to consider these aspects when creating their own projects, thus making their learning richer and more meaningful.

Children should be given lots of opportunities to develop their own creative learning. Too often they are given only one strategy to solve a particular problem. The activities in Chapter 2 of this book asked the children to give reasons for their ideas and strategies. This chapter, in contrast, focuses on the children deciding for themselves why certain things have been organised as they have, and on finding possible alternatives to solve a problem. Questions are used in the activities to enable you to guide their thinking throughout, and to encourage them to think imaginatively and laterally – the roots of creative thinking. A key to asking questions when trying to develop creative thinking is to give the children time to answer. You should never expect an answer within less than ten seconds.

The activities outlined here, while written within specific contexts, are organised so that the children can work together in groups. This allows them to collaborate and bounce ideas off each other, sparking further creativity. A key skill outlined in the National Curriculum involves the children working with others to meet a challenge. Part of the development of this key skill involves the children learning to appreciate the experience of others, considering different perspectives and benefiting from what others think. The topic contexts of the activities in this chapter can be adapted for all subjects.

The way you organise children's learning is crucial to giving them the opportunity to think about how they will organise their own learning. Group work gives them suitable opportunities to consider and negotiate which ideas will be accepted and developed.

Thought-sharing, or brainstorming, is one way to encourage children to volunteer ideas in an uninhibited way. If all ideas are accepted, everyone will feel confident to contribute. The ideas may be discarded at a later stage, but putting them through the process means that good reasons have to be given for this.

The creative thinking skills are:
- creating ideas
- imaginative thinking
- finding alternative innovative outcomes
- lateral thinking
- hypothesising
- extending ideas.

INTRODUCING CREATIVE THINKING SKILLS

Subject and QCA unit, NLS or NNS objective	Activity title	Thinking objective	Activity	Page
English. NLS objectives: To understand how writers create imaginary worlds; to understand how the use of expressive and descriptive language can create moods	Write an image	To extend ideas	Thinking of words to describe what they see and writing about an imaginary world.	89
Maths. NNS objective: To identify lines of symmetry in simple shapes and recognize shapes with no lines of symmetry	Central line	To think imaginatively	Building models with 3-D shapes and identifying lines of symmetry.	90
Science. QCA unit 4E: Friction	Balloon power	To extend ideas	Making a balloon rocket travel faster and further by decreasing the amount of friction.	90
History. QCA unit 18: What was it like to live here in the past?	Visiting castles	To hypothesise	Looking at castles and deciding how people used to live.	91
Geography. QCA unit 16: What's in the news?	World affairs	To extend ideas	Identifying how football impacts on the environment, places and people.	92
Design and technology. QCA unit 3B: Sandwich snacks	Sandwiches for lunch	To create ideas	Creating a sandwich.	93
ICT. QCA unit 4B: Developing images using repeating patterns	Tiles	To create and extend ideas	Making tiles suitable for a kitchen or bathroom decoration.	93
Art and design. QCA unit 3A: Portraying relationships	Facial expressions	To create ideas	Creating masks and totem pole figures.	94
Music. QCA unit 13: Painting with sound	Sound paintings	To think laterally	The children will listen to a piece of music and paint the picture in their heads.	95
RE. QCA unit 4C: Why is Easter important for Christians?	Palm Sunday procession	To hypothesise	Creating the Palm Sunday procession, hypothesising why people did this and what it must have been like.	95
PE. QCA unit: Dance activities – unit 4	Lowry scene	To extend ideas	Thinking about the characters in a Lowry painting.	96

WRITE AN IMAGE

SUBJECT: ENGLISH. NLS OBJECTIVES: TO UNDERSTAND HOW WRITERS CREATE IMAGINARY WORLDS; TO UNDERSTAND HOW THE USE OF EXPRESSIVE AND DESCRIPTIVE LANGUAGE CAN CREATE MOODS, AROUSE EXPECTATIONS, BUILD TENSION, DESCRIBE ATTITUDES OR EMOTIONS.

LEARNING OBJECTIVE
To think of words that make an impact and provide an image of the setting.

THINKING OBJECTIVE
To extend ideas.

THINKING SKILLS
The children will look at different settings and think of words that describe what they see. They will use a thesaurus to identify more descriptive adjectives, and will consider alliterative phrases and onomatopoeia. They will add these word effects to pictures for others in the class to conjure up an image in the mind and guess which picture is being described. They will then incorporate all their ideas to create and write about an imaginary world of their own.

WHAT YOU NEED
Pictures of various settings that show human activity, weather, seascapes and the sky at night (like the motivational pictures often found in offices); a packet of popcorn, bowl and microwave; Post-it Notes; large sheet of paper and pen; drawing materials; access to computers.

WHAT TO DO
Look at the pictures on the outside of the popcorn packaging and talk about what the children can see. Ask, *If you had to add words to try to sell the popcorn, what would be good ones to use?* (Pop, bang, explode, puffed, inviting, tasty.)

Make the popcorn and listen to the sound that it makes. Now ask, *What words can you think of to describe the sounds?* Write down their suggestions on a large sheet of paper.

When you have recorded all the children's words, look at them together and link those that start with the same sound or phoneme. If you do not have any, challenge the children to think of some to link up

with some of your favourite words. Stress that this does not have to be the same letter. Put some of these into phrases, with additional similar-sounding words, to describe the popcorn snack in an inviting way. For example, 'popping puffed up popcorn', or 'super smacking snack'. Introduce the term *alliteration* if the children do not already know it.

Now look at words that sound like what they describe, such as *bang*, *explode* and *pop*, which conjure up an image in the mind. Tell the children that the term for these is *onomatopoeia*. Explain that this means words that sound the same as, or echo sounds associated with, what they mean, so that they build up a picture in the mind of sounds, emotions and feelings. For example, discuss what the word *explode* means to the children. Ask them, *How does it reflect its sound? What sort of sound do you expect to hear when you listen to this word in a phrase? Does it produce any feelings and emotions, such as excitement, amusement or fear? Would this be a good word to use if we were selling the popcorn?* Discuss the range of feelings and emotions that this word may conjure up for different people and decide together whether it would be a good onomatopoeic word to use in this context. Agree that it probably would.

Organise the children into groups after telling them that you want them to look at the different pictures you have displayed around the room. Explain that you want them to think of alliterative and onomatopoeic words to describe what is happening in the pictures, to reflect the obvious and inferential sounds, smells and feelings that each one contains. Invite them to write the words on Post-it Notes and add these to the pictures. Encourage them to use dictionaries and thesauri to locate some of these words and to find more interesting words or synonyms.

When the children have finished adding their words, take down the pictures and describe them one at a time, using the children's words in your descriptions. Then ask, *Can you conjure up the picture that is being described in these words?* Invite some children to choose a picture and use the words to describe it for the class to guess.

Ask the children to work individually or in small groups to create a picture of an imaginary world. This could be a space or Wild West scape, or an enchanted forest scene. Computers are a suitable way to produce these. When the children are happy with the world they have created, ask them to label it with adjectives, alliterative phrases and onomatopoeia, and then develop these to write a description of their imaginary world.

CENTRAL LINE

SUBJECT: MATHEMATICS. NNS OBJECTIVE: TO IDENTIFY LINES OF SYMMETRY IN SIMPLE SHAPES AND RECOGNISE SHAPES WITH NO LINES OF SYMMETRY.

LEARNING OBJECTIVE
To identify symmetry in regular shapes.

THINKING OBJECTIVE
To think imaginatively.

THINKING SKILLS
The children will think about the faces on 3-D shapes and whether there are any lines of symmetry. They will use this information to build symmetrical models of structures like buildings and vehicles, but should let their imagination run wild. Finally they will give reasons why they used certain shapes for particular purposes, such as flat shapes to build, round shapes for wheels, pyramids for church spires, and so on.

WHAT YOU NEED
A collection of 3-D shapes; a digital camera; paper and pencils, pictures of real buildings in the area.

WHAT TO DO
Give the children a collection of three-dimensional shapes and invite them to build a model or make a building. Challenge them to make this symmetrical. Ask them to name the shapes they have used, including cube, cuboid, pyramid, sphere, hemisphere, cylinder, cone, prism, tetrahedron, polyhedron and any others you may have in your collection, but develop their thinking by asking:
- Is your model symmetrical?
- Can you tell me why?
- Which shapes are symmetrical?
- Did this help to make your model symmetrical?

Take photographs or draw pictures of the models and ask the children to draw all the lines of symmetry they can see.

Extend the children's thinking by considering the properties of the shapes that were suited to their purposes. Ask:
- Why did you choose the cuboids and cubes for building towers?
- Why did you decide not to use the sphere at the bottom of the model?

- Why did you choose cylinders for wheels? Could you use cones? What would happen if you did?
- Would cones make good chimneys?
- Which shapes would you choose for rolling, sliding or building towers? Can you place the cuboids in a different way to build a tower? What happens when you do this with cubes? Or even cylinders?

Compare the shapes in the models with pictures of real buildings in the local area and beyond. Give other groups the pictures and ask them to recreate the models using the solid shapes.

Extend the activity by removing one of the shapes, which the children will then need to build by combining two or more different shapes (for example, remove the cuboids, which can be made from two cubes, or the spheres, which can be made from two hemispheres).

With younger or less able children, fit four cubes together to see how many different new shapes they can make. For each one, identify the lines of reflective symmetry, and note those that do not have lines of symmetry.

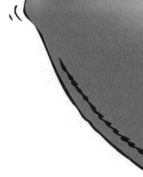

BALLOON POWER

SUBJECT: SCIENCE. QCA UNIT 4E: FRICTION.

LEARNING OBJECTIVE
To learn that air is a force that can make things move.

THINKING OBJECTIVE
To extend ideas.

THINKING SKILLS
The children will consider how well their balloon rocket moves along a line and how they can improve this. They will extend their ideas by decreasing the amount of friction that is occurring to make it travel faster or further along the line.

WHAT YOU NEED
A balloon for each child and a few spares; a plastic-coated washing line strung across the classroom; cardboard tubes, plastic straws or pen cases; empty plastic drink bottles or washing-up liquid bottles with a section cut out to allow the balloon to

expand; sticky tape; a timer; a tape measure; paper and writing materials.

WHAT TO DO

Make your balloon-powered vehicles out of different types of materials and objects – for example, an empty washing-up liquid or drink bottle, or a cardboard tube. The lighter the rocket, the less pull down on the line there will be, and the faster the rocket will travel. Attach the rocket to the line by threading the line through a second cardboard tube or plastic straw taped along the top of the rocket. Add a balloon so that the air is released at the neck

end of the bottle or the underside of the cardboard tube. If you attach it to a plastic tube (the sort on bathroom sealer containers are suitable), you can blow up the balloon while the tube is attached to the rocket. Test out the 'rockets' on the washing line to make sure that they work and to see how far they go.

Talk to the children about how you are going to find out which is the fastest and which one goes the farthest.

Test the speed first. Decide how far you are expecting the vehicles to travel before you start finding the speed (by timing how long it takes for each balloon to travel that far). Ask, *Do you want the vehicles to go to the end of the line? Why not?* Discuss that fact that some of the balloons may not reach the end of the line and therefore would not get a result. Ask, *How far do you think all the balloons will travel?*

How will you measure the speed? Who is going to record the results? Which balloon do you think will go fastest? Why? Test the balloons together, recording the amount of time it takes for each balloon vehicle to travel the designated distance. Disqualify those that do not finish the course. Now ask, *How do you think you could make the balloons go faster?* Test out their ideas to see if they were right.

Next, decide how you will find out which vehicle will travel farthest. Ask, *How will you measure the distance? Will you put a marker on the line, or make a mental note of which one went farthest?* Explain that if you put a marker on the line, it may stop those vehicles that are tested afterwards, especially if they are capable of going further. Find a way to record the distance, using either standard or non-standard measures, depending on the needs of your class. Ask, *Which vehicle went farthest? How do you know? Can you think of a way to make the balloons go farther?* Investigate their ideas, such as putting more air into the balloon, using bigger balloons, rubbing the line with soap to reduce friction, using a tube made from a more slippery material (like a plastic pen case).

At the end of testing, note the children's conclusions, then ask them to identify the factors which affected how fast and how far the balloons travelled. Talk about the amount of air, the size of the balloons, the friction of the washing line and cardboard tube. Ask, *Which factor made the winning balloon go the fastest and/or the farthest respectively? Was this because the friction was reduced?*

Apply the vehicles to model boats and test these on a paddling pool filled with water.

VISITING CASTLES

SUBJECT: HISTORY. QCA UNIT 18: WHAT WAS IT LIKE TO LIVE HERE IN THE PAST?

LEARNING OBJECTIVE

To use evidence to learn how people used to live in the past.

THINKING OBJECTIVE

To hypothesise.

THINKING SKILLS

The children will hypothesise about how people used to live in the past by evaluating evidence from visits, books and stories.

WHAT YOU NEED

A visit to a nearby castle, preferably one that was used in Tudor times, but one which has some buildings and ruins to spark the children's imaginations; pictures that provide evidence about the way people used to live; paper and pens.

WHAT TO DO

On a visit, or by looking at the pictures, talk about the different parts of a castle. Look at the gate, and the soldiers' quarters, and talk about what life would have been like for them. Ask, *Where would they eat and sleep? Did they have comfortable beds? Was it warm in the castle or would they have been cold in the winter? Where did they go to the toilet? What weapons did they use? How do we know?* Relate the answers to the evidence seen in the castle or the pictures. For example, the slits in the side of the castle will indicate whether the soldiers used bows or crossbows.

Do the same with the great hall. Ask, *What would this room have been like? Would the fire have been big or small? How do you know? What evidence is there to tell you this? What kind of events would have been organised in this room? How many floors were there? How close was it to the kitchen? Why?* If relevant, relate the various activities to the life of Henry VIII, or consider how the evidence gives us an idea of the way the castle inhabitants used to live.

Repeat this process with other rooms in the castle. Talk about the number of floors in the towers and ask how the children know. Ask where they think the sink and ovens would have been in the kitchen, all the time encouraging them to say how they know and relating this back to the evidence.

Back in the classroom, organise the children into groups to perform short plays demonstrating their hypotheses of how the different rooms would have been used and the people who would have used them.

WORLD AFFAIRS

SUBJECT: GEOGRAPHY. QCA UNIT 16: WHAT'S IN THE NEWS?

LEARNING OBJECTIVE

To learn about the impact people can have on the environment.

THINKING OBJECTIVE

To extend ideas.

THINKING SKILLS

The children will look at a newspaper article or TV report about a football match and think about how this activity impacts on people and the environment. They will extend their ideas by relating the information they have gathered to identify the impact people have on places and how this affects the way we all live.

WHAT YOU NEED

Any relevant newspaper article or TV extract about a football match; a large sheet of paper and pens; maps of areas around one or two famous football stadiums, such as Old Trafford, Villa Park, Highbury or Ibrox.

WHAT TO DO

Read the article and/or watch the TV extract and agree on what it is about. Think about the information that it gives about the area, and the way people there live, such as the types of houses local residents live in, whether there are front gardens and parking spaces, and whether there are any nearby shops and pubs. Ask, *Are there any bus stops or train stations close by, or are they at a distance from the ground? Is it usually a quiet place to live? Are there any local schools? Are there any clues about the environment or other geographical features? What can you see (or read) about the features of the place in the report? How does this help us learn about the place and people who live there? Is life there the same as everywhere else, apart from on match days?* List all the things that have been learned about the place under human and physical features and, next to the information, list the questions about how this affects people's lives. For example, how the number of spectators attending the football match will impact on the transport infrastructure and the lives of people who live around the ground. Think about the number of supporters, their route to and from the stadium, and how long it would take to get from the stadium to the car park, coach or train station. Ask, *How much noise would they make? How long would it take? How many people would there be? How would this determine when residents go out or return home on match days? Would there*

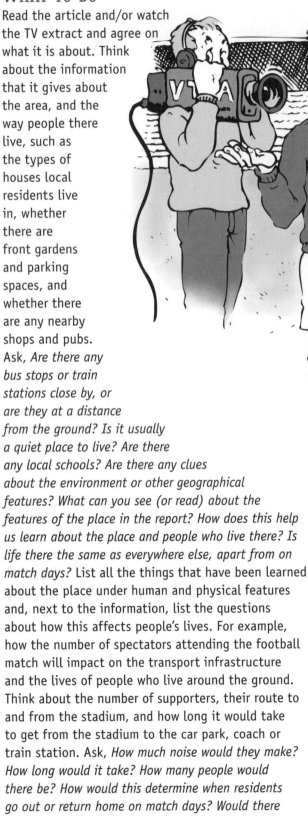

be any benefits to local businesses? Would there be any disadvantages? Would there be any environmental issues? What about litter? Would there be any? How could supporters be deterred from littering the local area?

Extend the children's thinking and ideas by using the information to investigate areas around well-known football grounds. Look at their position on maps and think about how the spectators will get there. Ask, *How might the area be improved or changed to reduce the impact of football crowds on people who live in this town or city?* Write a letter to the local planning committee with the children's ideas.

SANDWICHES FOR LUNCH

SUBJECT: DESIGN AND TECHNOLOGY. QCA UNIT 3B: SANDWICH SNACKS.

LEARNING OBJECTIVE
To create ideas for sandwich fillings.

THINKING OBJECTIVE
To create ideas.

THINKING SKILLS
The children will think about what they like and dislike in their sandwiches and why. They will then use this information to design and make a filling for a lunchtime sandwich. They will finish by carrying out a taste test to find which sandwich filling is most popular in the class.

WHAT YOU NEED
Plates; knives; bread; spread; the fillings identified by the children; a large sheet of paper.

WHAT TO DO
A week before you intend to do the activity, ask the children, as a homework task, to find as many different types of bread and sandwich fillings as they can, at home or in the shops. Put up a large sheet of paper within the children's reach so that they can list all the ones they have found.

The day before, carry out a survey of the ones the children have tried and like, and give these a tick. Note the fillings that contain one, or more than one, ingredient – such as chicken, cheese or ham, as opposed to chicken and salad, ham and cucumber or cheese and tomato. Use the children's preferences to buy the ingredients you will need for the lesson.

At the beginning of this lesson ask the children to volunteer which sandwich fillings they like best and why. Explain that you want them to think about the reasons why they like the fillings they have chosen and to use this information to create a new sandwich filling, perhaps by combining different or unusual ingredients. Ask the children to work individually, but to discuss their ideas with a partner. Once they have reached a final decision, including the type of bread they prefer, they should draw a picture of their new sandwich and label it clearly to show what they will need to make it.

Next day (or immediately if you have had time to buy the items chosen by the children), make the sandwiches for a lunchtime picnic. Check for allergies first. Evaluate which ones the children liked and why. Make the sandwiches again for other children to try.

Challenge the children, as a maths investigation, to find out how many different types of sandwich they can make with three types of bread, and three different filling ingredients. Make these to find the class's favourite combination.

TILES

SUBJECT: ICT. QCA UNIT 4B: DEVELOPING IMAGES USING REPEATING PATTERNS.

LEARNING OBJECTIVE
To copy and paste in a repeating pattern.

THINKING OBJECTIVES
To create and extend ideas.

THINKING SKILLS
The children will think about the style, colours and patterns for a kitchen or bathroom decoration design. They will make two or more tiles or stamps of actual size to repeat over a space to show how these would look in the finished room.

WHAT YOU NEED
Computers; suitable software to create and select stamps to make repeating patterns; sales catalogues, brochures, home improvement magazines.

WHAT TO DO
Look at different kitchen and bathroom tile designs in sales catalogues, brochures or home improvement magazines. Decide together why these are suitable

for kitchen or bathroom decoration. Ask, *What colours have been used? How suitable are these? Could the designer have been more adventurous? Would you change or adapt any designs or colours?*

Before you start, give the children five minutes to discuss with a friend the colours they want to use in their kitchen or bathroom. They should ask, *Do you want to use two or three contrasting or complementary colours, or as many colours as you can?* Let them decide how they will choose the colours. They might try lots of colours at first, and then limit themselves later to decide which combination they like best.

Show the children how to make a stamp or repeating picture by placing on the screen a suitable clip-art image of a kitchen or bathroom theme, changing the colour and size (and perhaps the orientation), and using the 'save as' tool to give it a name. The tile can then be repeated at intervals in a grid to make a design for a bathroom or kitchen. If appropriate, and without limiting their creative ideas, give lower attaining children a selection of stamps from which they can choose their pattern or picture. This will prevent them from becoming frustrated if they have difficulties creating their own.

Alternatively, children could create their own stamps by drawing shapes or pictures freehand, using 'save as' to give the outline a name, and then 'line' and 'fill colour' to produce different colours of the same theme. When they use these stamps to make patterns, they can decide whether to create repeating ones. Let them evaluate each other's work, agreeing how well colours go together, and use this information to make any changes to their pattern.

Finally, the children could try using 'fill colour' to place some of their stamps onto different coloured backgrounds, and then say which of these combinations they like best.

FACIAL EXPRESSIONS

SUBJECT: ART AND DESIGN. QCA UNIT 3A: PORTRAYING RELATIONSHIPS.

LEARNING OBJECTIVE
To learn how to create facial expressions using lines, shape, colour and position.

THINKING OBJECTIVE
To create ideas.

THINKING SKILLS
The children will look at how expressions are created in

pictures, on masks and on totem poles, and use this information to create their own ideas.

WHAT YOU NEED
Pictures of (or actual) African masks; pictures of totem poles from North America and Canada; pictures of the statues found on islands in the southern ocean such as Easter Island; paintings of faces, including *Symphony in Rose* by Alexej von Jawlensky (available from www.postershop.com or found in the Discovery Art series, published by Wayland) and *Weeping Woman* by Picasso; paper; boxes; adhesive; pastels and paints; resources to make papier mâché.

WHAT TO DO
Look at the painting *Weeping Woman* by Picasso and, as a class, spend no more than five minutes talking about how he has used line, colour, position and shape to create the expression of the woman weeping. Ask, *How does he create the impression of the tears falling? How does he make the woman look so sad? How do the lines create an angular look rather than a peaceful, happy expression?*

Now look at an African mask and, for no more than five minutes, talk about the material from which it is made. Discuss the expression that the artist has created. Ask, *Why has he used so few colours? How have the facial features been created? How are they different to those in Picasso's painting? Why have they been depicted in this way? Did the artist want to depict an actual face?*

Give out the pictures you have of the statues, totem poles and paintings of different faces. Ask the children to spend two minutes on each picture to discuss in pairs, or groups of three, how the faces have been created. Ask the children to focus on the materials from which they have been made, and the artistic elements of line, colour, shape and position of the features. Swap over the pictures so that the children can look at two different styles of creating faces.

Look at *Symphony in Rose* by Alexej von Jawlensky together and discuss how he has put together this picture of a face. Ask, *How has he combined the shades of colour? How are the eyes the same? How are they different? How has he used line and shape to create the effect? What about the nose? Does this line up with the centre of the picture? Why has he drawn the nose like this? Was it to give balance to the painting?* Ask questions in the same way about the mouth and cheekbones. Ask, *Is the person happy or sad? How do we know?* Talk about how the artist has created the expression on the face, which tells us how the person is feeling. Discuss his use of line, shape, colour and position of the facial features.

Give the children pastels and invite them to explore the colours and different ways of representing facial features before putting them together to create their own faces.

Extend the activity by creating masks, statues and totem poles, from papier mâché and boxes.

SOUND PAINTINGS

SUBJECT: MUSIC. QCA UNIT 13: PAINTING WITH SOUND.

LEARNING OBJECTIVE
To understand how music can describe images and moods.

THINKING OBJECTIVE
To think laterally.

THINKING SKILLS
The children will listen to two different styles of music and, for each, discuss the mood it evokes. They will then choose one of the pieces and paint a picture of the image that it makes them see in their heads. The children will produce a range of images because the music will inspire them with different feelings and moods, but some children will include things that are the same. By identifying aspects that are different and similar, the children will note how they have all thought in a different way – thought laterally – to create individual pictures from the same piece of music.

WHAT YOU NEED
A piece of loud pop music such as the instrumental section of Queen's *Bohemian Rhapsody*, and a quieter piece such as 'Morning' from *Peer Gynt*; paper and paints; pens; paintings by Constable that show peaceful, rural scenes; abstract art by more modern artists such as Turner, Jackson Pollock or Whistler.

WHAT TO DO
Listen to the piece of pop music and describe what the music is like. Ask, *Is it loud, quiet, fast, slow, tuneful, rhythmic? What instruments can you hear?* Talk about the musical elements that have been used to create the piece. Consider the dynamics, duration, timbre, tempo, structure, and the way the tune moves up and down (the pitch).

Ask the children what image the music brings into their heads? Ask, *How could you paint this image? Is it a calm picture or one with more movement?* Look at a piece of abstract art, for example by Jackson Pollock, and a landscape, for example by Constable, and decide which best reflects the music. Invite the children to give reasons for their choice, encouraging them to talk about the mood and feelings the music evokes for them. Ask, *Do you all think the same thing, or does someone have a different idea? Why have most of you chosen the abstract picture* (if they have)*? Does it reflect the mood of the music better?* Relate the movement in the picture to the elements in the music that evoke the mood and feelings.

Now listen to the quieter piece of music and ask about the image that this piece conjures up in their minds. Ask, *What does this make you see? Perhaps the sun coming up over the brow of a hill? What else could this calming piece of music reflect?* Look at the paintings again and consider whether the landscape is like the picture in the children's heads.

Ask the children to paint a picture to represent one of the pieces of music. Look at the paintings for each piece at the end of the lesson and compare the ways in which they are the same. *Have you all used a particular style? Are some more abstract than others? How are they different? Have some of you thought of different ideas? What prompted them?* Talk about how the children have thought laterally to produce different paintings from the same piece of music. Display the children's paintings, labelling them with words reflecting the music that inspired them.

Extend the activity by looking at other pictures and composing musical phrases to depict these.

PALM SUNDAY PROCESSION

SUBJECT: RE. QCA UNIT 4C: WHY IS EASTER IMPORTANT FOR CHRISTIANS?

LEARNING OBJECTIVE
To learn about the atmosphere and feelings of the crowd in Jerusalem on Palm Sunday.

THINKING OBJECTIVE
To hypothesise.

THINKING SKILLS
The children will consider the reasons why people took part in a particular procession, and think about the atmosphere, and their feelings and emotions. They will put together a piece of drama to reflect these aspects of the procession, hypothesising what it must have been like for an ordinary person.

WHAT YOU NEED

A story that details the modern-day Palm Sunday procession; pictures and/or video of the story of Palm Sunday representing the story from the Bible when Jesus entered Jerusalem.

WHAT TO DO

Use the pictures or video to tell the story of Palm Sunday. Discuss the people's beliefs and faith that Jesus was the Messiah and the feelings and emotions that people must have felt before, during and after Jesus arrived. Ask, *What did people do while they were waiting? What did they do as he passed? What did they do when he had gone by? How did they demonstrate their happiness and excitement?* Relate the people's actions to their belief and faith that Jesus was the Son of God.

Discuss the use of palms and why this tree was chosen to wave as Jesus passed through the town. Ask, *Was it simply because it was available? Did the people use other leaves? Why is this tree used in today's processions? What feelings does the palm evoke during today's processions? How does this symbol remind the people of the actual day when Jesus came to Jerusalem?* Organise the children into groups and let them put together cameos of the roles they might have played in the procession. Let them hypothesise their feelings and emotions, and consider the different ways that people demonstrated this. Refer to the Bible and other stories, if necessary, for the facts.

Perform the cameos, in groups, to the rest of the class, before putting them all together to depict what the procession must have been like.

Look at pictures and watch the video extract of the modern-day Palm Sunday procession and compare this to the children's own ideas and presentation. Talk about this afterwards and gauge whether the children think their hypothesis was right, and why.

LOWRY SCENE

SUBJECT: PE. QCA UNIT: DANCE ACTIVITIES – UNIT 4

LEARNING OBJECTIVE

To explore character traits and create characters in dance.

THINKING OBJECTIVE

To extend ideas.

THINKING SKILLS

The children will use a painting by LS Lowry as a stimulus for creating different characters. They will explore how to use actions and movements to depict their chosen character, and think about how they can extend their ideas through exploring pathways and changing speed and direction. They will use pause to create the painting effect.

WHAT YOU NEED

Any painting by LS Lowry containing a number of characters.

WHAT TO DO

Before the lesson, show the children your chosen painting and talk about and describe some of the characters. Wonder together where they may be going. Ask, *Do you think they will be walking quickly or slowly? Will they stop to talk to each other? What will they do when they find they have been talking so long that they may now be late?* Let the children explore their own ideas and use their imagination to plan and talk about different dance scenarios.

At the beginning of the lesson, warm up by exploring the different pathways that the people in the painting may take. Ask, *Will they move to the edge of the painting and exit, before re-entering after a short pause?* Explore this idea with the children.

Let the children work independently for five minutes to add actions to their pathways that will make their character unique, such as looking at a watch, holding onto a hat or looking around for a friend. Ask, *Will your characters be calm or moving frantically? Will they adopt different poses at different times?*

Share these ideas with each other and give the children an opportunity to reflect and extend them. Practise the sequences until the children have put together a travel, still cameo and travel phrase. Build the dance by asking some children to move at certain times and pause as a still picture, while others begin their pathways.

Dress up in different costumes or use props to add realism to the dance in later lessons. Introduce canon entrances and exits, where different children enter the painting at different times, from different sides, from the back or front and travelling across, diagonally or to the front or back so that there is an ever-changing landscape to create different paintings for a class or group freeze-frame. Take photos of these for a class display of the dance. The children may wish to add effects during an ICT activity.

EXTENDING CREATIVE THINKING SKILLS

Subject and QCA unit, NLS or NNS objective	Activity title	Thinking objective	Activity	Page
English. NLS objectives: To write poems based on personal or imagined experience; to list phrases and words; to experiment with powerful and expressive verbs	Tricks for scoring goals	To think imaginatively; to extend ideas	Listening to a poem and writing their own imaginative verses.	98
Maths. NNS objective: To solve mathematical problems and puzzles, recognise simple patterns and relationships, generalise and predict	Seating plan	To think laterally	Creating seating plans.	99
Science. QCA unit 4B: Habitats	Different worlds	To hypothesise; to create ideas	Creating habitats suitable for different creatures.	100
History. QCA unit 18: What was it like to live here in the past?	Living here	To hypothesise	Thinking about how people used to live in the local area.	101
Geography. QCA units 8 and 21: Improving the environment; How can we improve the area we can see from our window?	Beautiful world	To think laterally; to create ideas	Improving an area or areas within the school.	103
Design and technology. QCA unit 3A: Packaging	Pizza delivery	To create ideas	Making packaging for takeaway meals.	104
ICT. QCA unit 4B: Developing images using repeating patterns	Misfits	To hypothesise	Using images to create a piece of artwork.	105
Art and design. QCA unit 4C: Journeys	Journeys	To extend ideas	Using techniques and styles in Aboriginal art to inform and extend their own ideas for using symbols to depict a journey.	106
Music. QCA unit 9: Animal magic	Magical animals	To think imaginatively	Composing a piece of music to depict animal movements.	107
RE. QCA unit 3B: How and why do Hindus celebrate Divali?	Divali	To create ideas	Planning and holding a Divali celebration in school.	109
PE. QCA unit: Net/wall games – unit 1	Balloon antics	To think imaginatively	Making up a game to play with a balloon.	110

TRICKS FOR SCORING GOALS

SUBJECT: ENGLISH. NLS OBJECTIVES: TO WRITE POEMS BASED ON PERSONAL OR IMAGINED EXPERIENCE, LINKED TO POEMS READ; TO LIST BRIEF PHRASES AND WORDS; TO EXPERIMENT BY TRIMMING OR EXTENDING SENTENCES; TO EXPERIMENT WITH POWERFUL AND EXPRESSIVE VERBS.

LEARNING OBJECTIVE
To write new verses in the same style as a given poem.

THINKING OBJECTIVES
To think imaginatively; to extend ideas.

THINKING SKILLS
The children will listen to a humorous poem and relate this to their own experience. They will use their imagination to consider other possible ways to distract the goalkeeper's attention in order to score a goal. The children will then extend and elaborate their ideas, and add verses, over the next few days.

WHAT YOU NEED
A copy of 'How to score goals' by Allan Ahlberg from *Friendly Matches* (Penguin), enlarged so the whole class can see; paper and pens; Blu-Tack.

WHAT TO DO
Tell the children that you are going to write a poem together that follows a certain style and uses a range of ideas and devices to create interest and variety.

Read the poem together and talk about the humour and how the poem is structured. Ask:

◉ *How are the verses numbered?*
◉ *How does each verse start? Are they always the same, or sometimes different?*
◉ *Are the verses the same length, or are some shorter or longer? Why is this?*
◉ *How do the verses finish?*
◉ *Which word is used most?*
◉ *When the words 'shoot' and 'etc' are used at the end of some verses instead of 'goal', is a goal scored? How do we know? Can we infer this?*

Look at verses four, six and ten, which use brackets. Ask, *Why have these been used?* Explain that they are used to indicate an aside comment, like we sometimes have in play scripts. Talk about how the poem is written as if the poet were talking directly to us, as in a play.

Invite the children to follow the author's style and add their own ideas by writing additional verses to extend the poem. Share their verses at intervals throughout the lesson, and at the end, so that they can contribute to each other's ideas by editing and extending the description or effect.

Display the verses where the children can reach them to elaborate on and extend some of the ideas, possibly through using more interesting words, phrasing things in a more complex way, or by adding suitable expressive punctuation.

The poem can be added to over a number of days or until the children run out of ideas. They might even be motivated to carry on with this as a homework activity. Alternatively, they might like to e-mail another class to ask for additional ideas.

DIFFERENTIATION
Let the children work in pairs or small groups to share ideas and spark each other's imaginations. This will benefit lower *and* higher attaining children, either through working in mixed-ability groups or through pairing two higher attaining children together.

WHERE NEXT
Write other 'How to...' poems, such as 'How to win a race' or 'How to get to the front of a queue'.

ASSESSMENT
Keep the children's poems to note their imaginative ideas and how well they follow the poet's style to extend their thinking and presentation of ideas.

LEARNING OUTCOMES
All the children will be able to work together to develop a longer poem. Some will use their imagination to write their own verses, following similar ideas, and incorporating the style devices used by the author. They will go on to extend their ideas by elaborating and adding interest to them.

FURTHER ENGLISH CHALLENGES
No ears today
Read the poem 'Thirteen questions you should be prepared to answer if you lose your ears in school today' by John Coldwell, published in *Penny Whistle Pete and Other Pesky Poems* (Collins Pathway). Listen to all the excuses made for not having ears in school that day. Think of other possible excuses. Look carefully at how the poem is presented and how the illustrations support the text.

Encourage the children to use their imaginations to think about other things that could have been left at home that day (for example, their eyes, tongue or brain), and make up excuses for not having them with you.

Finally, invite the children to think of other things they do not have today (for example, their manners, sense of humour or smile), and write a poem in the same style, giving reasons for not having the chosen characteristic with you that day. Encourage the children to illustrate their poems, and to extend their ideas by editing and elaborating, introducing more interesting vocabulary and punctuation to get the meaning across effectively.

SEATING PLAN

SUBJECT: MATHS. NNS OBJECTIVE: TO SOLVE MATHEMATICAL PROBLEMS AND PUZZLES, RECOGNISE SIMPLE PATTERNS AND RELATIONSHIPS, GENERALISE AND PREDICT.

LEARNING OBJECTIVE
To find a way to solve a mathematical problem.

THINKING OBJECTIVE
To think laterally.

THINKING SKILLS
The children will consider the number of people who will be attending the school show and decide how to organise the seating so that everyone can have a seat, move around comfortably and see clearly. They will consider the size of the chairs and how they can perhaps raise some of them to improve the view for people at the back.

WHAT YOU NEED
Large sheets of paper scaled to fit the size of the space; 100 squares of paper cut to scale to repersent chairs; a prepared sheet of paper with squares attached in rows of ten; paper and pens; Blu-Tack.

WHAT TO DO
Talk about an occasion when parents come to school to watch a show or attend a presentation. Talk about the number of people who usually come, and the number allowed into the hall. Ask how many seats will be needed if 100 people attend, how many if 87 attend, and so on, to make sure that the children understand that each person will need a chair.

Start with 100 – a nice round number. Talk to the children about how the seats might be arranged to fit this number into the hall. Accept their

suggestions, probably organising them into rows of ten. Ask, *How many rows of ten will you need*?

Produce your pre-prepared sheet with squares of paper in rows of ten, attached with Blu-Tack so that they can be moved about. Explain that the paper is cut to scale, and that the seats are also cut to scale to represent the size of the space and seats. Look at your arrangement and discuss whether this is still what the children want. *How could you rearrange the seats so that they are still in rows of ten but give people a better view?* Talk about how rows can be staggered so that the people in the second row can look over the shoulders of those in front of them. Move this row slightly to show them what you mean. Now ask, *What about an aisle to allow people to leave without disturbing too many other people? Where can you make this? What about two aisles?* and so on.

Discuss the possibility of organising the rows in fives, perhaps leaving a larger gap in the middle of the first four rows so that those in rows five to ten can see better. Ask, *Will rows of 20 fit into the space? Should the rows be straight, or are they better in a semicircle?* Discuss the children's ideas before putting them into groups to investigate their own organisation.

Give each group of children their own scaled sheet of paper and seats and let them work to develop their own seating arrangement. Encourage them to think about larger numbers of seats in each row, perhaps 15 or 20, if these will fit. Share these plans at the end of the lesson, noting any different arrangements and discussing why the groups have decided to arrange them in the way that they have.

DIFFERENTIATION
Take the lower attaining children into the hall with 100 chairs and arrange these physically into rows. Count with the children how many seats are in each row, and reorganise them, if they wish, into different arrangements, with different numbers of chairs in each row. Give higher attaining children a different number of chairs that does not divide evenly. This will require them to think about odd and even numbers of seats in different rows.

WHERE NEXT
Let each group work with an adult, and use chairs to make and evaluate their arrangement during the next day's group work.

ASSESSMENT
Note the children who think laterally to solve the problem, perhaps by having different numbers to those expected to create a different arrangement of seats.

LEARNING OUTCOMES

Most children will think laterally to create their own arrangement of chairs. Some will copy your suggestion, or work with smaller numbers and think about the different ways these can be grouped.

FURTHER MATHS CHALLENGES

Jumbo jet

Create a seating arrangement for a Jumbo jet. (Depending on the size, this is usually done in a three-four-three or three-five-three format. Layouts and numbers of seats can be found on the Internet sites of various airlines, so the children can compare their ideas when they have finished.) Let the children think about how they can arrange the correct number of seats in economy class, then compare their ideas with how seats are actually arranged. Invite them to label the seat numbers in rows so that passengers can find their seats easily. Ask, *Can you think of a better way to do this than the conventional method?*

First class

Tell the children that the front of the aeroplane contains 39 first class seats. They take up the first six rows of the aeroplane. Ask them, *How could the seats be organised?* Invite the children to think laterally to investigate and solve the problem. Ask, *How many different arrangements can you find?*

DIFFERENT WORLDS

SUBJECT: SCIENCE. QCA UNIT 4B: HABITATS.

LEARNING OBJECTIVE

To learn that certain creatures and plants need certain conditions to live, and that these are found in particular habitats.

THINKING OBJECTIVES

To hypothesise; to create ideas.

THINKING SKILLS

The children will hypothesise what it would be like to be a creature living in a particular part of the school grounds. They will consider the life support systems and conditions that different creatures and plants need, before creating some habitats of their own so that they can study these life forms more closely.

WHAT YOU NEED

Glass or plastic tanks; soil; leaves; grasses; suitable lids with air holes; equipment to collect creatures, such as pooters and magnispectors; research materials covering the plants and creatures collected.

WHAT TO DO

List all the different habitats that the children can think of throughout the world. Write these on the board under headings such as *large habitats* (oceans, on land, underground), *medium habitats* (rivers, ponds, beaches, fields and rainforests), and *small habitats* (under a stone, hedgerows, trees and bushes).

Choose any one of these habitats and, pretending to be one of the creatures that live there, imagine with the children what it must be like to live there. Ask them, *What would the habitat be like? Why would you live here? What conditions does the habitat contain that you need to live? What other creatures would you be likely to meet? Would it be safe? Where would you sleep? What would you eat? Where would you find it? What plants are likely to be there? Would there be one or more than one in a group? Why would those plants be found here?* Repeat this with a different habitat.

Now think about habitats in the school grounds. Invite the children to work in pairs to choose one habitat and creature and discuss what it would be like for them to live here. Ask, *What dangers would you encounter? What would your day be like?* Ask them to present this as a short piece of drama that reflects their hypotheses about the habitats and conditions that different creatures need. Share some of these with the rest of the class.

Explain to the children that you want to create small habitats for little creatures so that you can study them in the school grounds and in the classroom. Research a range of sources for information about the kind of environment that different creatures like. For example, *Snails and worms like damp conditions, hedgehogs like dry conditions, and ants can live with either. Some creatures like wood and twigs, some prefer leaves and grass, others live in or near water.*

Ask different groups of children to choose one habitat and to plan and design one on a scale that they can care for. Discuss these together to see what hypotheses the children have used in their designs. Ask, *Why have you included these plants? Have you thought about predators? What about food sources? How does the habitat support the lives of your chosen creatures? Will it support other types of organism – both plants and animals?*

If possible, create some of the habitats in the classroom and others in the school grounds. Test the children's hypotheses to see if the finished habitats will support the life systems they are designed for. Ask, *Is there enough food? Will you need to monitor this and provide additional food occasionally?*

Habitats that are suitable to keep inside include wormeries, a snail or fish aquarium, stick insect or centipede tanks. Make sure that glass and plastic containers are large and airy and are not left in direct sunlight. Outdoors, you can develop hedgerows and ponds, and plant bushes such as buddleia, which attract insects like ladybirds and butterflies.

Where habitats are set up inside the classroom, note carefully where the creatures were found so that they can be returned safely at the end of the unit. Follow your LEA guidance for keeping and preserving creatures in school.

DIFFERENTIATION
Work with higher attaining children to design a pond suitable to sustain a variety of pond life. They should use secondary sources of information to inform their hypotheses. Lower attaining children should go out with an adult to explore the school grounds and locate different creatures. Ask them, *What are the habitats like? What conditions are there?* Set up another area in the school grounds to imitate one of these, and monitor the new area to see if it attracts similar creatures now that the conditions have changed. Hypothesise which creatures the children may find after a number of days. Note anything that creatures favouring damp or dry conditions have in common. Then hypothesise whether certain creatures (slugs, centipedes, hamsters, gerbils, and so on) would like damp or dry conditions based on these features.

WHERE NEXT
Monitor the habitats closely to make sure that they can sustain the creatures they have been designed for, and that no harm comes to the creatures.

Study one habitat in detail and note the needs of the creatures and plants. Pond life is particularly good for this, as there are so many different types of organisms, both plants and creatures.

ASSESSMENT
Note the children who hypothesise correctly which creatures like certain conditions, and reason why.

LEARNING OUTCOMES
Most children will understand that different creatures and plants need different conditions to thrive, and that they have certain features because of the places they live in.

FURTHER SCIENCE CHALLENGES
Plant world
Use growbags or a small patch of garden to create habitats for different plants, such as cacti, bedding plants, mosses, grasses and wild flowers. Talk about the plants that like dry habitats and those that like wet habitats in order to grow. Observe the plants as they thrive and note the conditions that have enabled this to happen.

Water world
Create an environment for water plants to grow. Think about the type and amount of water they need in order to grow. Try this out and create different types of water garden for your plants. Visit a garden centre to research the conditions first, if necessary.

LIVING HERE

SUBJECT: HISTORY. QCA UNIT 18: WHAT WAS IT LIKE TO LIVE HERE IN THE PAST?

LEARNING OBJECTIVE
To ask questions about an area's past from studying pictures.

THINKING OBJECTIVE
To hypothesise.

THINKING SKILLS
The children will examine a photograph of everyday life in the past and put together a performance of the events leading up to the taking of the photograph, and afterwards.

They will hypothesise about what people are saying to each other, based on their enquiries from a previous lesson – for example, 'Then and now, here and there', in Chapter 3 of this book – about the way people used to live in the local area.

WHAT YOU NEED
Photographs of people from the local area taking part in an everyday activity from the immediate past, and ones from further back in time, such as the sixties or seventies – perhaps of a family on holiday, a wedding, a street party or a carnival (Newspaper archives are good sources of these, if you want non-

family related photographs of local events in the past.); whiteboard and pen; paper and pens.

WHAT TO DO

In a previous lesson, carry out research into the period in which your photographs were taken. Find out about the fashions, the way of life, and the events that are depicted. Find out the reasons for any celebrations or activities taking place in the photographs. Carry out this lesson only when the children have a good knowledge and understanding of the way people lived in the chosen period. This fits well with what life was like during the recent past in the local area, or post-war Britain in the forties, fifties, sixties or seventies.

Look at one of the photographs and talk about what the people are doing. Ask, *Where are they? Are they going somewhere? Are they celebrating something?* Speculate together about what they may be saying to one another. Relate the children's ideas to what they know about the event from their previous research.

Ask them, *What do you think the people were doing before the photograph was taken? Why was the photograph taken? Why did the people decide that this would be a good place or time to choose? Is it because it will help them remember the day or the particular event? How does the photograph help us to learn about the way people used to live?*

Invite a group of children to act out the moment just before the photograph was taken, whether it was spontaneous or whether the people posed for it. When they have finished, invite another group to act out what may happen next. Discuss whether there could be other interpretations of this.

Organise the children into groups and ask them to interpret the photograph in a different way: to act out what they think happened immediately before the event and what happened afterwards. Perform the cameos in sequence, and note and discuss the different ways the event has been interpreted.

DIFFERENTIATION

Ask higher attaining children to think about any events that led up to the photograph but which took place a while before it was taken. This could include organising the event, or hearing about the end of the War, or the Coronation. Work with lower attaining children, questioning and prompting them to think about what the people in the photographs may have said, are saying, and may say to each other in the moments before, during and after the photograph was taken.

WHERE NEXT

Adapt and repeat the activity with other photographs and paintings for different historical periods with which the children are familiar, and for which they have carried out research into lifestyles and events, and the cause and effect for these.

ASSESSMENT

Watch the children's performances and note those who link historical facts they have learned during other enquiries to their hypotheses.

LEARNING OUTCOMES

Most children will learn to hypothesise about what might be happening in a photograph and how this relates to the way people used to live.

FURTHER HISTORY CHALLENGES

Ironing

Challenge the children to act out how they think different historical artefacts would have been used.

Ask one child to act out a short cameo of how a flat iron would have been used, before discussing how close this hypothesis was to the actuality. Repeat this with modern-day irons. Relate their hypotheses to the way people used to live, how long it took to do the ironing in the past, how the iron was heated, and so on. Repeat the activity, giving different artefacts to different groups of children to act out.

Street party

Find out all the facts that you can about a street party held locally in the past. Use the information to hypothesise what the party would have been like. Then let the children organise and act out their own interpretation of the party and enjoy the experience together.

Beautiful world

SUBJECT: GEOGRAPHY. QCA UNITS 8 AND 21: IMPROVING THE ENVIRONMENT; HOW CAN WE IMPROVE THE AREA WE CAN SEE FROM OUR WINDOW?

LEARNING OBJECTIVE
To express likes and dislikes about an area and identify how people affect the environment.

THINKING OBJECTIVES
To think laterally; to create ideas.

THINKING SKILLS
The children will select an outdoor area that they wish to improve. They will think about what they like and dislike about the area before using this information to make improvements. They will consider all the different ways that this might be achieved, thinking laterally, before putting their ideas into effect by creating their ideas physically.

WHAT YOU NEED
An area outside the classroom in need of improvement; a camera; large sheets of paper and drawing materials; adhesive; whiteboard and pen.

WHAT TO DO
Go for a walk in the school grounds and locate areas that look attractive and other places that do not – look for litter-strewn places, a lack of greenery, broken walls or furniture. Take photographs of these and print off copies for the children to use in their group work.

On returning to the classroom, note down where the photos were taken and discuss why certain places are nice to be in or look at, and others are not. Talk about how these areas might be improved. The children may suggest, *planting an area of garden, creating a place to sit and reflect, making a plain brick wall more attractive, or getting rid of litter or weeds.*

Share thoughts about how these places could be improved, and list them on a large sheet of paper to act as prompts to the children's ideas and to keep the thinking focused.

When the photographs have been developed, divide the children into groups and ask each group to choose a photograph of one area which needs improving. They can choose the same area as another group if they wish. Stick the photograph of this area in the centre of a large sheet of paper and ask the children to work together to select one small part at a time (perhaps a brick wall or a weedy flowerbed) and design new and improved views of these around

the photograph. Let the children's imagination run wild so that they create lots of new and exciting ideas for the space. Try not to direct their thinking.

At the end of the lesson, ask each group to outline their ideas and to say how they would improve the area.

When all the groups have finished their presentation, ask the class to suggest how they will sustain their improvements. Ask them, *What do you need to do to make sure it stays an attractive place?*

DIFFERENTIATION
Work with lower attaining children on one particular aspect that they have chosen themselves to develop, for example, improving a garden area or creating a raised flowerbed for a particular area of the playground. Focus on how you can make the area more attractive by painting or adding colourful sculptures or pots. Challenge higher attaining children to turn a blank brick wall into an attractive place. They can draw pictures, make flower boxes and containers, or add a mural.

WHERE NEXT
Choose the children's favourite ideas and transform the selected area. Transfer the activity to a local amenity, perhaps the local park or play area.

ASSESSMENT
Note the children who think laterally to create different ideas for improving their chosen place. Do they think of new ways to plant flowers or vegetables? Do they consider how litter can be collected? Do they have thoughts on how to brighten up a bare wall in new and interesting ways?

LEARNING OUTCOMES
Most children will suggest improvements to a particular area of the playground and come up with ideas for creating something new. Some children will think about how they can improve what is already there. Some will start to think about caring for the environment, and how they can encourage others to do so to sustain and maintain the place in its newly improved state.

FURTHER GEOGRAPHY CHALLENGES
A secret garden
Create a haven in an area of the school grounds. Include seats, flowerbeds and shade. Design a way of screening it off from the hustle and bustle of the rest of the playground, but allowing it to be seen and supervised. Think about how the garden can stimulate the different senses of sight, touch, smell and hearing.

Litter collection

Consider ways to keep areas litter free. Encourage the children to think laterally to create new types of bins – perhaps ones that operate electronically, with an arm that comes out and picks up the litter if it falls onto the ground in front? They might even create costumes for the bins to give them characters, such as Litter Letty, Garbage Gavin or Rubbish Rita.

PIZZA DELIVERY

SUBJECT: DESIGN AND TECHNOLOGY. QCA UNIT 3A: PACKAGING.

LEARNING OBJECTIVE

To generate ideas for an item of packaging, considering its purpose and uses.

THINKING OBJECTIVE

To create ideas.

THINKING SKILLS

The children will think about the purpose of the packaging used to transport pizza, considering the need to keep it warm and protected, so the packaging needs to be strong and insulating. They will also need to consider whether to advertise the pizza delivery service on the packaging and, if so, how information can be designed to attract the eye.

WHAT YOU NEED

Different pizza delivery boxes; card, polystyrene, plastic, wood and other materials from which the children can choose; scissors; adhesive; whiteboard and pen; paper and pens.

WHAT TO DO

Explain to the children that you want them to design and make suitable packaging for a pizza delivery service. Give out the boxes used by different companies for the children to look at in groups. Ask them to suggest adjectives that describe the properties of the boxes, such as *strong, sturdy, flat, easy to store*. Make a note of these.

Open one box out to show its net and talk about the way it is made. Ask, *How many faces does it have? Are they all the same size? How deep is the box? What shape is the net? How is it put together? Why has it got tabs? What are these for?*

Remake the box into its box shape and evaluate its depth. Ask, *How deep is it? Is it deep enough to hold a pizza with a thick base? How will the box need to be carried? What will happen to the pizza if the box is carried on its end or upside down? Has anyone ever found the pizza stuck to the top of the box when it is opened? How can we prevent this happening?*

Ask the children whether they like to eat pizza hot or cold. Then ask, *How can we make sure the pizza remains hot during its journey? Think about the different ways you know to keep food warm and how we can use this knowledge to insulate the box.*

Let the children consider the type of box they will need to transport and keep a pizza warm for fifteen minutes. Before they start making the box, their planning should take into consideration its shape, size, insulation, strength, and how they can stop the topping getting stuck to the top of the box during transportation. They should consider carefully the material from which they will make the box and, at the same time, make sure that it can be put together quickly and easily.

Let the children work individually as they are planning and making their boxes, but encourage them to talk together in pairs and small groups to evaluate and comment upon each other's ideas. Ask them, *Why have you chosen these materials? How have you constructed your box? Why have you made it this particular size? How have you prevented the topping sticking to the lid of the box?*

Next, consider how to make the boxes eye-catching. Ask, *How will other people know where the pizza came from? How will it encourage them to buy one for themselves?* Design symbols and decoration for the boxes.

DIFFERENTIATION

Give lower attaining children a ready-made box and ask them to decorate it with symbols and decorations that will catch the eye of a buyer. Higher attaining children should be encouraged to create a different shaped box that will be suitable for the pizza and provide a different design.

WHERE NEXT

Let the children test out the suitability of their boxes.

Look at other takeaway packaging and talk about how this is made, and the materials used.

ASSESSMENT

Note the children who create different ideas for the style, shape and way of transporting the carton. Note also the children who are particularly creative in decorating the box and understand how this advertises the shop's services and may prompt others to buy.

LEARNING OUTCOMES

Most children will design a basic box for transporting their pizzas. Some will think more creatively and come up with different ways to keep the pizza warm or to stop it sticking to the lid of the box. Most will think creatively to design suitable symbols and decoration to 'sell' their pizza delivery service.

FURTHER DESIGN AND TECHNOLOGY CHALLENGES

Jolly snacks

Design a box for transporting a snack from the classroom to the school playground for a picnic. The children should be challenged to create a way of carrying a drink, a sandwich and an apple, keeping each item undamaged, from the classroom to the playground. Some children may wish to include other food items to carry in their box. Consider the use of dividers, wrapping the food items in bubble wrap, or using a drinks container with a lid. Challenge higher attaining pupils to make a lid or some other way of covering the food.

Drinks carrier

Design and make a carrier that will transport two, three or four beakers of liquid so that they can be carried in one hand, thus leaving the other hand free to open the door. Let the children choose the materials from which to make the carrier. Challenge higher attaining children to make a carrier to carry drinks containers of different sizes.

MISFITS

SUBJECT: ICT. QCA UNIT 4B: DEVELOPING IMAGES USING REPEATING PATTERNS.

LEARNING OBJECTIVE

To use visual effects to create artwork.

THINKING OBJECTIVE

To hypothesise.

THINKING SKILLS

The children will think about how they can use visual images to produce a piece of artwork. They will consider a range of effects to hypothesise what their images will look like, before deciding for themselves which to use and combine to create an original piece of work.

WHAT YOU NEED

A digital camera or scanner; photo software, photographs of individual children; a video camera with the facility to change effects; a copy of the print *Marilyn Monroe* and other work by Andy Warhol.

WHAT TO DO

Make a short video sequence of the children taking part in an activity such as PE or playtime. Over lunchtime, or before the start of a day, link the video camera to a television to play this short extract back to the children. Discuss how clearly you can see their images, and note the colours, shade and light in the film. Play the extract through again, and this time engage the video effects, such as black and white, wide screen, sepia, mosaic and misty edges. Ask the children, *What do you think of these?* If possible, take a still photo of these to download into the computer and print out for the children to refer to.

Look at the print by Andy Warhol and talk about how he produced the different effects of the images of Marilyn Monroe. Discuss the colours and the way he has combined the different effects to make his picture. Ask, *Has he changed one or more things each time he has printed out the image?*

Show the children how to scan or download a photo of themselves into the computer and how to change the colours and background. Rotate and flip the image to create a different view. Work out together how you can create a picture in the same style as Warhol's. Copy the image and paste it in a tile pattern before changing each one in some way, for example changing the colour, blurring the edges or adjusting the size to create a different effect.

Organise the children into pairs so that they can talk about their work and choose the effects they want to try before they produce them. Move around each pair, encouraging them to create, in their heads, what they want their picture to look like before they alter the effect. Ask, *What colour do you want to use for the face or the hair? Do you want to flip the image? Do you want to rotate it?* Encourage them to think about what their finished picture will look like before they add the effect, so that they can evaluate how successful they have been. Ask, *Did you think it would look like this?* Save the finished pictures after each effect has been added and use the tiles to make a repeating pattern in the same style as Warhol.

Let the children make a second picture using the photograph of their partner. Use this second task as an assessment opportunity, to check whether the children are beginning to conceive their finished picture before they add the chosen effect. Encourage them to plan what they want their finished picture to look like before deciding where to place each different image. Note their conversations as they work to see if this consideration of the finished picture is happening before the effect is added to each image. Save the images each time and use them to create a second picture in the style of Warhol.

DIFFERENTIATION

Discuss the different effects created with the video camera with lower attaining children in a small group afterwards, while others are still working on the computers. Discuss how the effects change the way the footage looks. Press 'pause' and look at the still photo this creates.

Higher-attaining children should be encouraged to think of other possible effects they could introduce on a camera and write these ideas down.

WHERE NEXT

Take a photograph of a person and cut it up into small squares. Rearrange the pieces to recreate the photo.

Look at how portraits have sometimes been created by combining small photographs. This happens in the opening credits of the *Parkinson* TV programme, and has been done with characters from the *Star Wars* movies. Examples are found in most good poster shops.

ASSESSMENT

Assess the children as they work on the second task. Note those who hypothesise before they add their effect, and then evaluate together how successful they have been. Note the children who understand that the camera is portraying the same photo or video, but with a different effect. Keep the children's creations as evidence of who can transfer this idea to producing their own repeating pictures using a range of styles and effects.

LEARNING OUTCOMES

Most children will hypothesise what they think their photo will look like before they add their particular photo effects. They will understand that

applying visual effects to the same photo can create predetermined and planned, yet different, styles of painting and pictures.

FURTHER ICT CHALLENGES
Comic book art

Trace or draw comic heroes or characters. Hypothesise how you can create a picture in the same style. Ask, *How can you produce the image on the computer, and how can you make changes to it?* Ask the children to imagine what their finished picture will look like by reproducing the image several times in outline, drawing and planning the effects they intend to use before trying these out for themselves on screen.

Vases and bottle art

Take photos of everyday objects, such as vases or bottles. Choose objects with little detail so the changes are easier to make. Incorporate the flip, rotate, cut and flip skills learned in this and previous lessons to explore the range of visual effects. Imagine with the children how they think the finished picture will look if they use certain effects.

JOURNEYS

SUBJECT: ART AND DESIGN.
QCA UNIT 4C: JOURNEYS.

LEARNING OBJECTIVE
To develop ideas for their work.

THINKING OBJECTIVE
To extend ideas.

THINKING SKILLS
The children will look at the different techniques used by Aboriginal artists to create a story that tells of the journey of the animals. They will consider the symbols used and how they are arranged before using this to spark their own ideas. You may wish to link this to the next activity, 'Magical Animals'.

WHAT YOU NEED
A copy of an Aboriginal painting which shows symbols representing the movement of different animals; white, red and yellow paint; black or dark brown paper; paintbrushes.

WHAT TO DO
As a class, look at the painting and identify all the different symbols. Draw these on a separate sheet of

paper to show the children the designs. Ask, *What do they remind you of? Do they look like animal tracks?* Talk about how many times these are repeated, the different colours they are painted in, and the way that they have been translated or rotated on the painting. Ask, *What kind of animals do you think the symbols represent? How do you know? Has an animal been drawn?* Snakes are often favourites. Relate the different animals to the Aborigine Dreamtime stories.

Now look carefully at the way the symbols are painted. Ask, *Are they drawn, or produced with a series of dots? What colours have been used? Why are they these colours, do you think?* Explain how the Aborigine people made their paints from the earth and rocks they found around them, such as red Outback soil and white chalk. Tell them that people often borrowed ideas from each other's paintings, but did not copy them exactly, as this was considered offensive.

Together, make up the story of the journeys the different animals in the painting are making. How are they moving? Where are they going? From where have they started? Do they meet another animal on the way? Invite the children to think about animals they are familiar with and how they might represent these on a painting. Let them work individually to explore their ideas in sketchbooks before translating their ideas into paint. Invite them to use the Aboriginal ideas for producing the different symbols, and to use the same colours to create similar effects.

DIFFERENTIATION
Give lower attaining children a painting so that they can copy some of the symbols. As they produce them, ask them to say which animal is represented and which way it is travelling.

Higher attaining children should be encouraged to tell a story through their paintings, and to think about how many animals are travelling together and how many are alone. Ask, *How can you show on your painting whether the different groups meet up?*

WHERE NEXT
Make group paintings on large sheets of paper, incorporating several of the children's ideas. Mix paint with sand to create different textures.

ASSESSMENT
Look at the children's sketchbooks and note those who use the ideas to create their own unique symbols to represent a journey. Help those who tend to copy ideas from the painting to produce a different symbol to represent movement.

LEARNING OUTCOMES
Most children will be able to extend their ideas to depict animals going on a journey and develop these in a sketchbook for later use.

FURTHER ART AND DESIGN CHALLENGES
Doodling
Explore the shapes and designs made by doodling. Let the children 'take their pencil for a walk' and look at the finished 'scribble' to find shapes and pictures in it. Use a black crayon or felt-tipped pen to outline the shapes they have made. Look at paintings by Miro and talk about whether their doodles look like the characters in his paintings. Extend their ideas by repeating the activity, but perhaps with a particular character or object in mind. Ask, *How does the doodling add shape and form to the finished drawing?*
Border design
Create a paper frieze to act as a border for a display of the children's paintings. Challenge the children to 'take their pencil for a walk' to create a continuous design along a sheet of paper. Extend the idea by transferring this design to a printing block to create the finished border.

MAGICAL ANIMALS

SUBJECT: MUSIC. QCA UNIT 9: ANIMAL MAGIC.

LEARNING OBJECTIVE
To use musical elements to describe the movement of animals.

THINKING OBJECTIVE
To think imaginatively.

THINKING SKILLS
The children will think about the way animals move, both when they are going from one place to another, and when they are standing on the spot. This lesson develops the children's thinking about how the different elements of music could reflect the movements of different animals, for example through changes of tempo (speed), pitch (tune level), and duration (length of notes). They will then think imaginatively when considering various situations

that animals find themselves in, such as peaceful sleep or danger from predators, and use timbre (quality) and dynamics (loud and quiet) to reflect these moods and feelings. Some pupils will consider the structure of the finished piece and begin to tell a story of the animal's movements through music.

WHAT YOU NEED
Two large sheets of paper for each group; pens; a range of pitched and non-pitched musical instruments; whiteboard and pen.

WHAT TO DO
Explain to the children that the outcome of the lesson (or series of lessons) will be for them to compose a journey in sound for an animal of their choice. Decide whether you want to give the children complete freedom to choose, or whether you want to build on earlier work and restrict the choice to one continent – for example, Australia.

Brainstorm the names of all the animals that live in Australia. List the names on the board or a large sheet of paper that can then be displayed where everyone can see it, and write adjectives that describe the movement of each one. For example:

- ☉ Kangaroo – jumping, fast, high, strong, zigzag.
- ☉ Cassowary – slow, fast, jump, swerve.
- ☉ Lizard – very slow, low, crawl, pause.
- ☉ Snake – fast, slither, strike.
- ☉ Spider – scamper, run, scurry, stop.

Ask different groups to think of musical phrases for each of the animals that will depict each of these movements. Let the children explore the range of instruments before stopping them to talk about some of the sounds they have made. Evaluate which are most effective, before guiding them to think about changing some of the musical elements to make the sounds depict the movements more effectively. For example: *Does the kangaroo keep the same speed, or does he stop every so often and jump more slowly? Can these phrases be repeated a few times to give the music structure? Will the movement of the spider be more dramatic if a tune is used to depict the scurrying?*

Think about the different times of the day that these animals will move. Ask, *Will they always move in the same way? What will their movements be like when they are standing still? How can you depict these different times of day and movements musically?*

Perform the musical phrases to the other groups and evaluate together how the elements can

be further used to add more effect. On large sheets of paper, the groups record the music pictorially so that other groups who have not heard the music before will know how to play it precisely. They will need to include notes for tunes, rhythms for speed and duration, and directions for dynamics. Finally, they will need to think about when the different instruments are played in relation to each other, perhaps by overlapping the score. This will combine some of the sounds to add timbre to the piece.

DIFFERENTIATION
Ask higher attaining children to work out chords to depict some of their animals. They should consider how well the notes combine to make a concordant or discordant sound to depict the animals of their choice. Lower attaining children should think about rhythmic phrases and sound pictures only.

WHERE NEXT
Make a class performance of the finished piece, overlapping the times that each group starts and finishes to add timbre and interest. Tape the performance and use the music for a dance about animal journeys. Link this to the work in the art and design lesson 'Journeys' in this chapter.

ASSESSMENT
Assess each group to see how they combine the musical elements imaginatively to depict the various movements of the different animals. How effectively have these been used? Do the musical phrases give a clear picture of each movement?

LEARNING OUTCOMES

All the children will use their imagination to contribute to a group composition, which will build into a class performance. They will all use their imagination to combine musical elements to describe the movement of different animals musically.

FURTHER MUSIC CHALLENGES

Glockenspiel speaking

Consider the different sounds that glockenspiels make by using different types of beaters and playing single, and groups of, notes. Select an animal and challenge the children to think imaginatively to compose a piece of music that depicts its different movements. Tell them to think about the full range of musical elements and to structure the phrases logically. Use the pentatonic scale so that they can combine two or more notes successfully.

Repeat this for other instruments, such as drums, or woodblocks, guiros and maracas together.

Animal sounds

Think about the sounds animals make, such as the braying of a donkey, bird song, cockerels crowing, dogs barking. Ask the children to create these sounds using the instruments you have available, everyday objects and body percussion. Encourage them to alter the tempo (speed), pitch (tune level), and duration (length of notes) to depict the animals' sounds.

DIVALI

SUBJECT: RE. QCA UNIT 3B: HOW AND WHY DO HINDUS CELEBRATE DIVALI?

LEARNING OBJECTIVE

To learn about, and from, some of the customs and practices related to celebrating Divali.

THINKING OBJECTIVE

To create ideas.

THINKING SKILLS

The children will use information they have learned about Divali to create a timetable of activities to celebrate this festival in school. This will help them to understand the purpose and meaning of this celebration to Hindus and Sikhs.

WHAT YOU NEED

Recent research about some of the customs and practices involved in celebrating Divali, such as parties, food and sweets, cards, diva lamps, religious celebrations, Mendhi patterns; paper and pens.

WHAT TO DO

Invite a visitor into school to talk about the purpose and meaning behind celebrating Divali, and why it is so important to Hindus and Sikhs. Talk about all the practices that take place and the way that these should be celebrated. Ask, *What emotions are involved? Is it a noisy or a quiet celebration? What kinds of things do families do when they meet to celebrate Divali? How is this the same as or different to the Christmas parties held in many schools?*

Use this information to organise and create a plan to celebrate Divali. Devise and prepare a number of traditional activities in which the children will take part and let them work out their own timetable for the day, agreeing when, how and in what way these will take place. Make a list of the food, clothes and music that you will need and decide how the class will divide into groups so that everyone takes part in all of the activities.

DIFFERENTIATION

Work with lower attaining children on one activity at a time so that they understand the importance of the purpose and meaning of each one. They can then be fully involved in the planning and creation of Divali celebrations.

Give higher attaining children the job of acting as leaders in the group activities to ensure that they are carried out in the agreed manner.

WHERE NEXT

Plan similar celebrations for different faiths as they occur during the year. Focus on learning about the purpose and meaning of each celebration and making sure that they are celebrated in the correct manner.

ASSESSMENT

Note the children who understand the importance of mood when creating different activities through which to celebrate Divali. Note if anyone thinks of a new idea that fits well into the celebration and suits the intended mood.

LEARNING OUTCOMES

Most children will understand the importance of Divali to Hindus and use this to create a timetable for the day's events and activities when planning and holding suitable celebrations.

FURTHER RE CHALLENGES

Sweet delight

Gather together the ingredients for making sweets for Divali. Use the ingredients to make different kinds of sweets to enjoy at the end of the Divali celebrations.

Divali cards

Think about the symbol of light, as it is used at Divali time, and use this to create Divali cards and divas. Add appropriate designs to the cards and divas to reflect the purpose and meaning of the celebrations.

BALLOON ANTICS

SUBJECT PE: QCA UNIT: NET/WALL GAMES – UNIT 1

LEARNING OBJECTIVE

To make up a competitive team game that includes some kind of scoring.

THINKING OBJECTIVE

To think imaginatively.

THINKING SKILLS

The children will make up a game to play with a balloon or balloons, which could incorporate any other piece of equipment they choose to use. They will decide for themselves on the rules and scoring system, as well as how many players will be on each team.

WHAT YOU NEED

A large indoor space; inflated balloons.

WHAT TO DO

Put the children into small groups and give each group a balloon. Allow them to play for a short while (no longer than five minutes), before stopping them to talk about what they were doing. Ask, *What did you like about the activity? What did you think was going to happen?* Explain that you want them to think of a game they can play against another group. Remind them of the traditional games on which they may want to base their ideas, or suggest that they may want to think of a completely new game. Let the groups explore this for another five minutes before sharing their ideas so far. Introduce the idea of a scoring system. Tell them that at the end of the game there should be a winning team that has scored the most points. Discuss what the teams have to do to score points, and then let the children work together to try out their scoring system. After a short time, collect the children's ideas and summarise them.

Next, decide how much space each team will be allowed to use. Discuss the idea of fairness and how each team should have the same amount of space. Ask, *What happens when the balloon or a player goes outside the space? Are the teams only allowed in certain parts of the court, or can they move freely*

around all the space? Each group should decide whether they would lay out a court. Return to the classroom and allow the children to draw their games, with labels to show the rules and the equipment they will need. Record the scoring system and agree the number of people to have on each team.

Collate all the children's ideas orally before choosing one structure, and one set of rules. Ask, *Will there be a designated amount of time or is the winning team the one to reach a certain number of points?*

Play the game as a class or small group.

DIFFERENTIATION

Remind lower attaining children of some of the games they already know as a starting point for their ideas. Higher attaining children should be given the additional challenge of creating a scorecard for the umpire to keep during the games.

WHERE NEXT

Play the game over a number of weeks to practise the skills and try out tactics.

Set up a competition for the new game to find the class champions.

ASSESSMENT

Note down the children's ideas and whether they have used their imagination to develop a suitable game. Does the game interest the other children in the class, and if so, why?

LEARNING OUTCOMES

All the children will use their imagination to contribute to a new class game.

FURTHER PE CHALLENGES

Anyone for balloon tennis?

Introduce the idea of a bat and let the children use their imagination to develop a suitable game. They may decide to use a net or not, and for the bat to be a hand, a tennis or badminton racquet, a cricket bat or a hockey stick. They will need to think about the number of children on the court in all cases, especially for tennis or badminton-type games.

Balloon blow football

Create a blow balloon football game using a tabletop as the court. Let the children decide how to score the goals – getting the balloon inside a box, or hitting a target that is marked with squares which have different numbers of points to score. They should decide how many children to have in a team, and whether to have a time or goal or points limit to win the game.

EVALUATION SKILLS

INTRODUCTION

Evaluative thinking gives children useful insight by involving them in assessment of their own learning. This is one of the key skills in the National Curriculum; it acknowledges that children need to be able to identify what they should do to improve their work. Although many teachers do encourage children to say what went well, or what was good about something they have done, the children are rarely given opportunities to say what it was that made it good. This leads to an inability to make suggestions for improvement.

The activities in this chapter address this by offering the children opportunities to say what was useful, of good quality or value when identifying the strengths of a particular achievement. There are examples of how these evaluation skills can be developed and adapted to suit other contexts equally well.

The activity in which the children evaluate the usefulness of historical sources is equally valid for other research projects and encourages them to question what they are reading, seeing and hearing.

The skill of evaluating the usefulness of information for the required purpose is the starting point for identifying which information they should collect and which they should reject in any research project they encounter in later school life. This type of activity will help the children to think independently about why the information they are analysing is important to the task. In the activity 'Super gymnasts', the significance is in their planning the arrangement of apparatus to perform their sequences, deciding for themselves which will be useful to the task and which will not. This reinforces the necessary skills of organising, supporting their own learning needs independently, and helping them to develop initiative.

The skills are:
- ⊙ evaluating information, including
- ⊙ judging value
- ⊙ judging usefulness
- ⊙ judging quality
- ⊙ suggesting improvements by developing criteria for judging.

Introducing evaluation skills

Subject and QCA unit, NLS or NNS objective	Activity title	Thinking objective	Activity	Page
English. NLS objective: To evaluate advertisements for their impact, appeal and honesty; linguistic devices, such as puns, jingles, alliteration and invented words	Write it up	To evaluate information (judging quality)	Deciding whether the quality of titles, captions, headings and adverts make an impact.	113
Mathematics. NNS objectives: To read and begin to write the vocabulary related to position, direction and movement	Square co-ordinates	To evaluate information (judging value)	Using a memory game to practise co-ordinates.	113
Science. QCA unit 4F: Circuits and conductors	Does it light up?	To evaluate information (judging quality)	Deciding whether bulbs will light, buzzers will sound and motors will run in different circuit,s and saying what they need to do to make those that do not, work.	114
History. QCA unit 9: What was it like for children in the Second World War?	Children at war	To evaluate information by judging the usefulness of historical sources	Evaluating different sources of evidence.	114
Geography. QCA unit 16: What's in the news?	What's happening?	To evaluate information (judging value)	Looking at newspaper articles and evaluating their value for telling us about that part of the world.	115
Design and technology. QCA unit 4D: Alarms	Set it off and start it up	To evaluate information (judging value)	Evaluating the value of different switches to operate devices.	116
ICT. QCA unit 3D: Exploring simulations	Where to go?	To evaluate information (judging value)	Evaluating a favourite programme to promote to younger children in the school.	116
Art and design. QCA unit 3B: A visit to a museum or gallery.	Gallery tour	To evaluate information (judging value)	Evaluating an Internet site plan for planning a visit to an art gallery.	117
Music. QCA unit 14: Salt, pepper, vinegar and mustard	Jingles	To evaluate information (judging usefulness)	Listening to advertisement jingles and theme tunes and evaluating how the musical elements are used for effect.	117
RE. QCA unit 4D: What religions are represented in our neighbourhoods?	What does it say?	To evaluate the value of learning gained about a religion from a visitor who practises that religion	Considering the value of learning about religion from a visitor who represents that faith and developing the children's awareness of different religions.	118
PE. QCA unit: Gymnastics activites – unit 3	Super gymnasts	To evaluate information (judging quality)	Evaluating and judging the usefulness of particular pieces of apparatus to perform sequences.	119

WRITE IT UP

SUBJECT: ENGLISH. NLS OBJECTIVE: TO EVALUATE ADVERTISEMENTS FOR THEIR IMPACT, APPEAL AND HONESTY, FOCUSING IN PARTICULAR ON HOW INFORMATION ABOUT THE PRODUCT IS PRESENTED; EXAGGERATED CLAIMS AND TACTICS FOR GRABBING ATTENTION; LINGUISTIC DEVICES SUCH AS PUNS, JINGLES, ALLITERATION, AND INVENTED WORDS.

LEARNING OBJECTIVE
To identify the linguistic devices used in advertisements that persuade us to buy products.

THINKING OBJECTIVE
To evaluate information (judging quality).

THINKING SKILLS
The children will judge the quality of captions, jingles and names of products in advertisements. They will give each advert a mark out of ten, before explaining how and why they have given this score. They will relate this to the advertisement's impact, appeal and persuasive argument, deciding how honest the information is and how well it is presented. They will use this information to suggest improvements and develop their own ideas on computer.

WHAT YOU NEED
Adverts cut out of magazines (with the name of the product removed); video extracts of a range of adverts that use jingles, commentary and features that are visually attractive; a video recorder.

WHAT TO DO
Look at the range of paper adverts, with the name of the product removed. Ask if the children can recall what they are. Ask, *How do you recognise the product that is being advertised? Does the slogan or the catchy jingle spark your memory? Does it use colours or shapes that catch your eye? Which ones do you not recognise? Why? How are they different? Are they less memorable because the name is easy to forget, the caption less memorable, or the design less eye-catching?*

Choose one of the adverts and evaluate it in more detail. Look at the labels and captions and decide why these attract the eye. Ask, *Is it because of the style or the catchy title? What message is being given? Is this an honest appraisal of the product or is it exaggerated? How do you know? How effective is the advertisement in persuading you to want to buy that product? What linguistic devices are being used – for example, jingles that rhyme or refer to the product to make the advert stick in your memory; use of imagery that sparks a particularly happy memory or reminds you*

of the product; alliteration to help you remember the name of the product and make you want to buy it, or a pun or play on words.

As a class, give each advert a score out of ten to reflect its quality and how effective it is in advertising the product.

Watch some of your video extracts at this point and evaluate the adverts in the same way. Ask, *Which is your favourite? Why?*

Challenge the children to improve these or make up their own captions, using the quality criteria they have identified. Some may wish to use a computer to do this. Give them a context to guide their thinking, perhaps promoting a forthcoming school event, or asking them to think of a new name for a favourite product. When they have finished, let them give their own and others' captions a score out of ten.

SQUARE CO-ORDINATES

SUBJECT: MATHS. NNS OBJECTIVE: TO READ AND BEGIN TO WRITE THE VOCABULARY RELATED TO POSITION, DIRECTION AND MOVEMENT, FOR EXAMPLE: DESCRIBE AND FIND THE POSITION OF A SQUARE ON A GRID OF SQUARES WITH THE ROWS AND COLUMNS NUMBERED.

LEARNING OBJECTIVE
To describe the position of a square by using co-ordinates.

THINKING OBJECTIVE
To evaluate information (judging value).

THINKING SKILLS
The children will play a simple game using co-ordinates to pair up hidden pictures. They will consider whether the game is useful and valuable in helping them to remember how to use co-ordinates.

WHAT YOU NEED
A pelmanism-type game with up to 18 pairs of matching pictures; a large sheet of paper with horizontal and vertical grid lines numbered.

WHAT TO DO
Organise eight pairs of pictures into a 4 x 4 square and note the co-ordinate label of the square where each one is placed. Revisit how to locate squares using co-ordinate references if the children have forgotten. Turn the pictures face down. Tell the children that there are pairs of pictures hidden in the squares for them to find. They should do this, with a partner, by naming the co-ordinates. So, for example, if a child says (4, 3) and (2, 1), her partner should

turn over the pictures on those squares. If the two pictures match, the first player keeps the pair and has another turn. If not, the pictures are turned over again and the partner has a go. Continue until all the pictures have been paired. The person with the most pairs is the winner. The person selecting the co-ordinates should check that the correct picture is being turned over, and the turner should check with the chooser that they are turning the correct card.

Extend the game by having pictures that match in fours, and making the square or rectangle bigger.

Afterwards, lead a class discussion and ask the children to judge the value of this game in helping them remember how to use co-ordinates. Ask, *Did it make you think carefully about the position of the picture, rather than just which picture it was?* Challenge them to think of other games they could play to help them remember how to use co-ordinates.

DOES IT LIGHT UP?

SUBJECT: SCIENCE. QCA UNIT 4F: CIRCUITS AND CONDUCTORS.

LEARNING OBJECTIVE
To learn that some materials conduct electricity and others do not, and that some are better conductors than others.

THINKING OBJECTIVE
To evaluate information (judging quality).

THINKING SKILLS
The children will construct an electrical circuit and judge whether it is able to make a bulb light, a motor run, or a buzzer sound. They will then think about materials that might substitute for the switch and allow the circuit to work. They will evaluate which materials do nd do not make good conductors, before agreeing that metals make the best conductors.

WHAT YOU NEED
Wires, batteries, bulbs, buzzers and motors, switches; materials of a suitable size to substitute and make home-made switches including aluminium foil, coins, pencil-lead, plastic, steel strips, fabric, rock, paper, and wood.

WHAT TO DO
Put the children into pairs, and ask each pair to make a circuit from wires, a bulb, a battery and a switch. Revise with the children what they have learned about complete circuits, and how the electricity is conducted around the circuit to make the bulb

light. Remind them what happens when the circuit is broken, or when the switch is in the 'off' position.

Tell the children that you will be evaluating different substances together to discover what makes a good conductor of electricity and what does not. Talk about how you can find this out by substituting another material for the switch, and using it to make and break the circuit. Explain that if the material is a suitable conductor, when it is put together to complete the circuit the bulb will light. If it is not, the bulb will not light.

Make a simple switch from foil to demonstrate. Invite someone to push the switch together and note what happens to the bulb. When the foil comes apart and the circuit is broken, note how the bulb goes out. Explain that this is what happens inside a push switch in an electrical circuit.

Organise the children into small groups or pairs and ask them to construct a circuit. Use motors, bulbs or buzzers depending on whether you want to extend the learning to another form of electrical device, and whether your nerves can stand it! Invite the children to use different materials to make the switch and evaluate how effective each one is as a conductor of electricity. Use the materials in your collection, as well as letting the children suggest others to test.

After the children have tested all the materials, ask them, *How can you record which ones will and which will not conduct electricity?* (A *yes/no* list will do.) *How can you show which material is the best conductor?* Relate this to the material used in houses to wire electrical circuits. *Why is metal used?*

Finish with a quiz, asking the children to evaluate whether a bulb will light when different materials are used as conductors.

CHILDREN AT WAR

SUBJECT: HISTORY. QCA UNIT 9: WHAT WAS IT LIKE FOR CHILDREN IN THE SECOND WORLD WAR?

LEARNING OBJECTIVE
To find out how World War II affected children.

Thinking objective

To evaluate information by judging the usefulness of historical sources.

Thinking skills

The children will evaluate a range of information which will help them research the effects of the Second World War on children. They will decide which resources are useful and which are not.

What you need

A wide range of sources of information for the children to evaluate, including accounts of evacuees, memorabilia, reference books, CD-ROMs or websites, videos, films, stories or poems; a whiteboard or large sheet of paper.

What to do

Look at the evidence in your collection and discuss the kinds of things the different resources will help you to find out. Ask, *Will it tell us about the evacuation of children during the war, the things they ate, the clothes they wore, how rationing affected them?*

Together, make a list of questions for planning research about what life was like for children during the Second World War. Write these on a large sheet of paper or the board. Suggestions for questions include, *Where were children who were evacuated sent? How did they get there? What was rationed and why? What was life like for children who were evacuated? What were clothes like at the time?*

Split the children into groups and give each group one of the questions they listed to research. Identify the topic to which it relates – for example, location, transport, food, lifestyles, and clothes. Ask the children to locate all the resources that would be useful for their research. Ask, *Which books are likely to tell you something about your topic? Are there any CD-ROMs or websites that you can use? Are there any videos, films, stories or poems that help describe what life was like? How does the memorabilia help?*

Gather the groups together and, by the side of each question on your list, note all the sources of evidence that were useful to them in finding answers to their queries. Use this information to carry out research into the range of topic areas identified by the children through their questions.

What's happening?

SUBJECT: GEOGRAPHY. QCA UNIT 16: WHAT'S IN THE NEWS?

Learning objective

To decide whether a given newspaper article is useful for finding out about different parts of the world.

Thinking objective

To evaluate information (judging value).

Thinking skills

The children will look at different articles from a range of newspapers and evaluate photographs and written accounts to judge how valuable they are in giving us information about a particular part of the world. They will evaluate information on topics such as place, weather, physical and human features, population, lifestyle and transport processes. They will then decide whether newspapers are valuable resources for research into a particular topic.

What you need

A range of newspaper articles which reflect the geographical features and processes of a particular place, either at home or abroad, such as a football match or other sporting commentary, an account of the Eurovision song contest, the Oscars or a film premier, or a report about a natural disaster; a chart with a list of features and processes (including human and physical features, weather and population statistics, transport systems, environmental issues and lifestyle); large sheets of paper; pens.

What to do

Select a newspaper article to look at with the class to model the process of evaluation. Read the article together and look at the photograph and additional graphics. Agree what the article is about and note some of the information it gives about its locality.

Produce your chart at this point and discuss the headings that you have listed. These should include human and physical features, weather statistics, date/time of year, population, transport systems, environmental issues and lifestyle – you can add any others that occur in your chosen article. Read the beginning of the article again and, against each heading, record any relevant information you have found out from the article. Look at the photograph and make notes of any information that is evident in this. When you have finished and checked that you have noted all the significant facts, look at the amount of information you have gleaned from the article. Ask, *How valuable was this article in finding out about that particular locality?*

Organise the children into groups of two or three and give each group one article and a large sheet of paper. Make sure they can all see the article clearly, then ask them to work through the same process with this new piece of writing. Group higher attaining children together and give them articles about the same event from different newspapers. After they have gathered the initial details, challenge them to compare and contrast the information gleaned. Ask, *Which newspaper article was most valuable for gaining information about that particular locality?*

Share the information at the end of the lesson and agree whether newspapers are valuable resources for researching a new locality.

SET IT OFF AND START IT UP

SUBJECT: DESIGN AND TECHNOLOGY. QCA UNIT 4D: ALARMS.

LEARNING OBJECTIVE
To learn that there are different types of alarm which are used to attract attention.

THINKING OBJECTIVE
To evaluate information (judging value).

THINKING SKILLS
The children will evaluate how effective different alarms are at attracting people's attention. They will use the information to agree the types of switches used to set off alarms, and the value of these for the purpose of the alarm. For example, whether it is strong enough to detect small movement or breaks in the light quality; whether it picks up a small sound.

WHAT YOU NEED
A range of items (plus pictures and video clips of these) that use a switch to set off an alarm to attract the attention of the person using them. Include microwaves, alarm clocks, sirens, burglar alarms, telephone tones, pedestrian crossing lights and sounds, car alarms and timers; a range of different switches attached to a circuit to set off an alarm; a large sheet of paper and a pen.

WHAT TO DO
Set a timer to sound an alarm after five minutes. While this is ticking away, invite the children to suggest all the items they can think of which use an alarm to attract people's attention. List these down the left-hand side of a large sheet of paper.

When the timer goes off, talk about how it works. Ask, *What kind of switch is used to set off the alarm? What is the outcome, or reflex action, caused by the joining of the circuit?* Review the list of items that use alarms and identify how attention is attracted. Is it through sound, or bright flashing lights? List the outcome on the right-hand side of the paper opposite the appropriate item. In the centre identify the likely switches that could be used to set off each alarm. Show these to the class and demonstrate their use.

Finish the lesson by watching the video extracts and looking at the items or pictures of things that set off an alarm when a switch operates a break or join in a circuit. Evaluate the effectiveness of the different types of switches in setting off the alarms, as well as each alarm's quality in terms of how well it attracts people's attention.

WHERE TO GO?

SUBJECT: ICT. QCA UNIT 3D: EXPLORING SIMULATIONS.

LEARNING OBJECTIVE
To evaluate the suitability of an adventure program for younger children.

THINKING OBJECTIVE
To evaluate information (judging value).

THINKING SKILLS
The children will look carefully at an adventure program and judge its value for teaching younger children how to make decisions. They will evaluate its motivation and fun value by forming opinions about the quality of the program's graphics and interest. They will then develop a presentation to promote the program to children in a younger class.

WHAT YOU NEED
Any new adventure program that younger children in the school have not yet used – this could be one used by the children in Year 2 that the new Year 2 are meeting for the first time (*Snow White and the Seven Hansels* is suitable.); any story-maker software that invites the children to select and create a setting, characters and props for an adventure story; large sheets of paper; access to a computer and printer.

WHAT TO DO

Let the children revisit the program and think about how much they enjoyed the challenge and fun of completing it.

Gather them together and make notes about what they learned from the program. Ask, *How valuable was it in teaching you facts and knowledge? Did the program help you to develop decision-making skills? Did it help you to learn skills that allowed you to approach other programs with confidence? How did it do this? Was it fun to play? Why? Did you find it interesting? What do you think of the graphics, the content and the storyline? Is there a good range of options in the menu from which to select and make decisions?*

Organise the children into groups and give each group a large sheet of paper. Explain that you want them to prepare an oral presentation to encourage children who are now in Year 2 and have not yet worked with it, to use and enjoy this program. Tell them that you want them to write their own notes to inform this presentation. Explain that, although the presentation will be oral, they may wish to include a demonstration of the program on computer screen or some visual aids on large sheets of paper. Ask the children to think about the adjectives that they could use to promote this program. Ask, *How will you show the Year 2 children what you are talking about? Will you demonstrate the program? Will you print off some screens that you can pass around for the children to see?*

Rehearse each presentation in turn, asking the rest of the class to provide feedback about its quality and interest. Make improvements before presenting the program to the younger children.

GALLERY TOUR

SUBJECT: ART AND DESIGN. QCA UNIT 3B: A VISIT TO A MUSEUM OR GALLERY.

LEARNING OBJECTIVE

To allow the children to find out what they can see and do in art galleries.

THINKING OBJECTIVE

To evaluate information (judging value).

THINKING SKILLS

The children will visit the National Gallery website to plan a tour around the gallery. They will evaluate how well the site helps them to plan their tour.

WHAT YOU NEED

Computers; access to the Internet; some knowledge of the National Gallery website (www.nationalgallery.org.uk), including any current special exhibitions and the whereabouts of specific paintings you want the children to 'visit'.

WHAT TO DO

Log on to the National Gallery website and negotiate your way around it for a few minutes, looking at the different pages and facilities. Locate the site plan and discuss as a class how you can use this to plan a guided tour around the gallery. Pose different situations and, with the children working in pairs if you have enough computers, ask them to look at the website and consider where they would go first.

For example, tell them you want to go to the 'special exhibition' first. Ask, *Where would you need to go when you get to the gallery? Might you decide to go to the shop first, while it is empty? Is it possible to go there at the start, or do you need to walk around the gallery first, as you do in some attractions?*

Give pairs of children the task of looking at particular paintings, using at least two different lists so that you can give children sitting next to each other different ones, and ask them to plan a suitable route. If some children need help, suggest they locate the gallery each painting is found in before looking at the site map and planning the route accordingly. Ask, *Did you all decide to use the same route or did someone think of a different one? Why did they choose the route they did? Was it the shortest and most direct?* Evaluate the different routes that the children have planned and discuss how useful the site map was in helping them to do this. Ask, *How useful was this web page in helping you to plan your visit? Do other galleries have useful websites?* These can be found at the back of the QCA document and will support any unit you are planning to follow.

JINGLES

SUBJECT: MUSIC. QCA UNIT 14: SALT, PEPPER, VINEGAR, MUSTARD.

LEARNING OBJECTIVE

To learn that jingles have specific musical characteristics that contribute to their success.

THINKING OBJECTIVE
To evaluate information (judging usefulness).

THINKING SKILLS
The children will evaluate why particular jingles are successful by thinking about the catchiness of the tunes, which help consumers to recall the advert easily. They will consider how rhythm is used to gain attention, and use this information to compose a jingle of their own. This will help them to understand the value of different musical elements in making tunes interesting.

WHAT YOU NEED
A videotape of advertisements that use electronic sound effects, jingles and songs to support the products that they are selling; recordings of jingles and theme tunes from TV and radio programmes, such as the news, sports programmes and the weather forecast; keyboards and mobile phones (switched off!) with a range of electronic sounds.

WHAT TO DO
Listen to the jingles, sound effects and theme tunes you have collected. Talk about the musical elements that are used in each one. Ask, *Is the tune short and repetitive? Is it based on a recent pop song? Is it loud and dramatic, or quiet and pleasant to the ear? Does it move slowly or is the tempo fast? Is it played by one or more instruments?* Identify these, and note how the effects have been created. Ask, *Were these effects produced with musical instruments or electronically?* Listen to the tones made by a mobile telephone keypad and note the tunes that these create.

Talk about adverts that use popular songs, such as recent chart hits and classical music themes. Talk about songs that have become famous because they started life as adverts – there are obvious examples related to soft drinks and fast food. Ask, *Do these help us to remember what is being advertised? Why?* Evaluate how useful the musical elements are in helping us to remember the product or programme that is being advertised. Ask, *Is the tune catchy? Does it spark memories of pleasant and happy occasions? Does it create a certain mood? Is it exciting and does it make us want to watch?*

Ask the children to work in groups to write an advert to sell a product, such as a car, sports equipment or hair accessories – let them choose. Encourage them to use their imaginations, to add sound effects and jingles to support their advert, and to think about the tune and the different elements they could use to add interest. Allow them to use electronic keyboards to add different rhythms and sounds (sometimes called voices) to any simple tunes they have composed. Perform the jingles to the rest of the class and evaluate how effectively each one sells the chosen product.

WHAT DOES IT SAY?

SUBJECT: RE. QCA UNIT 4D: WHAT RELIGIONS ARE REPRESENTED IN OUR NEIGHBOURHOODS?

LEARNING OBJECTIVE
To learn about the Sikh religion from a practising Sikh.

THINKING OBJECTIVE
To evaluate the value of learning gained about a religion from a visitor who practises that religion.

THINKING SKILLS
The children will consider the value of learning about a particular religion from a visitor who represents that faith. In this lesson the focus is on the Sikh religion, which links closely to the other QCA units in Years 3 and 4 about Hinduism. It can easily be adapted to learn about any other religion found in your particular neighbourhood, or used to develop the children's awareness of different religions if you are a single-faith school.

WHAT YOU NEED
A visitor; religious artefacts from the visitor's religion; videos and books.

WHAT TO DO
Before the visit, ask the children what they want to find out about Sikhism. Start by recalling with them what they already know. Use books and videos to spark their memories if necessary. Check that they remember the facts, and are able to talk about the purpose and meaning behind Sikh practices and artefacts, and the way these are used. Look at any artefacts and discover the depth of the children's knowledge and understanding of their meaning and purpose. Ask, *Can you tell me about the meaning and purpose of the five Ks to Sikhs?* Agree where they think there are gaps in their knowledge and understanding. Think about the things that people learn from their religions, such as the way that they should lead their lives, the rules that they need to follow, and the way their religious artefacts are used. Ask, *Do you think that Sikhs have similar rules, values and religious practices that they learn from their religion?*

If you do not know a suitable visitor, consult your LEA or write to your nearest Gudwara explaining what you want to do, and asking if a suitable person could visit the school to answer the children's questions and talk about their religious beliefs, practices and artefacts. Prompt your visitor so that they address the areas where the children require information in a short talk. Ask them to include a description and an explanation of the five Ks, as well as what these mean to Sikhs and how they guide them to lead their lives. Talk about the beliefs these promote and what Sikhs learn from them.

After the visit, look again at the areas where the children had gaps in their knowledge and discuss what they have learned from the visitor that they would not have learned from books, or by looking at artefacts without an explanation. Ask, *How valuable was a visit from a practising Sikh in helping you to learn more about the practices and beliefs of this religion? Why was it more valuable than other sources* (if it was)?

Discuss the possibilities of inviting another visitor to talk about a different religion.

SUPER GYMNASTS

SUBJECT: PE. QCA UNIT: GYMNASTICS ACTIVITIES – UNIT 3.

LEARNING OBJECTIVE
To decide which apparatus is most useful in supporting gymnastic movements and sequences.

THINKING OBJECTIVE
To evaluate information (judging quality).

THINKING SKILLS
The children will judge the usefulness of the equipment available to support their individual gymnastic performances. They will suggest ways in which the apparatus can be adapted or made more challenging to support them further as they make improvements to the quality of their movements.

WHAT YOU NEED
Large sheets of paper and pens; a video recording of the children's gymnastics sequences; access to gymnastic apparatus.

WHAT TO DO
As a class, watch video footage that has been taken earlier of each pupil's gymnastics sequence and, through a class discussion, note the components

and strengths of these. Ask, *How could these be further improved? Could you add more variety, greater strength and boldness in the movements, more control or balance in the rolls? How might you perform these successfully?*

Look at the range of apparatus available for the children to practise and refine their sequences, and discuss how these can be used to support their suggested improvements. Take one aspect and discuss it in detail. Ask, *How useful are the ladders for improving the quality of rolls? Are they useful at all? Perhaps they would provide more challenge to the travelling part of the sequence? Would benches and planks be useful to make the suggested improvements to the rolls? How? Would they provide more challenge if they were inclined? Could a roll be incorporated into the opening movement onto a table or platform?*

Organise the children into groups and let them develop their own ideas for the arrangement of apparatus to allow group members to extend and improve the performance of their sequences. For example, they will need to identify suitable apparatus to support a range of travels, a roll, jump and balance. They need to discuss how this should be arranged to build an interesting sequence of moves. Some children may need to adapt their sequence to fit. They should draw their ideas on large sheets of paper so that they can share these with the rest of the class. Encourage them to label the individual items by name and say how each one will support certain parts of their gymnastics sequences. They should also indicate the start and finish of their sequence. Ask, *How useful is this piece to develop jumps? How can this piece help you to build in a more controlled and interesting travel?*

Gather the children together at the end of the lesson and ask them to share each other's apparatus plans. Ask individual children to say whether each one would suit their sequence, and why. Ask, *Would you all start in the same place? Could some children start at the opposite end of the apparatus arrangement and travel over it in a different direction? Would this make a difference? Do any of you not have a suitable piece of apparatus on which to perform and develop your sequence?* (If the group work brief was followed, everyone should have at least one.) Use a show of hands to choose the four arrangements that the children think are the most useful for performing each of the sequences. Take each idea in turn over a number of lessons for the children to explore and evaluate. Let them make and try out any suggested improvements during the lessons by adapting and reorganising the arrangements. The children can vote for those that will support their particular gymnastics sequence and organise them all for a final lesson.

EXTENDING EVALUATION SKILLS

Subject and QCA unit, NLS or NNS objective	Activity title	Thinking objective	Activity	Page
English: NLS objectives: To choose and prepare poems for performance; to rehearse and improve performance	All at sea	To evaluate information (judging quality); to suggest improvements	Considering the quality of a performance before deciding how to add variety to make their own performance more interesting.	121
Maths: NNS objective: To recognise reflective symmetry in 2-D shapes, reflections and translations	Balloon curtains	To evaluate information; to suggest improvements	Creating a design by reflecting, rotating or translating simple balloon designs and evaluating how well they have used these devices to make the design more attactive and appealing.	122
Science: QCA unit 3F: Light and shadows	Shadow puppet show	To evaluate information (judging usefulness and quality)	Investigating a range of materials to see which are best for making puppets to perform a shadow puppet show.	123
History: QCA unit 10: What can we find out about Ancient Egypt from what has survived?	Pyramids	To evaluate information (judging usefulness and value)	Deciding how valuable are Egyptian remains, such as the Pyramids, for finding out what life was like in Ancient Egypt.	124
Geography. QCA unit 18: Connecting ourselves to the world	Keeping in touch	To evaluate information (judging quality)	Listing occasions and methods needed for communication and evaluating how these systems can provide information about geographical queries.	125
Design and technology. QCA unit 4E: Lighting it up	Light it up	To evaluate information (judging usefulness)	Looking at a range of different lamps and discussing the design features and how these features are for a particular purpose.	126
ICT. QCA unit 4C: Branching databases	Branching out	To evaluate information (judging usefulness)	Classifying information about cars by identifying similarities and differences in order to construct a branching database.	127
Art and design. QCA unit 3C: Can we change places?	Frog city	To evaluate information (judging quality)	Looking at garden and indoor ornaments and considering their tactile and visual qualities.	129
Music. QCA unit 11: The class orchestra	Orchestra practice	To evaluate information (judging quality)	Adding vocal, instrumental and percussion accompaniment to a familiar song. Recording performance and evaluating. Practising and then performing to an audience.	130
RE. QCA unit 3B: How and why do Hindus celebrate Divali?	Religious facts	To judge usefulness and value	Considering the value and usefulness of a range of books in providing answers to predetermined questions about a religion. Deciding which book is the most useful for research.	132
PE. QCA unit: Swimming activities and water safety – unit 1	Getting my feet off the bottom	To evaluate information (judging usefulness)	Playing games to try out different swimming movements with swimming aids to decide which are the most useful.	133

ALL AT SEA

SUBJECT: ENGLISH. NLS OBJECTIVES: TO CHOOSE
AND PREPARE POEMS FOR PERFORMANCE, IDENTIFYING
APPROPRIATE EXPRESSION, TONE, VOLUME, USE OF
VOICES AND OTHER SOUNDS; TO REHEARSE AND IMPROVE
PERFORMANCE, TAKING NOTE OF PUNCTUATION AND MEANING.

LEARNING OBJECTIVE
To identify expression, tone, volume and use of
voices to plan a group performance of a poem.

THINKING OBJECTIVES
To evaluate information (judging quality); to suggest
improvements.

THINKING SKILLS
The children will work together in small groups to
plan and assemble a performance of 'The Jumblies'
by Edward Lear. They will consider the quality of a
performance when it is read in a 'boring' voice before
deciding how they can add variety and make their
own performance more interesting by changing the
tone, volume and expression in their voices. They will
need to use other thinking skills during this process,
including analysing the structure of the poem, and
using imagination to add voices and change the tone
and volume.

WHAT YOU NEED
A copy of the poem 'The Jumblies' by Edward Lear for
the class introduction, and a copy for each group.

WHAT TO DO
Read the poem out loud with as little expression
as possible, but not quite in a monotone. Ask the
children what they thought of your performance:
*What did you think of the way it was read? Was it
interesting to listen to? Was it boring? Why?*

On the left side of the board, list all the words
the children used to describe your performance. Then
think of antonyms for each word, and write these
down on the right. Perform the poem again, this time
in the way described by the children's antonyms.

Organise the children into groups of six or
seven. Tell them that you want them to plan a
group performance of the poem. Challenge them
to think of a way to make their own performance
more interesting. Explain that they should make
sure that it is not boring – that it grabs listeners'
interest and keeps them attentive throughout. Give
the children freedom to decide how they will do
this for themselves. They may wish to use the list
of antonyms as a prompt, to consider changing the

volume for different phrases and words, performing
it with actions or props, or in some other innovative
way.

Let the groups plan and practise the performance
of the poem. Initially, give each group a different
verse and the chorus to begin rehearsing, as this will
prevent the activity becoming overly long. Prompt
the children to think about the meaning of the words
and how they may need to adjust their performance
to reflect the mood these depict. For example, how
will they perform 'They went to sea in a sieve' – with
quaking voices to reflect the danger, or with a
snigger to reflect the stupidity?

Gather the groups together to perform each
verse and chorus in turn until the whole poem is
performed. Ask, *How did the performance style add
interest to the performance? How did the style support
the words?* Ask the children to evaluate the quality of
each group's performance and suggest how they can
make even more improvements. Agree a class style
and perform the poem as a whole.

DIFFERENTIATION
Work on the chorus with lower attaining pupils so
that they can perform this at the end of every verse.
Encourage higher attaining children to think of a
range of ways to layer the voices by coming in at
different times, and by combining several voices to
distinguish different parts.

WHERE NEXT
Develop a performance of the whole poem as an
independent group activity over a series of literacy
lessons.

ASSESSMENT
Note the children who can say what they like about
each other's performance. Listen to them as they
work in groups, and note down those children who
suggest how the group can make their performance
more interesting by changing the volume and rhythm
of the stanza, and having voices coming in at
different times.

LEARNING OUTCOMES
All the children will be able to perform the poem in
an interesting way. Many will evaluate each other's
performance in terms of quality, and some will be
able to suggest how improvements can be made.

FURTHER ENGLISH CHALLENGES
Jumblies rap
Plan and perform the poem as a rap. Ask the
children to evaluate the quality of this performance
by thinking about the rhythmic structure, the use

of syncopated rhythms, and the patterns of vocal contrast created by layering voice entrances.

Chorus
Plan and perform the chorus, in groups, changing expression to reflect the various antics that the Jumblies get up to, and the places they visit. Evaluate the different performances and select the styles that the children like best to use in a class performance.

BALLOON CURTAINS

SUBJECT: MATHS. NNS OBJECTIVE: TO RECOGNISE REFLECTIVE SYMMETRY IN 2-D SHAPES, REFLECTIONS AND TRANSLATIONS.

LEARNING OBJECTIVE
To recognise reflective symmetry in 2-D shapes, reflections and translations.

THINKING OBJECTIVES
To evaluate information; to suggest improvements.

THINKING SKILLS
The children will make a design for fabric or wallpaper by reflecting, rotating or translating simple balloon designs, and evaluate how well they have used these devices to make the design attractive and appealing. They will think about whether they have changed too much and made the finished design too 'busy', before improving their ideas and making a finished design. A simple computer art package can be used to make and rotate stamps.

WHAT YOU NEED
Large sheets of paper; card; tracing paper; drawing materials; a completed pattern that shows two different clusters of balloons repeated at equal distances and reflected in alternate sequence; computers; a simple computer art package such as *Dazzle* that can be used to make and rotate stamps.

WHAT TO DO
Look together at your finished balloon design and evaluate how appealing it is. Ask, *Would you like to have this pattern on wallpaper or curtains in your bedroom? Why? Do you like the colours and design? What is special about it? What do you notice about the way the clusters of balloons have been repeated?*

Note that the distance between the clusters is always the same, and that some clusters are reflected and others translated. Ask, *What colours have been used? Are the balloon clusters always in the same colours?* Can the children suggest how the

design can be improved, perhaps by adding a third, smaller cluster of balloons, or by rotating one of the repeated designs?

Show the children how to design balloon clusters by drawing freehand or round oval-shaped templates onto tracing paper, and tracing these onto card to make templates. When they have made their templates, they should decide where and how they will transfer these to paper. They need to evaluate the distance between each cluster and whether they will translate, rotate or reflect each one.

When the children have finished their individual designs, they should share them with a friend to talk about what they like about them and how the design might be improved. During an independent group activity, let the children make improvements to their designs, possibly creating a different cluster, or repeating it in a different style.

DIFFERENTIATION
Sit with the lower attaining pupils at the beginning of the group activity to make sure they understand the evaluation process in deciding how many clusters to use in their patterns, and how often they will be repeated.

Encourage more able children to measure precisely the distances and angles of position between the different clusters.

WHERE NEXT
Use woodblocks and string to transfer the balloon design and print it onto paper for a wallpaper pattern, or white fabric for soft furnishings.

Use these improved furnishings to create a balloon corner in the classroom.

ASSESSMENT
Notice how well the children limit their ideas to make sure that the finished design has some sort of structured pattern created by rotation, translation and reflection.

LEARNING OUTCOMES
Most children will be able to evaluate their finished designs and make improvements based on these evaluations.

FURTHER MATHS CHALLENGES

Wallpaper patterns

Evaluate different wallpapers, deciding whether the patterns are repeated using translation, reflection or rotation, and how often these repetitions occur. Copy one of the designs and use it to make a different wallpaper pattern.

Crockery

Look at the way crockery designs use repeating patterns. Note how these are rotated, reflected or translated. Ask, *Which is used most often? Why are repeating patterns used more often in crockery, while translation of shape is used more often in larger areas such as wallpaper and fabrics? Is it because there is less available space on crockery?*

SHADOW PUPPET SHOW

SUBJECT: SCIENCE. QCA UNIT 3F: LIGHT AND SHADOWS.

LEARNING OBJECTIVE

To learn that some opaque materials do not let light through.

THINKING OBJECTIVE

To evaluate information (judging usefulness and quality).

THINKING SKILLS

The children will investigate a range of materials in terms of how much light they let through – none, a little or a lot. They will use the results to evaluate which materials are best for making puppets to perform a shadow puppet show.

WHAT YOU NEED

A range of materials that let through different amounts of light, such as Cellophane, tissue, sugar paper, fabrics, Clingfilm, plastic, card, metal foil; a strong light, such as a projector or a powerful torch; a large white sheet; sticks; scissors; adhesive.

WHAT TO DO

Tell the children that you want to find the best material for blocking out enough light to make shadow puppets for a play. Set up an investigation to find out which materials let through no light (opaque materials), a little light (translucent materials) or lots of light (transparent materials). Record the results as a table. Link the column titles to the scientific terms: *transparent*, *translucent* and *opaque*.

Encourage the children to suggest their own ideas for which materials to test, and to plan how they will carry out the investigation, incorporating reasons for making it fair. Talk about the range of materials, using the same light source at the same distance away from the screen, and measuring the light (light sensors linked to a computer will do this accurately).

Use the results to conclude which materials would be good for making puppets to perform a shadow puppet show. Ask, *Why will these materials be the best ones to use? Is it because they let through no light? How easy are they to shape and manipulate to make puppets? Will there be moving parts? Which of the selected materials would be best for this? What objects could be used as props?*

In groups, make the puppets and begin to work out a puppet show. You may wish to link the context to a current topic – for example, the Viking Invasions or the story of Rama and Sita. Hang a large white sheet in front of a powerful light source to test out the puppets and evaluate whether they make good shadows. Test the characters as they move across and away from the curtain. Ask, *What happens to the shadows when the puppets move farther away from the curtain? What happens when they are close to the curtain?* Evaluate how well the puppets create changes in perspective and size as they move closer to or further away from the curtain. Ask, *Would they be more effective if they were bigger or smaller?*

Perform the shadow puppet show to each other and evaluate the quality of the shadows. Ask, *Why are the shadows successful? Is it because of the quality of the materials for making good shadows?*

DIFFERENTIATION

Organise the children into mixed-ability groups so that higher attaining children can help those who might struggle. Make sure that they take turns to test out the materials so that everyone is included in the investigation. The conclusions should all be group decisions. Check that all the children are able to agree which materials let through no light, a little light, or lots of light, and to give reasons why. Check they understand that this is why these materials make a good shadow that can be seen clearly.

WHERE NEXT

Ask some children to act out a mime of a favourite poem or story behind the curtain as a shadow play for the rest of the class to guess. Evaluate their effectiveness at making good quality shadows.

ASSESSMENT

Note those children who select suitable materials for their puppets based on the results of their investigation, and understand that a material makes a good shadow because it lets through no light.

LEARNING OUTCOMES

Most children will evaluate materials in terms of whether they let through a lot of, a little, or no light. They will use their evaluation to make effective puppets for a shadow play.

FURTHER SCIENCE CHALLENGES

Ghost story

Investigate the quality of materials that could be used for making faded shadows to represent ghosts. Ask, *Which materials are best for this? Why? Are the shadows lighter than those made by opaque materials? Why?* Relate the children's evaluations to the information recorded in the table created at the beginning of the main activity about the amount of light each material lets through.

Shadow play

Ask the children to plan a group shadow play with themselves as the characters. One good context is a surgical operation with a saw and hammer – plastic, of course! Have about six children in each group. Ask them to evaluate the distance the light needs to be away from the curtain to pick out their shadows clearly. Ask, *How can you add variation to your performance in terms of changing your size, position and perspective? What props will you use? Where will these be positioned? How can you be certain you make a shadow?* Encourage them to take turns to watch three people perform the same sequence behind the curtain, and then to suggest how they can make the actions clearer and more dramatic.

PYRAMIDS

SUBJECT: HISTORY. QCA UNIT 10: WHAT CAN WE FIND OUT ABOUT ANCIENT EGYPT FROM WHAT HAS SURVIVED?

LEARNING OBJECTIVE

To understand what life was like in Ancient Egypt.

THINKING OBJECTIVE

To evaluate information (judging usefulness and value).

THINKING SKILLS

The children will look at different Egyptian remains, such as the Pyramids and the Sphinx, and decide how valuable these are as resources for finding out what life was like in Ancient Egypt.

WHAT YOU NEED

Pictures and photographs of modern Egypt, especially tourist spots and places of interest; models and pictures of some of the people and treasures that existed in Ancient Egyptian times, including photographs taken outside and inside the Pyramids; computers; access to the Internet; paper and pens.

WHAT TO DO

Ask the children what they already know about Egypt, both modern and in the past. Explain that you want them to think about the everyday lives and beliefs of the groups of people who lived in Ancient Egypt.

Look at a photograph of modern Egypt that shows the Pyramids, and ask the children to describe what they can see. Wonder with them how they were built, and why. Ask, *Who built the Pyramids? For whom were they built? How does this information help us to identify the different groups of people who would have lived in Ancient Egypt? Are there still kings and queens in that country today?* Encourage the children to infer other information from the photograph. *How long would it take to build a pyramid? How would the people get the stone to the top of the pyramid? Where is the door? Was there a door? Where are the Pyramids built? Why are they built next to the River Nile? What was the importance of this river to the Ancient Egyptians?*

Now look at a photograph of the inside of a pyramid and think about why they were built with separate chambers to carry out daily functions. Relate this to the beliefs of the Ancient Egyptians. Identify the different chambers and the valuable items that were put inside. Ask, *Why were they put there? Who were they for? Were other people entombed in the pyramid with the body of the dead person?* Explain how a person's servants were entombed with the body of the Pharaoh so that they could look after them in the afterlife. Think about the mixed feelings that these people would have had, which would have ranged from fear to privilege. Discuss why this was so. Ask, *How would they have felt? What does this tell us about the beliefs of the people who lived at that time?*

Divide the children into groups and ask them to work together to glean as much information as they can from photographs and models of famous people who would have lived at that time, such as Tutankhamun or Nefertiti. Challenge them to use the photographs and artefacts to identify questions for research. Ask, *How well does the picture spark ideas for questions for future research?* Give some groups identical pieces of evidence so that they can compare notes.

Consider each source of evidence and agree how valuable it is for their research. Reaffirm to the children that many of these items survived for hundreds of years and can help us to learn about and understand the way people used to live.

DIFFERENTIATION

Put the children into mixed ability groups for this activity so that higher attaining children can help others who are finding the work difficult. Move around the groups, prompting them to infer additional information from what they see.

WHERE NEXT

Show the children photographs of hieroglyphics that have survived and ask them to discuss the value of these in finding out about Ancient Egyptians.

Give groups of children a topic to research, asking them to begin by identifying the range of surviving historical sources that will help them with their research. In your discussions, try to move the children's thinking towards using the Internet.

ASSESSMENT

As the children are working, listen to their discussions to find out how well they are using the sources of evidence to glean information. Note those who are beginning to understand how valuable this type of evidence is in finding out about the way people used to live.

LEARNING OUTCOMES

Most children will learn to evaluate the importance of historical sources in helping them to find out about the way Ancient Egyptians lived. Some will understand how they can infer additional information to tell them about the Egyptians' beliefs and customs.

FURTHER HISTORY CHALLENGES

Egyptian display
Make an end-of-topic display to show off all the things that the children have found out during this unit of work. By the side of each piece of work, display the pictures of all the things left in modern Egypt today that the children found useful in their research.

Today and yesterday
Evaluate the resources according to whether they help to find out about modern or Ancient Egypt. Ask, *Are there any sources of information that are useful*

for both? How valuable are they for helping us to understand the way people live today and the way they lived in the past?

KEEPING IN TOUCH

SUBJECT: GEOGRAPHY. QCA UNIT 18: CONNECTING OURSELVES TO THE WORLD.

LEARNING OBJECTIVE
To learn about the different methods of communication used across the world.

THINKING OBJECTIVE
To evaluate information (judging quality).

THINKING SKILLS
The children will list all the occasions when they need to keep in touch with other people and discuss the possible ways to do this. They will use this information to evaluate the quality of the communication systems used around the world. They will then consider how the same systems can be used to find information about a range of geographical queries, such as weather and climate, or routes and methods of transportation.

WHAT YOU NEED
Computers; access to e-mail and the Internet; telephones, including mobile phones; fax and video machines; letters and newspapers; televisions with Teletext; whiteboard and pen; paper and pens.

WHAT TO DO
Talk to the class about the different ways to communicate with people and places that are too far away to visit. If children in the class have relatives in a distant country like Australia, they can talk about all the ways they use to keep in touch, such as sending letters or cards, by e-mail or by telephone.

List the variety of ways that people are able to keep in touch today, noting with the children how many of these are relatively new. Talk about how news reporters use videophones to send their reports to the news programmes and newspapers, and the possibility of sending photographs as attachments to e-mail.

Look at a mobile phone and talk about the different ways of sending messages on this, including text, pictures and by speaking. Consider the other items on your list. Ask, *Is any other single means of communication as versatile as the mobile phone?*

Divide the children into groups and give each one a different means of communication to consider. Ask them to think of all the ways that it can be used to find information. After about five minutes, ask the groups to share their findings with the rest of the class. Display the children's suggestions prominently so that they can refer to them during the next task.

Now choose one geographical location anywhere in the world and give each group a topic to research – possibly its climate, its physical and human features, its transport systems and the routes to get to it.

Explain that the children need to consider the topic they have been given and then explore and evaluate the communication systems that allow them to find the information they need. They should discuss how successful each means of communication is at finding relevant information for their particular topic. After about ten minutes, share what the children have found out. Evaluate the quality of each system in terms of the number of topics it could support. Ask, *Does any one communication system come out better than another? How do you know? Agree with the children how they can use these systems when planning their research in geography.*

DIFFERENTIATION

During the first group task, help lower attaining children to send fax and e-mail messages so that they understand how these can be used. Encourage them to discuss the range of information that can be sent and received in this way, making sure that they mention photographs and various forms of written communication. Ask higher attaining children to consider how different systems are used in everyday life (for example, Internet in offices, or telephones to connect alarm systems to police stations). Encourage them to take a mental walk down their nearest High Street and think about the communication systems that would be in use inside the different businesses.

WHERE NEXT

Plan research into a geographical topic and list the ways that communication systems can help the children to find information. Carry out and share the research into your chosen topic or place.

ASSESSMENT

Assess how diverse the children's thinking is when they are identifying the quality of the different communication systems. Note those who think about the wider uses of the different systems.

LEARNING OUTCOMES

Most children will recognise the quality and value of the different communication systems and link this to

how they can be used in their research about people and places.

FURTHER GEOGRAPHY CHALLENGES
Mobile messages

Send text messages to someone you know, asking them questions about where they are. Use the information to pinpoint their position. Evaluate the quality of the phone to support this activity. Ask, *Can you think of a better way of communicating with this person, or is the area too remote for other things to be used?* Identify different places around the world and, for each one, list the possible ways of communicating with a relative or friend who lives there.

Holiday destinations

Work in groups to research holiday destinations. Challenge the children to identify the best way of finding holiday bargains using the different means of communication. Include the Internet and Teletext, as well as faxing the local Travel Agent. Evaluate the quality of each system in terms of speed, and the range of information received. Make sure to follow the school's policy for Internet security and communicating with people outside the school.

LIGHT IT UP

SUBJECT: DESIGN AND TECHNOLOGY.
QCA UNIT 4E: LIGHTING IT UP.

LEARNING OBJECTIVE
To identify which lamp is most useful for its function.

THINKING OBJECTIVE
To evaluate information (judging usefulness).

THINKING SKILLS
The children will look at a range of different lamps and discuss the importance of certain design features to the purpose of each one. They will evaluate how useful these different design features are for a particular purpose, and recognise any features which are less important.

WHAT YOU NEED
A collection of lamps including a desk lamp that can change the direction of the light in some way, reading lamps, table lamps, nightlights, uplights and spotlights; whiteboard and pen; paper and pens.

WHAT TO DO

As a class, look at a desk lamp and take some time to discuss its design and how it is made. Talk about the brightness of the light and the way the lamp can be moved and bent into different positions to direct the light to precise places. Discuss why and how this design feature is important to the lamp's purpose and function. Ask, *Why is it important that the user can direct the light onto a precise spot?* Talk about the colour of the lamp and discuss whether this is an important feature. *Why? Is it more or less important than the need to direct the light? Is it more or less important than the strength of the light?* Then talk about the way the lamp looks, and discuss whether this is important to its function.

Look at other desk lights and compare and contrast the design elements. Make a table with five columns on the board and note for each lamp: colour and style, strength of light, whether it is possible to direct the light, and how easy it is to change the direction.

Ask the children to find a partner and give each pair a lamp. Explain that they should evaluate the design and function of their lamp and decide how effective this is in supporting its purpose. Ask them to prepare a short written evaluation and to give the lamp a mark out of ten.

Bring the class back together to discuss and agree the marks given to each lamp. Make a 'Top Ten' list to display alongside the lamps and the children's written evaluations.

DIFFERENTIATION

Work with lower attaining children to evaluate what each lamp is used for. Once they have identified the purpose, match it with the design features that are useful in supporting that purpose. They will then begin to link the design features to the lamp's intended use.

Higher attaining children should think about lights used in other situations (such as traffic lights, streetlights, floodlights, spotlights, car headlights, zebra crossing lights, and so on) and evaluate the effectiveness of their design. They should record as a table the usefulness of different design features for each one, such as coloured light, flashing lights and the way light can be flooded over a large area.

WHERE NEXT

Look at other things that give light, such as torches, candles or oil lamps, and evaluate the usefulness of these for different occasions and purposes (during a power cut, when camping, or to create a different atmosphere).

ASSESSMENT

Listen to the children's comments as they evaluate the different types of light, and note those who relate the quality of each one to its use and purpose.

LEARNING OUTCOMES

Most children will be able to evaluate the quality of each lamp in terms of its brightness and whether the design suits its function and purpose.

FURTHER DESIGN AND TECHNOLOGY CHALLENGES

Spotlights

Design a sequence of spotlights to use in a puppet show by placing coloured acetates over a bright light. Combine the colours, and note how coloured light can be mixed to make other colours.

Evaluate the usefulness of the colours in adding interest to the show and making certain characters stand out. Look at a short video clip of a stage show and evaluate how the spotlights support the quality of the performance. Ask, *How well do they suit their purpose?*

Bedtime lights

Evaluate different lights that are used in babies' nurseries. Make a table to note the value of the design features used in each one, such as dim light, attractive colours, whether it is interesting to look at and has a stable structure so it does not fall over.

BRANCHING OUT

SUBJECT: ICT. QCA UNIT 4C: BRANCHING DATABASES.

LEARNING OBJECTIVE

To use a database to sort and classify information and present findings.

THINKING OBJECTIVE

To evaluate information (judging usefulness).

THINKING SKILLS

The children will learn how to classify information about cars by identifying similarities and differences in order to construct a branching database, which will help identify each car.

WHAT YOU NEED

A collection of five model cars; photographs of cars; a computer database; a large sheet of paper; felt-tipped pens; Yes/No labels; whiteboard and pen.

WHAT TO DO

Look at the collection of cars and identify things about them that are the same, and other things that are different. For example, some may be the same colour, but different a make, model, or engine size. Continue until every car in your collection has been identified orally by clear definitions and classification. Challenge the children to determine the fields that will eventually identify the cars individually.

Model a question based on one of the fields that will divide the group of cars into two, such as, *Is the car blue?* On a large sheet of paper, put all the blue cars on one side, and the rest on the other, with lines labelled 'Yes' and 'No' to indicate the classification. Write the question above the lines.

Identify another question that will define the cars further, such as, *Is the car a BMW?* The children may start to realise that you are asking questions that match the fields identified earlier. If they do, invite someone to think of the next question that will help to classify the cars; if not, note how the questions relate to the fields the children identified earlier. When you are sure they understand how the field titles will help them to write suitable questions, ask them to think of further questions until each car has been identified individually and is at the bottom of its own line.

Explain that this is what a computer does when it sorts information to find the answer to a given question. Encourage the children to think about how important it is to put the correct information into the computer in the first place.

Ask the children questions such as, *Find the car that is blue, has a 2-litre engine, is convertible and made by BMW.* Use the branching classification to find the car. Ask, *How useful is this way of classifying cars in helping you to locate a car of a particular colour, model, make and engine size?*

Give the children the photographs of cars and ask them to input similar information into a pre-prepared computer database organised into the same fields. Set this up with the children if you wish to consolidate

their understanding of what they need to do. When all the information has been entered, interrogate the database to find particular cars – for example, a red hatchback car made by Fiat with a 2000cc engine. Ask, *Can you find a car like this? Why not? Is it because Fiat does not make one, or is it because you have not put the information into the computer, so that it cannot find one?* Note with the children that unless the information is put into the computer – and put in correctly – the computer will not be able to locate what you want to find.

DIFFERENTIATION

Help lower attaining children to put the information into the computer. Talk to them as the computer searches for the requested car, reminding them that it is sorting and comparing each one against the fields until it finds the correct one. Ask them to say how useful this method is for finding a particular car quickly. Higher attaining children can input additional vehicles and consider whether the computer takes longer to find the information when it has a larger number of vehicles to sort.

WHERE NEXT

Discuss the usefulness of this type of database for people planning to buy a car.

ASSESSMENT

Note the children who understand the value of this type of computer program to help them find a given item (in this case a car) quickly. Note those who understand the significance of sorting by fields.

LEARNING OUTCOMES

Most children will learn the usefulness of branching as a way of organising information to find a given object quickly.

FURTHER ICT CHALLENGES

Jewellery store

Look at the range of jewellery in a particular catalogue or shop and construct a branching database to distinguish the different pieces. Identify the fields, such as type of jewellery, type of stone or metal, and price, and put the information into a database. Then interrogate the computer to locate a particular piece of jewellery, such as a silver necklace with a blue sapphire stone costing less than £100. Judge the usefulness of the branching database to classify and locate the necklace quickly. How useful would a jewellery store find this software in locating the availability of a particular piece of jewellery for a customer?

Christmas list

Make a database to collect ideas for Christmas presents the children would like to send to relatives, so that they can select which one they would like to order. Identify the fields – type of present, price, place of purchase – and put the information into the database. Let the children interrogate the database to find a particular item at a certain price that can be bought from a local store. You may need to adapt the activity to accommodate any children in your class who do not celebrate Christmas, and be wary to prevent the destruction of Father Christmas beliefs.

FROG CITY

SUBJECT: ART AND DESIGN. QCA UNIT 3C: CAN WE CHANGE PLACES?

LEARNING OBJECTIVE
To talk about the qualities of sculpture.

THINKING OBJECTIVE
To evaluate information (judging quality).

THINKING SKILLS
The children will look at a collection of garden and indoor ornaments shaped like frogs and consider their tactile and visual qualities. They will consider these qualities when evaluating other garden ornaments and sculptures in the local area, and realise that beauty is often in the eye of the beholder! They will then use the descriptions and evaluations they have prepared to make their own garden ornaments.

WHAT YOU NEED
A collection of frogs made from different materials and with varied shapes, sizes, colours and textures; other garden ornaments; paper and writing materials.

WHAT TO DO
Look at the collection of frogs and ask the children to decide which they like best, and why. Ask, *Is it because of the expression on its face, its colour, the material from which it is made, or some other reason? Do you all like the same frog, or does anyone prefer a different one? Why?* Explain that people like different things because we all have diverse tastes and may prefer different colours, styles and materials.

Pass the frogs around the class and invite the children to feel and stroke them. Ask, *How does stroking this make you feel? Does it have a calming effect on your mood? Does it make you grit your teeth?* Talk about the line and form of each frog, and how these send messages and create moods that will affect different people in a range of ways. Discuss how the different frog ornaments make the children feel and note orally the variety of their responses.

Divide the children into groups and give them a few minutes to talk about their favourite frog from the collection. Ask them to list the reasons why they like the one that they have chosen as a group, on a sheet of paper. Does anyone in the group have a different preference?

Refocus the children's attention and try, as a class, to identify the qualities of the ornaments that the children like. Ask, *Is there one quality that they all have in common, such as their texture, line, material or design? How do these make this frog beautiful?* Note how many different frogs have been chosen as favourites, and reinforce to the children that beauty is in the eye of the beholder.

Introduce other garden ornaments made from a range of materials and, with the children working in pairs with a different ornament, identify the qualities of each one. Ask, *Is it good to touch? Why do you like touching it? How does the sculptor use lines to add interest? How are the expressions created, if there are any?* Ask each pair to write a description of their ornament, building in an evaluation of its tactile and visual qualities, and whether they like it or not.

DIFFERENTIATION
Spend time with lower attaining children sorting the frogs into groups according to their attributes and qualities to help them focus on these elements when they are evaluating the quality of each one. Focus their attention on the colour and style first. Higher attaining children should be encouraged to plan a presentation to describe their favourite frog to the rest of the class. They should include one statement for each quality they have identified.

WHERE NEXT
Let the children use clay and other materials to mould and sculpt their own frog or other garden ornaments.

If possible, take the children to a sculpture park and evaluate the qualities of the sculptures there. Write a leaflet giving the children's opinions of the sculptures that are (and are not) interesting to them.

Visit a garden centre with a good range of garden ornaments and evaluate the qualities of each one. Invite the children to choose a favourite ornament, sketch it and write a short evaluation of its qualities.

Make sculptures from different materials, such as wire and plaster of Paris.

ASSESSMENT

Listen to the children's conversations and note those who understand the qualities of the different sculptures that influence whether we like or dislike a particular example.

LEARNING OUTCOMES

Most children will learn to talk about the qualities of sculptures in terms of their texture, line and form. They will all appreciate the qualities of colour and style.

FURTHER ART AND DESIGN CHALLENGES

Natural sculptures

Make sculptures from natural materials and evaluate together the qualities of each one. How have the children combined the qualities of form, colour and texture to add interest for the observer? What mood does each sculpture create when it is touched and stroked? Invite the children to give their sculpture a name.

Rock garden

Make a group sculpture with rocks and stones. Encourage the children to talk about the qualities of each group sculpture and how they have combined the textures and forms to give it tactile and visual qualities. Give the rock gardens names to reflect the qualities of the stones and rock.

ORCHESTRA PRACTICE

SUBJECT: MUSIC. QCA UNIT 11: THE CLASS ORCHESTRA.

LEARNING OBJECTIVE

To learn how to prepare a class performance.

THINKING OBJECTIVE

To evaluate information (judging quality).

THINKING SKILLS

The children will take a familiar song and add vocal, instrumental and percussion accompaniment. They will record their performance and listen carefully to decide how good the quality is, and why. They will use this information to suggest and make improvements to the performance by changing the speed, duration and dynamics in certain parts to reflect the words and sentiments of the song. They will then practise and rehearse until they are happy that they have a finished piece suitable for performance to an invited audience. This activity may take several lessons to build up a useful evaluation and allow time to make and practise the suggested improvements.

WHAT YOU NEED

A copy of the song 'Jamaica Farewell', words and music by Lord Burgess (Irving Burgie), arranged by Graham Westcott from *Ta-ra-ra Boom-de-ay* (A and C Black ISBN 0 7136 1789 6), or another familiar song; a range of pitched and non-pitched musical instruments, including a glockenspiel or keyboard; a tape recorder; paper and writing materials.

WHAT TO DO

Explain to the children the outcome of the lessons: that you will work together to develop a good quality performance for your intended audience, probably the rest of the school. Talk about the process you will go through.

Start by revisiting the song and talking about its structure. Identify the verse and chorus, then look at the rhythm and decide if some sequences are repeated in the tune and chorus – for example, 'sad to say', and so on. Ask half the class to clap this as an ostinato while the other half sings the song, swapping over to give each half a turn.

Concentrate on the tune next and think about how it moves up and down, and how the rests add interest. Think about how the different parts of the song can be sung. Ask, *Which bits are smooth and which bits need to be sung with a crisp or staccato rhythm?* Let the children decide.

Organise the children into groups of four and let them practise the tune on a glockenspiel, keyboard or other pitched instrument to work out the tune. Write down the note names in order, line by line, under a copy of the words for other children to follow. They should be able to keep the rhythm from memory.

When the tune is secure, add accompaniments on appropriate instruments. For example, the children may decide that maracas are more suitable than tambourines. Ask them why they think this. Select the instruments that the children think compliment the mood and style of the song.

Rehearse and practise the song, making improvements to the expression by changing and improving the use of musical elements until the children are happy with the finished performance. Evaluate the different stages of performance by listening together to a recording of the children's performance.

DIFFERENTIATION
Organise the children initially into mixed-ability groups so that they can all share their ideas. Talk to each group in turn and discuss how the changes in tempo, duration and dynamics can make certain parts more dramatic. This will focus less able children's attention on evaluating the musical styles and elements. Invite any children who can play a musical instrument, such as a recorder or a violin, to compose simple melodic phrases to accompany the piece. The rest of the group can evaluate how these affect the timbre, texture and pitch of the piece.

WHERE NEXT
Perform the song to the school, to another class, or to parents.

ASSESSMENT
Assess how well the children evaluate their performance and make improvements from each other's suggestions. Note how well they use their knowledge of musical elements to make changes to the quality of their performance to reflect the mood and style of the song.

LEARNING OUTCOMES
Most children will adjust and improve their performance to add emphasis to different parts of the song by changing the elements of speed, pitch, duration and dynamics.

FURTHER MUSIC CHALLENGES
Harmony
Challenge the children to add a harmonic accompaniment to the song. This can be an ostinato on the note of the chordal accompaniments identified above the music. They can evaluate the quality of the notes they play by listening to whether they fit harmonically to the tune. Some children may be able to sing the verse a third note higher or sixth note lower than the tune. This is one of the other notes in the accompanying chord.

Technical note: Chords are made up of a bottom note, and notes three and five notes higher. The song is written in the key of D, therefore the three chords are D with notes DF#A; G with notes GBD; and A with notes AC#E.

Fill the gaps
Listen to the chorus and think about a rhythm or melodic accompaniment that the children could play in the spaces created by the longer notes or the rests.

RELIGIOUS FACTS

SUBJECT: RE. QCA UNIT 3B: HOW AND WHY DO HINDUS CELEBRATE DIVALI?

LEARNING OBJECTIVE
To research for religious facts.

THINKING OBJECTIVE
To judge usefulness and value.

THINKING SKILLS
The children will work in groups or pairs to consider the value and usefulness of a range of books in providing answers to predetermined questions about a religion. This activity can be adapted to research any religion that you are studying at the time. The children will share what they have found out and decide which book is the most useful for their research.

WHAT YOU NEED
A list of questions that you want answered about Divali; a range of non-fiction books, including a Big Book; poems; videos and CD-ROMs; paper and pens.

WHAT TO DO
Talk to the children about what they already know about Divali. Look at the questions that you have already listed and read these together to remind the children what they say.

Show the children the Big Book and follow your usual practice of talking about the front page, index and contents pages. Flick through a few pages and look at some of the pictures it contains.

Look at your first question and ask the children how you might go about deciding whether the book contains the information you are looking for. Ask, *Do you think the contents, index or pictures will provide the most useful clues to this?* Follow the children's lead and look at all the places they suggest in turn before deciding which was most useful. Agree that it is probably best to try the index first and then look at the listed page to evaluate how much relevant information there is. Ask, *Can you find the answer to the question on this page? If so, how useful is this resource? What other sources might be useful in helping us to find the answer to the question?* Agree how useful the book is in providing material to answer the first question, and whether it holds valuable information.

Continue with the other questions on your list, using the Big Book, CD-ROMs, poems and video extracts to find the answers, until you are sure that the children understand how to evaluate each source of information.

Put the children into groups or pairs and give each group a different book to evaluate, using the same set of three questions. Ask them to evaluate how useful their book is in providing relevant information to answer the questions. Include some questions which cannot be answered from all of the books. If possible, give one group a relevant CD-ROM to evaluate.

Bring the class together again and share what they have found out about the different sources of information. Ask, *Which books are the most useful? Why? Is it because they provide valuable information to help answer the questions you want to find answers to? How useful was the CD-ROM? Can you think of other sources which might be useful in helping you to find out more about Divali?*

Finish by watching another short extract from the video and identifying together the questions it provides answers for.

DIFFERENTIATION

Give lower attaining children books with lots of pictures so that they can use these as a means of locating the information. If necessary, provide someone to help with reading, so that they can concentrate on evaluating the information, rather than using time reading what it says. Higher attaining children can be given the more challenging task of evaluating the CD-ROM.

WHERE NEXT

Watch a short extract from the video together and consider its usefulness in the same way, evaluating the relevance of the information it provides in answer to the questions on your list.

ASSESSMENT

Note the children who evaluate the usefulness of the books and the value of the information each one provides.

LEARNING OUTCOMES

Most children will understand the importance of evaluating books and other sources of information when using them to research for facts to answer questions.

FURTHER RE CHALLENGES

For and against

Give each group of children an encyclopedia and ask them to evaluate the worth of the information it provides to answer their questions. They should write a 'for and against' list to help them reach their final evaluation. For example, under 'for' they could write that the book provides useful contents and index pages to help locate the information quickly; under 'against' that the information is not detailed enough. Ask, *Is the information in the encyclopedia as detailed as that you have found in the non-fiction books you have evaluated so far?*

Pictures and poems
Look at pictures and listen to poems about Divali celebrations. Evaluate the information that can be gained from these sources and how useful this is for learning about the festival of Divali. For example, some pictures may show henna designs on hands; others may show the food that is eaten. Poems may describe the presents and clothes that are worn at this special time.

GETTING MY FEET OFF THE BOTTOM

SUBJECT: PE. QCA UNIT: SWIMMING ACTIVITIES AND WATER SAFETY – UNIT 1.

LEARNING OBJECTIVE
To work with confidence.

THINKING OBJECTIVE
To evaluate information (judging usefulness).

THINKING SKILLS
The children will play a series of games and try out different swimming movements with swimming aids to help them decide for themselves what is most useful and of most value in helping them to gain self-confidence for getting their feet off the bottom of the swimming pool.

WHAT YOU NEED
A swimming pool; a range of swimming flotation aids in line with your school and LEA policy.

WHAT TO DO
Talk to the children at the side of the pool and ask them to hold on to the bar and raise their feet so that they are sitting in the water. Ask them, *How safe do you feel? What do you notice about the way you float in the water?* Ask them to push their feet back to the floor of the pool. Ask, *Was this easy or did the water put up some resistance?* Repeat this until the children are confident that they can push down to get their feet back to the floor of the pool.

Give each child a float, or two floats (one to go under each arm), and ask them to sit in the water again but this time without holding on to the bar. Ask, *How well do you float? How easy is it to push your feet to the bottom? How well do the floats help you*

to get your feet off the bottom? Repeat this exercise with one float, if you have used two previously, and think about how these can be held in front of or on the chest to help the children sit in the water.

Explore pushing the water in different places to change direction in the water. This will help the children to understand how to push against the water to move in certain directions. Ask, *What happens when you push down? Do you always stand up?* Explore this for the rest of the lesson, letting the children gain in confidence.

Back in school, evaluate how the floats helped them to stay afloat. Ask, *How did kicking your legs and moving your feet help you to stay afloat? Was it easier to sit with the floats or when you were holding on to the bar at the side of the pool?* The children's answers will depend on their degree of confidence.

DIFFERENTIATION
This activity is for starter swimmers, so there will be no improving or competent swimmers in the group.

WHERE NEXT
Develop games which help the children to move around, using floats to help them move with their feet off the bottom.

ASSESSMENT
Watch the children closely and assess who is ready for games that take them farther away from the side of the pool. Some may begin to feel confident to venture into slightly deeper water.

LEARNING OUTCOMES
Most children will learn how floats help us to get our feet off the bottom of the pool and therefore allow us to practise the moves we need to make to help us learn to swim.

FURTHER PE CHALLENGES
Across the pool
Evaluate games that the children can play to get from one side of the pool to the other. The aim of these games is to increase the amount of time, or the length of the pool they cover, without touching the floor with their feet. Note the floats that they need to use, and whether they will have their feet and legs beneath, behind or in front of them. Again the evaluation will depend on the children's individual skills and confidence.

Water tag
Identify a range of games for the children to play to gain confidence in the water – for example, water tag or 'ring of roses'. Make a list of rules to help the children evaluate how to play the games safely.

CROSS-CURRICULAR PROJECTS

INTRODUCTION

This chapter draws together the full range of thinking skills into activities which can be taught together as a complete project. The chapter offers two themed projects, 'Shipwrecked' and 'A school library', within which all the subject areas can be taught. Although one main thinking strategy is identified in each activity, often more than one is being used. In the activity entitled 'Island delights', for example, the children will create ideas and evaluate what they have done before extending these ideas further.

The purpose of this chapter is to highlight the thinking skills, and it is the questioning and organisation of learning which carries most importance. The individual activities are flexible enough to address several different learning objectives or to develop different thinking skills, so you may wish to change the focus in some of the lessons.

SHIPWRECKED

The first topic covers several activities from the QCA units of work for Years 3 and 4 and shows how these can be approached in different ways to support learning across the curriculum. Some are extensions of the main activities which link naturally to the context of the subject units – researching pirates links well to different periods of history, while the mapping activity develops geographical skills.

Set the context for the activities by telling the children that you have all been shipwrecked and washed up on the shore of an island in the middle of the ocean. Wonder with them the sorts of things that may have been washed ashore from the ship, such as materials they could use to construct a shelter, food to cook a decent meal, and items to make a rescue signal. There may even be tools which the children could use to make some comforts.

A SCHOOL LIBRARY

The second topic addresses all the thinking skills across a number of activities, but focuses on developing the children's evaluative and creative thinking. In many of the activities they will be evaluating the local public library and using some of the ideas they gain there to create a new, or develop the existing, library in school.

The activities 'Materials on loan', 'People of importance' and 'Music library' all use evaluation skills initially, before developing enquiry skills or creating new ideas for book collections and other materials for loan. Creative thinking is developed in the activities 'Bookstands', 'Book location' and 'Story-teller' where they are invited to create new ways of displaying books and information, and creating furniture for different activities that take place in the library. Again reference has been made to the relevant National Literacy and Numeracy Strategy objectives, as well as the QCA units of work which provide a suitable context.

In this series of activities, some subjects provide contexts for English activities rather than subject-discrete objectives. So, for example, the activity 'People of importance' is an English activity set within RE and PE contexts.

SHIPWRECKED

Subject and QCA unit, NLS or NNS objective	Activity title	Thinking objective	Activity	Page
English. NLS objective: Note making – to edit down a sentence or passage by deleting the less important elements.	Message in a bottle	To evaluate, by judging how successful their finished writing is in getting the message across effectively	Judging the quality and effectiveness of messages and thinking about what they need to include to get across the imperative nature of the message.	136
Maths. NNS objective: To begin to use ideas of simple proportion – Year 4 to use fractions and decimals.	Distance calculation	To deduce	Deducing the position and distance between two points on an island. Considering the position of different features on the island using the points of a compass.	137
Science. QCA unit 4C: Keeping warm	Sleeping bag	To test conclusions	Evaluating materials for keeping things warm. Measuring the temperature of water that has been kept warm by different materials.	138
History. QCA unit 6: Invasion and settlement	Famous pirates	To plan research	Investigating the lives of pirates and why they lived the life they did. Identifying sources of relevant information and writing a factual account of their chosen pirate.	140
Geography. QCA unit 25: Geography and numbers	Where am I?	To locate	Locating features on a map of the island using knowledge and understanding of positional language. Using co-ordinates to locate features.	141
Design and technology. QCA unit 3B: Sandwich snacks	Island delights	To create and extend ideas; to evaluate information	Creating recipes from a given set of ingredients. Evaluating likes and dislikes to produce a meal that their friends like.	142
ICT. QCA unit 3B: Manipulating sound	Rescue me	To create ideas; to evaluate information (judging quality)	Thinking about the sound needed to attract attention and developing ideas for a rescue signal. Considering the musical elements and evaluating the quality of sound.	143
Art and design. QCA unit 3B: A visit to a museum or art gallery.	Island landscapes	To analyse line and colour	Analysing how artists use line and colour to create certain moods and feelings. Looking at different landscape effects and use of perspective.	144
Music. QCA unit 13: Painting with sound	Mood music	To analyse; to evaluate information (judging quality)	Listening to and analysing the elements composers use to create particular moods. Classifying pieces of music to make different tapes of mood music.	145
RE. QCA unit 3D: What is in the Bible and why is it important for Christians?	Rules to live by	To extend ideas	Considering the Ten Commandments and why they are important to Christians. Writing a set of rules for behaviour on the island.	146
PE. QCA unit: Outdoor and adventurous activities – unit 2	Chicken rescue	To make judgements	Working with a set of equipment to rescue a chicken stranded on an island in the middle of a piranha-infested lake. Thinking about how to transport people across the water and bring back the chicken safely.	148

Message in a bottle

Subject: English. NLS objective: Note making – to edit down a sentence or passage by deleting the less important elements.

Learning objective

To consider which elements are truly essential in getting a message across quickly and effectively.

Thinking objective

To evaluate, by judging how successful their finished writing is in getting the message across quickly and effectively.

Thinking skills

The children will judge the quality of their messages by thinking carefully about what they need to include, and how they need to present important information so that the reader gets the message quickly. They will also consider how effectively their writing gets across the imperative nature of the message.

What you need

Sheets of paper or small torn pieces; pens; plastic bottles; whiteboard and pen.

What to do

Talk about the island where you have been washed ashore after the shipwreck. Set this up as a drama lesson if you wish, and act out events that may have occurred since the ship started to sink.

Think about the likely terrain, and the things you might find and use to make shelters – fire, food and so on. Discuss the predicament that you are all in and the possibility of rescue. Ask, *How can we let people know where we are? Do we actually know where we are? How do you know this? What can you see? How might we gain the attention of potential rescuers?* Talk about all the ways you could attract attention. Discuss the use of beacons, sirens and making messages from stones and natural materials on the beach.

If it has not already arisen, introduce the idea of writing a message and putting it into a bottle. Point out that the message needs to be clear and concise so that the person finding it will know immediately

how vital it is to act on the information it contains. Ask, *What sort of things would we need to include?* Write these as a list on the board. Prompt the children's ideas and thinking by questioning them about how they could alert the finder to the fact that they need help desperately and want to be rescued. Ask, *How would you write this particular part of the message? Would you write it in larger letters? What colour would you use? Where on the paper would you write this piece of information?* Include ideas such as HELP, SOS, and EMERGENCY. Check some of these words in a thesaurus or dictionary to get additional ideas for high-impact words. Ask, *What other things would it be useful to say?* Again question the children to develop their thinking: *How can you explain where you are? What can you describe? What clues are there to explain the exact position of the island? Is the ship's log available, or charts from the ship, which will help?* Develop the children's imagination in this way by encouraging them to think of plausible reasons why they might have certain clues to their whereabouts.

List all their ideas, then think about the size of the bottle and the paper that is available. Ask, *How can you make sure that the reader's attention is drawn to the very important nature of your message without using too many words? How will you fit all the essential information on this piece of paper?*

Let the children choose for themselves the resources they want to write their message, experimenting with different colours and sizes of letters. Remind them that they need to grab the reader's attention, but must also include all the important parts of the message in a limited space. If some children would prefer to do their work on computer, point out that there is a very slim chance of one being available on a remote island! Challenge them to use their imaginations to come up with a feasible reason why one may be there.

Plan a class message, in sentences first, to judge its effectiveness. Then show them how to edit one sentence down to a few words. Allow the class to judge the quality of the edited message in terms of how quickly it gains the attention of the reader, and whether it gets the important message across. Ask the children to follow the same process to edit their own messages, and to ask a partner to evaluate its effectiveness. Test a few of the messages in bottles to see if they will float, and whether they remain waterproof.

DIFFERENTIATION
Draft possible messages for lower attaining children to edit down to a smaller number of words. Write out the finished, edited version for them to copy, and evaluate the quality together as a smaller group. Challenge the higher attaining children to produce a map of the island, showing its geographical location, and where you are shipwrecked. Consider the value of this information before inserting the map into the message.

WHERE NEXT
Pretend to be rescued and send postcards home with the rescuers, explaining that you intend to stay on the island and giving your reasons why.

ASSESSMENT
Assess how well the children evaluate the effectiveness of their edited messages. Ask, *Have you left out any important information? How quickly will the reader understand the importance of acting on your message?*

LEARNING OUTCOME
The children will learn to judge the quality of their writing in terms of whether it gains the attention of its intended audience. They will learn how to edit sentences to reduce the number of words, without losing the impact of the message.

FURTHER ENGLISH CHALLENGES
SOS
Use pebbles, sticks and other natural materials to write messages on the 'beach' (an area on the field or playground). Photograph the finished messages and evaluate them together afterwards. Ask, *How well can they be seen? Is the message clear? Which word(s) make the message clear?* Give each message marks out of ten for quality.
Seed messages
Sow wild grass seeds on a patch of earth in the school grounds to spell out a message. It is probably best not to use words like SOS or HELP. Challenge the children to think of words that will attract attention but will not alarm anyone in the locality, such as HELLO or HI THERE.

DISTANCE CALCULATION

SUBJECT: MATHS. NNS OBJECTIVE: TO BEGIN TO USE IDEAS OF SIMPLE PROPORTION – YEAR 4 TO USE FRACTIONS AND DECIMALS.

LEARNING OBJECTIVES
To calculate distances in kilometres and metres; to use four and eight compass directions.

THINKING OBJECTIVE
To deduce.

THINKING SKILLS
The children will be asked to deduce the position and distance between two points on their island. In order to do this, they will consider the position of the different features on the island, using either four or eight points of the compass, depending on their learning levels. They will also learn to use the proportional scale, again matched to their learning levels, to work out the distance between two given points. This will help them to develop an understanding of measures and space, as well as fractions and decimals, and start to use this information to solve simple problems.

WHAT YOU NEED
A map of your imaginary island, with a scale measured in kilometres or metres and a compass symbol showing north; tape measure and ruler.

WHAT TO DO
Before the lesson, draw a large A2-size map of your imaginary island with the children, including physical features that should be positioned according to four and eight points on a compass.

Look at the map and identify the features. Talk about the positions of the different features and deduce their compass positions. For example: *The tallest mountain is north-west of our campsite.*

Look at the scale and talk about what this means with the children. Explain that they need to pretend that for every centimetre, the actual distance is one kilometre or one metre. Choose one feature and measure its distance in centimetres from the campsite. Question the children to help them use the scale to deduce the actual distance. Ask, *If each centimetre equals one kilometre, how far away is the feature? If one centimetre equals one metre, how far away is the feature now? Which scale represents the greater distance?*

Once the children understand the ratio of the scale, introduce other scales for them to interpret, such as one centimetre equals ten or a hundred metres or kilometres.

Give pairs of children two named features and ask them to deduce and describe the position of each one using the four or eight point compass, as appropriate, as well as working out the distance between them.

DIFFERENTIATION

Keep the scale simple for lower attaining children so that they can use their knowledge and understanding of one-to-one correspondence or multiplying by ten to help them work out the distance. Higher attaining pupils can work out distances using measurements that include 0.5 or 0.25 of a centimetre. They will need to use their knowledge of fractions and decimals to deduce the distance.

WHERE NEXT

Look at a range of actual islands in different oceans and use the scale to work out how far they are from the nearest mainland. Start with the islands around Scotland before moving on to others farther afield.

ASSESSMENT

Assess how well the children deduce the distance between two features using a simple understanding of proportion and their knowledge of the four or eight points of a compass.

LEARNING OUTCOMES

Most pupils will begin to deduce the distance and position of the different features on their island map.

FURTHER MATHS CHALLENGES

School island

Go outside into the school playground and note the features around you. Stand in one spot and ask the children to identify the feature which is north-west, south-east, and so on. Ask the children to identify features themselves for the rest of the class to deduce. Return to the classroom and plot the features on a plan of the school.

Feature plot

Give the children a map of another fictitious island, with an eight-point compass symbol showing directions in one corner. Make sure the measurements on the map are in whole centimetres, to match the one centimetre to one kilometre ratio. For example, if the map shows the island to be 20 centimetres long, the actual length will be 20 kilometres. Mark the centre of the island with a cross and ask the children to draw a tree four kilometres to the south-west, a cave five kilometres to the north-west, and so on. You can extend the activity by asking the children to use the scale to draw a feature of their choice a given

distance away from a named feature. For example: *Draw a ruined castle six kilometres away, south-west of the cave.* The children will need to deduce both the direction and scale to work out the position and distance of one feature from the other.

SLEEPING BAG

SUBJECT: SCIENCE. QCA UNIT 4C: KEEPING WARM.

LEARNING OBJECTIVE

To learn that some materials are good thermal insulators.

THINKING OBJECTIVE

To test conclusions.

THINKING SKILLS

The children will consider the range of materials they think would be good for keeping things warm. They will then plan a fair test to find out the best material to use to make a sleeping bag. They will test out their predictions by measuring the temperature of water that has been kept warm by the different materials. They will use these results to draw a conclusion. They will then test their conclusions by planning and carrying out a further test.

WHAT YOU NEED

At least four sleeping bags of different materials and thickness; identical water-tight containers; warm water; thermometers; a range of materials that may keep things warm, including polythene, plastic, bubble-wrap, sponge, fleece and other fabrics; aluminium foil; paper and writing materials.

WHAT TO DO

Tell the children that it gets very cold on the island at night and it is important for them all to keep warm. Invite them to think of all the ways they could keep warm at night, considering both comfort and how well the materials they use will insulate their body heat.

Look at the sleeping bags and ask the children to say how you might find out which one would be best for keeping you warm. Ask, *What do you need to find out? What will you use? How can you make the test fair?* Ask them to plan a fair test in small groups. Discuss this and decide how to carry out the test. The following is a suggestion.

Give each group a sleeping bag to test, an identical container of warm water (the same temperature in each one), and a thermometer. Explain that they should carry out the test by wrapping the container in their sleeping bag. Then, every five minutes, they should take the temperature of their water and record the number of degrees in a table. After the test has been completed, look closely at the materials in the winning sleeping bag and talk about how these make it so good at retaining heat. Ask, *What is special about the fabric and how it is put together?* Collect the children's ideas and record them on the board.

Now explain to the children that no sleeping bags were washed up on the shore after the shipwreck, so they will have to find other materials that they can use to make warm sleeping bags. Ask them to use their conclusions to test out which will make the best sleeping bag from a range of materials that have been washed up on the shore (see 'What you need'). Ask, *Can you think which materials we could use to make an effective sleeping bag? Do you think these materials might keep you even warmer?* Try out the children's ideas by making simple sleeping bags with the materials they have suggested and repeating the investigation with the containers of warm water and thermometers. Find out whether the children's predictions are right by noting the differences between the temperature readings for each material. Ask, *Which one cools down most quickly? How do you know? Which of the materials you have tested would be best for keeping you warm?* Conclude which is the best sleeping bag.

DIFFERENTIATION
Talk to lower attaining children in small groups to probe their understanding of what they found out from their investigation. Support their understanding of how well they are testing out their conclusions when testing alternative materials by asking direct questions about the comparative rate at which the temperature is falling for each material. Higher attaining children should be encouraged to plan their own second investigation to test out their conclusions.

WHERE NEXT
Pretend that the school grounds are your island. Ask the children to nominate places they think will be suitably sheltered and warm for them to set up camp. Test out the children's predictions by repeating their investigation in these places. Listen to their conclusions and check these out.

ASSESSMENT
Assess how well the children test out their conclusions and note those who understand that the results tell them how good their conclusions are.

LEARNING OUTCOME
Most children will learn how to test out their conclusions fairly. Some will need some direction, while others will realise that the results gained by measuring the falling temperature allow them to evaluate how effective their chosen material is.

FURTHER SCIENCE CHALLENGES
Keep it cool
Apply the children's ideas to keeping things cool. Ask them to set up an investigation to test out their predictions about which materials insulate cold, and keep things cool. Allow them to think up for themselves what they will try to keep cool, how they will do this, and how they will measure the changes in temperature. Check that they realise that the lowest temperature shows the most effective material. Test out their conclusions by using the material to see if it will stop an ice-lolly from melting over a longer space of time. Note those who apply their knowledge and understanding of insulation to form and test out their conclusions.

Sheltered places
Find the warmest spot in the school grounds to build a shelter. Let the children reason this for themselves by planning and carrying out their own investigation. They may choose to use the same equipment or to find out in some other way. Let the children decide. If they use the falling temperature of water to measure the effectiveness of each place to draw their conclusions, record the results as a line graph. These can then be photocopied onto transparencies to lie on top of each other to compare the results of different places. This way the children can draw

conclusions about which is the warmest place to build a shelter by choosing the place where the temperature dropped the least.

FAMOUS PIRATES

SUBJECT: HISTORY. QCA UNIT 6: INVASION AND SETTLEMENT.

LEARNING OBJECTIVE
To learn that one reason why people invaded countries and attacked ships was to acquire wealth.

THINKING OBJECTIVE
To plan research.

THINKING SKILLS
The children will consider the lives of different pirates and why they led the life that they did. They will think of questions to inform their research and identify all the places where they can find relevant information. They will list a range of facts about different pirates in note form, before writing a factual account of their chosen pirate.

WHAT YOU NEED
Access to the Internet, fiction and non-fiction books about pirates; CD-ROMs; paper and writing materials.

WHAT TO DO
Set up a search on the Internet to find websites that have information about different pirates. Vet the websites before the lesson so that you can choose the ones that are most suitable. List these websites for the children to use – www.piratehaven.org and www.ecani.com/pirates have lists of pirate names and child-friendly pictures if you stick to the gallery rather than the action; the BBC website also has links, although not on the children's page. You could start with a well-known pirate such as Blackbeard, Captain Kidd or Mary Read.

Make sure, too, that there are suitable books in the library. You may be able to ask your local library to prepare a topic box and secrete the books it contains in different, but relevant, sections of the library for the children to locate.

Tell the children a story about a pirate you have chosen. Ask them to think about why they boarded other ships or attacked settlements. Ask, *What were their reasons for this? Why did they like this sort of life? How did they live?*

Make a list of questions as a research plan:
◉ *How could we find out about pirates?*
◉ *What is the first thing you need to identify?* (The names of pirates for researching.)
◉ *What can you use?* (Books, posters, Internet, CD-ROMs.)
◉ *What key words can you use to locate the information in books, CD-ROMs and on the Internet?* (Names of pirates, ships and places where they were pirates.)

◉ *What information are you looking for? How will you record this?*
◉ *What will you do with the information afterwards to make it easy to read?*

Divide the class into groups and give them their first task: to locate and find out the names of different pirates from books, CD-ROMs and the Internet. Emphasise that the children should only use the websites you have looked at and show them where these are listed.

Once they have found some possible names, ask groups of children to use key words to research one name each. Each group should have access to the Internet, books and CD-ROMs, so that they learn how to use each of these research tools to find information. Ask them to make notes from their research and to write these up as a group account of the pirate they chose.

Make a timeline to show when these pirates lived in comparison to other famous historical figures you have already studied.

DIFFERENTIATION
Carry out the research plan with lower attaining children so that they are clear about what they are trying to find out (and why), and the places where they can find information. Higher attaining children

should be encouraged to develop a research plan for finding out about famous pirate ships.

WHERE NEXT
Set up a research plan for the children to use to find out about famous battles and voyages, setting the research around the explorations of, for example, Christopher Columbus or Ferdinand Magellan.

ASSESSMENT
Assess the children who set up their own research plan to find out about a particular pirate. Note those who need additional practice at this type of activity to extend their understanding of what to look for, and where to look.

LEARNING OUTCOME
All the children will learn to follow a research plan to find out about at least one pirate. Some will be able to apply this process to other research projects.

FURTHER HISTORY CHALLENGES
Jolly Roger
Set up a research plan to find out who or what the Jolly Roger is. Develop a set of questions for the children to follow to find out what they can about this flag. Include ideas such as, *What is it? Why was it used? What message did it send to other people? Where should we look for information? What are the key words? How should we record what we have found out?*

Pirates of the Caribbean
Plan research to find out about the famous pirates of the Caribbean. Ask the children to find the names of some of the pirates and identify key words that will help. Ask, *How will you know which sources of evidence to eliminate?* (The Disney website may well appear.) *Which parts of books and CD-ROMs will help you to locate the information you need? Can this be found in the resource you are using?*

WHERE AM I?

SUBJECT: GEOGRAPHY. QCA UNIT 25: GEOGRAPHY AND NUMBERS.

LEARNING OBJECTIVE
To understand compass directions.

THINKING OBJECTIVE
To locate.

THINKING SKILLS
The children will revisit their knowledge and understanding of positional language before using it to locate features on their map of the island. They will use co-ordinates to locate the features and will then choose other co-ordinates to challenge their friends to find further features.

WHAT YOU NEED
A map of your imaginary island that includes a compass symbol (A2-size for the class activity and enough smaller copies for each group to have one).

WHAT TO DO
Look at the map of the island together and identify some of the features. Pretend that you are standing somewhere on the island and describe your position, using compass bearings to help describe this in relation to the features that you can see. For example: *From where I am standing I can see the stone cave to the south-west. The mountain is to the north and the campsite is behind me. Where am I?* When the children have correctly identified where you are, ask them further questions: *Can I see the beach? What else can I see from my position? Which direction am I facing?*

Select individual children and invite them to describe where they are, again using the points of the compass for the rest of the class to locate their position. When you are sure that the children know how to use positional language to describe where they are, let them play this as a game in pairs or small groups. Use questions as prompts, such as, *What can you see and in which direction does it lie? What is behind you or to the side of you? What else can you see and where is it?*

After about ten minutes, draw grid squares on the map, giving each line a number. Explain longitude (lines down) and latitude (lines across) to the children.

Pair the children up to find the co-ordinates of the different features for visitors to the island to locate, using the lines down and across.

DIFFERENTIATION
Ask lower attaining children to use co-ordinates for the squares rather than the lines so that they develop an understanding of how to locate the different features within particular squares. Higher attaining children could use four-figure references to locate the position of particular features.

WHERE NEXT
Look at OS maps of the local area and use the co-ordinates to locate features and places.

Look at atlases and locate longitude and latitude lines. Show the children how to use these to locate the different countries of the world.

ASSESSMENT

Assess how well the children use the co-ordinates, and their knowledge and understanding of the four or eight points of a compass, to locate different features on a map.

LEARNING OUTCOMES

Most children will gain an understanding of the strategies they can use to identify the locations of different places on a map.

FURTHER GEOGRAPHY CHALLENGES

Island adventure

Recreate the island in an area outside, using chalk on the playground, or ropes and string on the field. Mark this with a co-ordinate grid by placing ropes or string to make the lines. Give each line a number, then add three-dimensional features at certain points, such as a pile of sand or earth for mountains, blue fabric for a river, and so on. Ask individual children to move to certain co-ordinates and to say what they can see from that point if they face north, south or another direction. Repeat this as often as you like.

ISLAND DELIGHTS

SUBJECT: DESIGN AND TECHNOLOGY. QCA UNIT 3B: SANDWICH SNACKS.

LEARNING OBJECTIVE

To design and make snacks.

THINKING OBJECTIVES

To create and extend ideas; to evaluate information.

THINKING SKILLS

The children will create recipes from a given set of ingredients. They will evaluate the class's likes and dislikes and use the information to create and extend the recipes to produce a meal their friends like.

WHAT YOU NEED

A wide range of food ingredients of your choice – potatoes, vegetables, jam, flour, butter, milk, eggs, sugar, baking powder (check for any food allergies before you start); a place and equipment for cooking the dishes that are created; a tasting table.

WHAT TO DO

Explain that it's lunchtime on the island and the children have several ingredients from which they can choose to make a variety of meals for the other shipwreck survivors. Show them the ingredients that are available. As a class, sort these according to their type, for example potatoes and vegetables for a main course, and other ingredients for a pudding.

Organise the children into groups of six and ask them to create recipes for a main course and a pudding. Some may invent new recipes, while others may work with ones they are familiar with. Record these on large sheets of paper to share with other groups. Listen to the evaluations of each recipe before organising an opportunity for each group to make them. Encourage them to select the equipment they will need to make the recipes for the other groups to try, and provide additional adult support.

Set up a tasting table, asking each child in the class to say which recipe they like best and why. Even if some of the recipes are disasters, this will still form part of the evaluation.

DIFFERENTIATION

Support the lower attaining children by talking about previous recipes they may have made, such as vegetable soup or cakes and biscuits. More able children should be challenged to invent a new recipe.

WHERE NEXT

Challenge the children by providing them with ingredients that they might find on the island, such as coconut and banana. Ask them to create recipes that include these.

ASSESSMENT

Note the children who create new recipes and evaluate these to extend and improve their flavours.

LEARNING OUTCOMES

Most children will be able to prepare a recipe, choosing from the range of ingredients available. Some will think of new and inventive ideas and give reasons for their choice by considering the flavours and texture.

FURTHER DESIGN AND TECHNOLOGY CHALLENGES

Exotic sandwiches

Ask the children to create different sandwiches by combining a wide range of different fillings. Evaluate the sandwiches together, making sure that the children do not eat anything that will cause a reaction or make them sick. Ask each child to give the sandwiches marks out of ten, and add these up to evaluate which new sandwich is the class favourite. Check that the children realise that the one with most points is the favourite, and the one with fewest points the least favourite. Ask, *Can we make the sandwiches tastier by toasting them?*

RESCUE ME

SUBJECT: ICT. QCA UNIT 3B: MANIPULATING SOUND.

LEARNING OBJECTIVE
To compose a sound sequence on keyboard and percussion instruments.

THINKING OBJECTIVES
To create ideas; to evaluate information (judging quality).

THINKING SKILLS
The children will think carefully about the type of sound they need to use to attract attention when developing their own ideas for a rescue signal. They will consider the musical elements – the pitch, rhythms and timbre of sounds – and evaluate the quality of these sounds before using them to create their own rescue signals using computer software or a keyboard.

WHAT YOU NEED
Computers; music software such as *Music Explorer*; keyboards; a tape recorder; a mobile phone with a range of ring tones or access to a suitable Internet website; percussion and other instruments.

WHAT TO DO
Think together of the different ways you could attract the attention of rescuers. You could use a large banner, a message written in stones on the beach, a fire beacon – you could even wave your arms madly in the air! Encourage the children to use their imagination.

Now explain to the children that there may also be a need to attract the attention of the shipwrecked mariners on the island when help finally arrives. Tell them that you want them to think of a musical sequence that will attract everyone's attention, no matter where they are on the island, to let them know that help has come. This will ensure that no one will be left behind on the island.

Talk about how they can do this, reinforcing that the only element they cannot use is excessively loud noise because this can damage the ears. Listen to, and then discuss, the different mobile phone ring tones and evaluate each one in terms of how good it is at attracting attention. Ask, *Why? What elements do they contain which makes listeners tune in and gains their attention?* Note the repeating patterns used in some, as well as any unusual rhythms or sounds that would be very different from their surroundings.

At this point, consider the sounds the children are likely to hear on the island and, for each one, think of a contrasting type of sound. For example, there may be sounds of leaves rustling, which are continuous and quiet, so a contrasting sound would have to be loud and sudden. Think about the musical elements of pitch, timbre and rhythm to describe possible island sounds and identify those that will contrast.

Listen to all the other different sounds you have available, using the keyboards and computer software. Let the children explore the different sounds before composing a sound sequence of their own, in groups, which they think will attract attention. Let them decide what they want to use, including percussion and other instruments, computers and keyboards.

Ask each group to record their musical sequences. If possible, find another adult to operate the tape recorder, and then take the children as far away from the tape as you can to listen to the sounds at a distance. Listen to all the sounds, then ask the children to say how well they can hear each one, and whether they think it would be effective in attracting attention from a long distance away. Ask, *Why do you think a particular tune attracts attention better than another? Is it because of the pitch, the volume or the style chosen?*

Evaluate the sequences together, judging the quality of each one in terms of how well it attracts attention, and deciding why.

DIFFERENTIATION
Give lower attaining children a sound sequence to start with. Concentrate on changing its pitch, volume and style on a keyboard, recording the finished tune when the children have agreed on its quality for attracting attention. Higher attaining children should be encouraged to use repeating patterns to make their signals, varying the pitch. They should evaluate the quality of their signal by comparing the quality of sound produced on a computer and a keyboard. Ask, *Which is most effective for attracting attention?*

WHERE NEXT
Find other tunes and sounds in the computer or keyboard memory, giving each one marks out of ten for their effectiveness in attracting attention.

ASSESSMENT

Assess how well the children consider the quality of their sequences in terms of how effective they are at attracting attention when they change the pitch, volume and styles of their signals and tunes.

LEARNING OUTCOME

Most children will learn to create a tune by varying the pitch, style and volume on a keyboard. Some will develop their ideas on computer software. They will all evaluate to some degree the quality of their tunes in terms of how well they attract attention, and give reasons for this.

FURTHER ICT CHALLENGES

Drum signals

Use a drum synthesizer to create a rescue signal using repeating patterns or a sequence of drum sounds. Discuss how the same sounds could be reproduced on items found on a deserted island.

144 **SOS**

Investigate Morse code and how this was used in the past to send messages. Develop a rescue signal using dots and dashes and reproduce these on a drum synthesizer or keyboard. Evaluate the quality of the rescue signal and think about the difficulties that arise with this method of communication.

ISLAND LANDSCAPES

SUBJECT: ART AND DESIGN. QCA UNIT 3B: A VISIT TO A MUSEUM OR ART GALLERY.

LEARNING OBJECTIVE

To consider how line and colour are used in paintings to create mood and feelings.

THINKING OBJECTIVE

To analyse line and colour.

THINKING SKILLS

The children will analyse how artists use line and colour in paintings to create certain moods and feelings. They will look at different landscape effects and analyse how merging lines and overlapping colour have been used to create them. They will look carefully at how different artists use colour to achieve certain effects. They will consider tones and tints (blues and greens in particular) and note how artists use these to create perspective and movement in their paintings. They will also look at how artists use contrasting colours to depict certain moods.

WHAT YOU NEED

Painting materials; paintings of landscapes by different artists that show the use of tones and tints of the same colour, for example *Lake Thun* by Ferdinand Hodler or *Nocturne in blue and silver* by Whistler; the work of artists who use contrasting colour and line to depict mood and feelings, such as the various views of France painted by Cézanne or *Landscape with cypresses near Arles* by Van Gogh – try to find four or more suitable landscapes if possible, and build this activity into a work focus for a visit to an art gallery.

WHAT TO DO

Look at four varying landscapes by artists in different styles. Talk about how each one recreates the features and colours in the landscape. For example, you could mention how colour creates distance and form in Whistler's studies or in Ferdinand Hodler's *Lake Thun*. Ask, *How has the artist used shade, tones and tints? From which direction is the light falling on the features? How do you know?*

Now look at landscapes by Van Gogh and Cézanne and talk about how they use line to create certain moods and feelings. Ask, *How does the use of line create an image of the cypress trees moving? How does the merging of line create the heat and sunshine in Cézanne's landscapes?* Encourage the children to think up and express their own ideas when describing the feelings and moods that the lines and colours evoke.

Now talk about the features on the island and, if necessary, look at the map together again before asking the children to create a painting of what they think it actually looks like. They should each choose one of the styles to copy, and then experiment with colour in the same way as Hodler or Cézanne to recreate landscape paintings that reflect the moods of the island. Ask them to give their paintings a title to reflect these moods and feelings.

DIFFERENTIATION
Work with contrasting colours with lower attaining children first, and talk about how this creates effects. Move on to discuss how Van Gogh uses curved lines to apply the colours to create movement. With higher attaining children, move directly to talk about how colours create mood and effect, for example: *Hodler creates the peace and tranquility of Lake Thun in his painting through the use of blue tints and tones and the gentle ripples of the water in the lake.*

WHERE NEXT
Choose one style and develop it over a number of weeks for different contexts, such as looking at how colour is used to camouflage animals, or in painting seascapes or night scenes. For each style, analyse the way colour is used before starting to plan and paint your own pictures.

ASSESSMENT
Note those children who are able to analyse the paintings in terms of the way colour is used to create certain effects. Look at the children's work and note who uses contrasting colour, and who uses tints and tones of the same colour to create certain effects. Record the children's words and descriptions to note who understands how the element of colour can create emotion in observers.

LEARNING OUTCOMES
Most children will analyse how colour is used in different paintings and understand how to use this in their own landscape paintings. Some will do this by using contrasting colours, while others will think about how the tones and tints of the same colour create certain effects, moods and feelings.

FURTHER ART AND DESIGN CHALLENGES
Digital landscape
Take photographs of landscapes in the surrounding area. Analyse the images in terms of their line, colour and tone. Download them into computer software, and add effects and change colours to create a different mood and/or feeling. Analyse the effects and describe how changes to the colour and pattern have changed our feelings towards different images.

MOOD MUSIC

SUBJECT: MUSIC. QCA UNIT 13: PAINTING WITH SOUND.

LEARNING OBJECTIVE
To describe the mood and effects created by different pieces of music, using relevant musical vocabulary.

THINKING OBJECTIVES
To analyse; to evaluate information (judging quality).

THINKING SKILLS
The children will listen to each other's favourite pieces of music and analyse the elements composers use to create a particular mood. They will evaluate their quality in terms of the moods they create. They will analyse and classify the pieces, and consider which ones to put together to make different tapes of mood music to play at different times of the day while on their desert island.

WHAT YOU NEED
A selection of the children's favourite pieces of music; a tape recorder.

WHAT TO DO
Explain to the children that you are going to make tapes of music to support the different activities that take place on the island at different times of the day.

Talk to the children about the kinds of things they might do while they are on the island. This will include lively things, like walking up a hill, digging and planting, making shelters, fishing; and quiet activities, like keeping watch and sleeping. Talk about the kinds of music that would be suitable to accompany these different activities. Listen to the children's favourite pieces of music, which will probably be pop music, and talk about how these make them feel. Analyse each one to identify which elements in the music create these feelings. Ask, *What musical elements does the composer use? Are there slow and simple rhythms or fast repeated semiquavers? Does the music have the loud and very full* texture and timbre of many instruments? Classify the different pieces of music into groups according to whether they are fast, slow, loud, quiet, have full or empty sounds, and so on. Then reclassify them in terms of the moods and feelings that each piece creates.

Encourage the children to think about the times when they would want to listen to music. Ask, *Which pieces of music would you play at night when you are trying to get to sleep? Why wouldn't you play loud or lively music? What would you play to encourage others to hike to the top of the mountain to look out for rescue ships? What kind of music would they need to keep them moving?* Match the activities identified at the beginning of the lesson to the types of music you have classified.

DIFFERENTIATION

Give lower attaining children particular pieces of music to analyse and evaluate against a given activity. For example, listen to *La Mer* by Debussy and say whether it would be suitable to play when sawing wood. Repeat this evaluation for 'The Anvil Chorus' from *Il Trovatore* by Verdi. Analyse the musical elements to decide what makes this second piece of music a more suitable match for a wood-sawing activity.

Introduce higher attaining children to pieces of modern music that do not necessarily have a regular scale or tune. Music by Bartok, Schoenberg or Copeland would be suitable.

WHERE NEXT

Over the next few weeks, make compilation tapes to reflect the different times of day and moods for which you want music to listen to. Give each tape a title. Use commercial compilation tapes and CDs for inspiration on which pieces to combine and ideas for titles.

Listen to a piece of music and ask the children to paint what they feel. They might paint a piece of abstract art in response to loud and challenging pop music, or a calm beach scene when listening to *La Mer* by Debussy.

ASSESSMENT

Assess how well the children analyse the elements of music and how well they select pieces to support certain island activities.

LEARNING OUTCOME

Most children will learn to analyse the musical elements in different pieces of music, and will be able to choose those which are most suitable to support the different activities.

FURTHER MUSIC CHALLENGES
Island cameo
Use extracts that the children have chosen and evaluated to build a dance cameo of all the activities the children think they will do while on the island. Paint a picture in dance and music of the mood and feelings created by the pieces of music chosen.

RULES TO LIVE BY

SUBJECT: RE. QCA UNIT 3D: WHAT IS IN THE BIBLE AND WHY IS IT IMPORTANT FOR CHRISTIANS?

LEARNING OBJECTIVE
To understand the importance of rules.

THINKING OBJECTIVE
To extend ideas.

THINKING SKILLS
The children will consider the Ten Commandments and why they are important to Christians. They will use these as a basis for writing a set of rules or commandments for behaviour on the island. They will include what are, and what are not, acceptable actions, and the way they must treat one another at all times. They will learn that because these rules must be obeyed, they are called commandments. They will extend their ideas about the consequences of their actions by phrasing the rules in a positive way. This will help them to guide particular behaviour and develop a growing sense of treating each other with respect.

WHAT YOU NEED
The Ten Commandments (Exodus, Chapter 20); paper and pens; drawing materials.

WHAT TO DO
Read the Ten Commandments and consider together what they mean. Discuss why they are important to Christians, and confirm with the children that they are rules that tell Christians how to live their lives and give them guidance on how to treat each other. Explain that the term 'commandments' means that they are commands, and must be obeyed.

Ask the children to think about how they would want people to behave on their island. List these on the board for the children to consider. Compare the children's list of the way they would like others to behave on the island with the Ten Commandments. Ask, *Would the Ten Commandments be relevant to this situation? Are there any you think you could leave out?*

Talk about the school rules and whether any of these are relevant to the way you would like people to behave towards one another on the island. Ask, *Would the school rules be more relevant that the Ten Commandments? Which ones would be suitable for people on the island? How would these rules help them to behave well?*

Model how to formulate a list of rules by writing a rule to help guide the behaviour of people who have to live together. Organise the children into groups and ask them to write rules for the other things on the list. Gather together and talk about these, and which ones possibly overlap. Edit them down to a maximum of ten to make a set of Ten Commandments for the island. Suggest that they could phrase their rules in a positive way so that, instead of making the rule 'You should not steal', they could write 'Always leave people's possessions where they are'.

Now challenge the children to consider the consequences if people break any of the agreed rules. What will be the consequence, for example, of stealing a treasured possession? Decorate the rules with relevant symbols to help people who read them to appreciate their importance immediately.

DIFFERENTIATION

Work with lower attaining children in a group and base their set of rules on personal experience. Talk with them about how they would like people to behave in school and apply these to how they imagine life on the island would be. Before defining a rule, talk to them about particular scenarios of what might happen as a consequence of certain actions. Model each rule in a positive way for the children to record. As they record the rules, higher attaining children should be encouraged to link each one with identified consequences if it is broken. For example, if someone calls another person an unpleasant name, this could link with the rule 'Always call someone by their proper name'.

These children might also like to identify possible consequences of not keeping particular rules, such as washing up that person's dirty dishes for a whole day.

WHERE NEXT

Look at the rules and commandments of other religions and investigate how the believers and followers show that they are keeping them.

ASSESSMENT

Note the children who are able to extend ideas of the Ten Commandments to identify rules and the consequences of certain actions, and can phrase their rules or commandments in a positive way.

LEARNING OUTCOME

All the children will learn to write rules to detail the expected behaviour of people who live on the island. They will build on their work on the Ten Commandments and extend these ideas to everyday situations. Some will do this independently, while others will need support in a small group.

FURTHER RE CHALLENGES

In court

Debate what action the children will take if any of the rules or commandments are broken. Put together a set of rewards and consequences for each rule, in terms of when they are obeyed and when they are not. Set up a court drama scene with children playing the different parts of judge, jury, defendant, prosecutor and defence lawyer to put forward evidence as to whether a rule has been broken and what action should be taken.

School rules

Extend the children's ideas by evaluating the school rules in light of this work. Ask the children, in groups, to adapt, change or add some rules of their own choice. Share the rules as a class and eliminate any that the children think overlap. Produce a set of agreed rules that the children can refer to easily. Encourage them to phrase these in a positive way and to limit the number to ten.

CHICKEN RESCUE

SUBJECT: PE. QCA UNIT: OUTDOOR AND ADVENTUROUS ACTIVITIES – UNIT 2.

LEARNING OBJECTIVE
To work together to solve a problem.

THINKING OBJECTIVE
To make judgements.

THINKING SKILLS
The children will work together with a set of equipment to rescue a chicken stranded on an island in the middle of a piranha-infested lake. They will make judgements about what to use and how to work co-operatively to rescue the chicken. They will think about how they can transport people across the water and bring the chicken back safely.

WHAT YOU NEED
Six PE benches, six planks, twelve crates (stable and strong enough to hold the children's weight safely), six buckets and six 'chickens' (these could be footballs); space outside to create a 'lake' and small 'island'. Use long ropes to mark out the area. Make the distance between the edge of the lake and the island in the middle longer than the bench and plank, so that the children are obliged to make stepping-stones to get to the other side.

WHAT TO DO
Explain the problem to the children. Tell them that they have to rescue a chicken from the middle of the lake. Tell them that they must be very careful because the lake is full of piranhas, which will eat them and the chicken if they fall in. The only person that the piranhas will not eat is you (the teacher), because then you can legitimately help to take one end of the benches to the middle of the lake. Challenge the children to use the equipment provided to reach the other side of the lake.

Divide the children into six groups of about five to solve the problem. Give each group a PE bench, a bucket, and access to one plank and two crates. Spread them out around the perimeter of the lake. Place a chicken for each group to rescue on the island. Explain that all the members of the group must reach the island in order to rescue the chicken.

Challenge them to find a way to reach the middle of the lake to bring the chicken back in the bucket.

DIFFERENTIATION
Extend the activity by removing the plank and challenging the children to rescue the chicken again, using only the bench and the crates. Higher attaining children should be put in larger groups so they have more bodies to get across the lake. Less able children should have extra equipment and work in smaller groups.

WHERE NEXT
Let the children think of other equipment from which they can select to find another way to rescue the chicken. They should be encouraged to make judgements about why they have chosen a particular piece of equipment in terms of how they will use this in their rescue attempts.

ASSESSMENT
Note the children who make judgements about which equipment they will use, and can explain how and why.

LEARNING OUTCOME
Most children will learn to make judgements about how they will use the equipment, and some will begin to say why they have used it in the way that they have. A few children will make judgements about the other things they could use in their rescue attempts.

FURTHER PE CHALLENGES
Collecting eggs
Tell the children that the chicken has laid eggs at the top of a tree, and ask them to plan how to get the eggs down without breaking them. Provide a picture of the tree, detailing the height of the first branch from the ground – it should be just out of reach from the top of a ladder. Encourage the children to make judgements about which equipment they will use and, if they decide to use a ladder, how they will do so safely, bearing in mind that they will still be unable to reach the first branch. Ask, *How will you make the ladder safe if you put it on top of a crate? How will you pass the eggs down safely to the ground?* It is not suggested that this activity is carried out in practice!

THINKING SKILLS: AGES 7–9

148

A SCHOOL LIBRARY

Subject and QCA unit, NLS or NNS objective	Activity title	Thinking objective	Activity	Page
English: NLS objective: To locate books by classification in class or school libraries	Titles for all	To sequence and locate	Learning how to sequence books in the correct order and using the classification system to locate a book of their choice.	150
Maths. NNS objectives: To use all four operations to solve word problems involving numbers in 'real life' using one or more steps; to check results of calculations by rounding to the nearest ten or hundred	Choices	To make decisions	Choosing which books they would like to buy with a set amount of money. Negotiating with another group to buy books they cannot manage to pay for themselves.	150
Science. QCA unit 3C: Characteristics of materials	Material uses	To locate and collect; to evaluate information	Evaluating different materials used in the local library in the manufacture of seats, shelving and furniture, and how their properties make them suitable for a particular purpose.	152
History. QCA unit 18: What was it like to live here in the past?	Annuals	To ask questions	Looking at the content of some of the strip cartoon stories in annuals of the past and comparing with present day cartoon strips.	153
Geography. QCA unit 6: Investigate the local area	Library location	To define a problem	Locating the nearest library and defining the difficulties people may have in getting there.	154
Design and technology. QCA unit 3D: Photograph frames	Bookstands	To evaluate information (judging usefulness)	Looking at the stability of different bookstands, the materials used and structure of the frame. Evaluating the bookstands in terms of the size and weight of books they can hold.	155
ICT. QCA unit 3A: Combining text and graphics	Book location	To create ideas	Creating a poster to show the classification of books in the school library.	156
Art and design. QCQ unit 4B: Take a seat	Loose covers	To think imaginatively	Designing and making loose covers to decorate a story-teller's chair and thinking about the different themes of stories.	157
Music. QCA unit 14: Salt, pepper, vinegar, mustard	Music library	To plan research; to improve ideas	Planning a tape of singing games which can be borrowed from the library. Investigating the range of musical games available in the local library. Focusing singing games on support for younger children's history learning.	158
RE and PE.	People of importance	To evaluate information; to suggest improvements	Evaluating the range of books available in the local library, catalogues and websites to support RE and PE.	160

TITLES FOR ALL

SUBJECT: ENGLISH. NLS OBJECTIVE: TO LOCATE BOOKS BY CLASSIFICATION IN CLASS OR SCHOOL LIBRARIES.

LEARNING OBJECTIVE
To learn how to use a library classification system.

THINKING OBJECTIVE
To sequence and locate.

THINKING SKILLS
The children will learn how to sequence books in the correct order and use the classification system to locate a book of their choice.

WHAT YOU NEED
A library which is classified in some sort of colour and/or number system; a chart detailing the reference for each colour; a computer with all the titles on disk.

WHAT TO DO
Visit the school or local library and look at how the books are organised. Ask, *What do you notice? Are all the books that belong to a similar topic grouped together?* Talk about the colours, if such a system is used, and locate these on a chart to find out what subject each one refers to. Ask the children, *Which colour section would you look in to find a book about football? Where would you look to find out about Van Gogh?* Give pairs of children a different book section to locate. Match the colours with the labels and evaluate whether the sections are correctly labelled.

Note with the children that all the books have a number. Ask them, *What do you think this number refers to?* Now give each child a book number to locate and watch them to see if they use their sequencing skills to locate the right book.

Allow the children to find a book about a favourite topic. Encourage them to use the chart and number system to locate their book. Give the children time to browse their favourite books for a few minutes while you work with the higher attaining children on their differentiated task.

DIFFERENTIATION
Show the higher attaining children how to use the library computer system to locate a title or author. Show them how to locate the matching reference number so that they can find the book they want on the shelves. Work alongside the lower attaining children to help them sequence the number of the books to find the one they want.

WHERE NEXT
Let the children take turns to go individually, and in groups, to find the books they need for a current class topic.

ASSESSMENT
Note how well the children understand and use the sequence of numbers and colours to locate the book they need.

LEARNING OUTCOMES
Most children will use a colour system to locate a book about a particular topic. Some will be able to refine their searches to locate specific books by following a number system.

FURTHER ENGLISH CHALLENGES
Find the author!
Challenge the children to locate books by a specific author. This will be easy if they are classified in alphabetical order. Some will need to use the school or library system to look up these names and find the corresponding number.

CHOICES

SUBJECT: MATHS. NNS OBJECTIVES: TO USE ALL FOUR OPERATIONS TO SOLVE WORD PROBLEMS INVOLVING NUMBERS IN 'REAL LIFE' USING ONE OR MORE STEPS; TO CHECK RESULTS OF CALCULATIONS BY ROUNDING TO THE NEAREST TEN OR HUNDRED.

LEARNING OBJECTIVE
To calculate how many books can be bought for a given amount of money.

THINKING OBJECTIVE
To make decisions.

THINKING SKILLS
The children will consider which books they would like to buy with a set amount of money. They will need to make choices, deciding which books they will buy and which they cannot afford. They may also choose to negotiate with another group to buy books that they cannot manage to pay for themselves.

WHAT YOU NEED
Books that have been selected for disposal, such as out-of-date atlases, topical books that are more than five years old and others with old-fashioned illustrations; book catalogues; coins; calculators; paper and writing materials; whiteboard and pen.

WHAT TO DO

Tell the class that you are planning to replace some of the old books in the library and that you want them to decide which books to buy in place of those that are being put out. Look at the books that are to be discarded and note the topics that they cover. Ask, *Would it be a good idea to replace some of these and provide additional books for these topics?* Make a list of the topics involved.

Ask, *From your own experience, what topics is it difficult to find books for?* Hobbies, sports, music and art are often badly represented in school libraries. Add these to the list. Finally, make a list of all the topics that the children cover over the year or two-year cycle in your school.

Divide the topics between groups of children and give them a set amount of money to spend. Depending on the ability groups of your class, make these totals between £50 and £250. Ask them to look through the catalogues and find books that they would like to buy. Tell them to make a list of the books and write the price next to each one.

Add up the total that each group has spent. Give them a calculator, if you are sure they are competent, or use the exchanging game process to put coins into hanging pennies for pounds as each one is made. Increase the number of prices to add for more able children. Others can add one more book price on each time. Alternatively, use a spreadsheet format on a computer.

When all the group totals are calculated, add them together to find the total amount spent. Ask, *Is it within the budget that was set?*

Agree as a class which books to order and purchase for the library.

DIFFERENTIATION

Ask lower attaining children to find fiction titles which cost less than five pounds. Keep a running total with this group until they have reached their budget limit. If they then find another book they like, they will need to decide which one to discard. Higher attaining children can be asked to estimate the total by rounding prices to the nearest pound before adding the total in their heads. Challenge them to find books of the same price and to calculate the total by multiplying.

WHERE NEXT

Set up book selection as an independent group activity during numeracy lessons for the rest of the week.

ASSESSMENT

Assess how well the children use their deduction skills to exchange totals of money to find the overall total spend. Note how well higher attaining children in particular are able to use the skill of rounding to estimate in their heads before checking their answers.

LEARNING OUTCOMES

Most children will find books for the new library, making choices and decisions based on cost. They will deduce how much they have spent by exchanging coins, and will decide whether they have spent too much or too little.

FURTHER MATHS CHALLENGES

Fiction library

Set up a fiction library by evaluating the existing books and adding to the collection, deciding whether to spend more money on books for younger or older children. Different groups should each concentrate on one particular age group. They must keep within budget and decide which books to include and which to reject.

Challenge higher-attaining children to look at the complete list of books the class have identified for purchase and work out how much more money is needed to buy all the books on the list. Alternatively, note that many of the books are the same price and point out that, by dividing the total amount available, the children will be able to calculate how many they can buy with the money.

Computer library

Decide which computer material, perhaps a CD-ROM like *Encarta*, would be suitable for use on the library computer. Use some that you already have in class and include additional titles from catalogues. The children should be challenged to include the software licences and annual subscriptions in their calculations.

MATERIAL USES

SUBJECT: SCIENCE. QCA UNIT 3C: CHARACTERISTICS OF MATERIALS.

LEARNING OBJECTIVE

To survey materials used in the local library and note their suitability for their purpose.

THINKING OBJECTIVES

To locate and collect; to evaluate information.

THINKING SKILLS

The children will carry out a survey of how different materials, such as plastic, wood, paper, fabric, rock and metal, are used in the local library in the manufacture of seats, shelving and other furniture. They will locate and identify the names of all the materials and use them to set up a table. Against each type of material, the children will record all the items made from it. On their return to the classroom, they will evaluate the information to consider which materials have been used for a particular purpose, and how their properties make them suitable for these purposes. They will use this evaluation to say which are most suitable for use in the decoration, furniture and accessories in the school library.

WHAT YOU NEED

A visit to the local library, or a video or virtual tour of one – these are sometimes available on county council websites; large sheet of paper divided into rows – one for each material property, and a column for the items found; large sheet of paper and pen.

WHAT TO DO

Explain to the children that you want to research the range of materials used in libraries and why these have been chosen. Explain that you want to consider the properties of each one and whether the materials are suited to the uses they have been put to. Visit, or look at photographs or video of, a library, paying particular attention to the furnishings and shelves. Ask, *Which materials have been used to make the shelves? What about the design? Are they solid, straight and able to support heavy loads? Have particular materials been used because of their properties? Which property makes this material most suitable? Can you think of another material with the same property that would be equally suitable?*

With the children, think about all the materials being used in the library. They should be able to find examples of all the materials they know and identify these in their material state, rather than as artefacts.

On the prepared sheet of paper, make a list of the materials you can see in the library. Against each one, list the items in the library that are made from this material. Then, for each one, identify the properties of the material and the reason why one or more of its properties suits this particular purpose. For example, next to 'paper' you may have 'posters' and 'flexible, smooth, waterproof so that it can be made flat and written on easily with a water-based pen' as properties that make the paper suited to its purpose. For 'fabric', you could have 'cushions', with 'soft, colourful and pliable' for properties and 'because they make the library attractive and can be plumped up for comfort' as reasons for using fabric. For 'windows', include 'transparent so that light can come in and you can look out'. Other items to list include partitions, book covers, bookshelves, tables, and bookends. Write these next to the material from which they are made.

Evaluate the information in terms of what it tells you. Ask, *How valuable is it in telling you about the range and types of materials that are used in the library? How valuable is it in telling you about how the materials have been chosen because they are suited to their purpose?*

Now ask, *Apart from paper, which material is used most in the library? Why? Which materials could be replaced with something different which has the same property?* For example, shelves can be made from wood, metal, rock and plastic because they are all rigid and will hold heavy loads. *Ask, Which material do you think is best suited to this purpose – the one already in use, or the new one you have thought of? Why?* Repeat this for some of the other items in the library, such as chairs, bookends, boxes and so on.

Make a new table. List all the properties you have identified, and against each one list all the items that have these properties. Now ask the children, *Do the same properties support the same function? For example, are all the soft items there for your comfort? Are the inflexible items there to support something or keep it in place?*

Use this information to plan and design items for your school library, such as bookstands and soft furnishings.

DIFFERENTIATION

Encourage lower attaining children to think about one material at a time, or list the items and name the material alongside it. Discuss the properties of the materials and consider why they have been used for their particular purpose. Higher attaining children can start by locating the properties and using this information to consider the reasons why this property is important to the particular item it is used to make.

WHERE NEXT

Carry out a survey of the school library and note any items you would like to add, such as posters, soft furnishings, cuddly toys or interesting bookends.

ASSESSMENT

Watch the children as they locate and collect the information about the materials used and make links with their properties. Note in particular the children who use evaluation skills to understand that the properties of the materials are important for the uses to which they are put.

LEARNING OUTCOME

Most children will locate and collect the names of the items and the materials from which they are made. Some will go on to evaluate the properties of the materials from which different items are made and use this information to consider how the property suits the items' purpose.

FURTHER SCIENCE CHALLENGES

Property game

Look at the information you have collected and note which material is used most in the library. Consider the reasons for this. Ask, *Is it because of the types of items used, or is it because of the use and purpose of the library?* Evaluate other areas of the school for the properties of the items it contains and note whether the ones that are most evident suit the use of the space. For example, look at the school playground and note how many items are strong and rigid because of the number of children who use them at one time.

ANNUALS

SUBJECT: HISTORY.
QCA UNIT 18:
WHAT WAS IT LIKE TO
LIVE HERE IN THE PAST?

LEARNING OBJECTIVE

To learn that life for children in the past was different from life today.

THINKING OBJECTIVE

To ask questions.

THINKING SKILLS

The children will look at the titles and content of some of the strip cartoon stories in annuals of the past and compare these with those of the present day. They will ask questions and use the answers to inform their research about how children used to live.

WHAT YOU NEED

Annuals, recent and from the past, suitable for the children's reading ability. Go back as far as you like – the only limitation will be what is available – but include some that contain new characters (the Tweenies or Bob the Builder) and others that have been available for a long time (*The Dandy*, *Blue Peter* or *Rupert*). Paper and pens; whiteboard and pen.

WHAT TO DO

Look at a modern annual. Note its title and content. Ask the children about the style of the pictures and whether it appeals to them. Ask, *Who would have read this annual? Do you think it was available in the 1990s? The 1980s? Why do you think that?*

Now look at a modern version of an annual that has been available for many years, perhaps *Blue Peter* or *Rupert*. Look in detail at the way it is presented, and at the articles and puzzle pages it contains. Look then at an older version of the same annual. Ask, *What kind of questions could you ask to identify what is the same and what is different about the two books?*

One way to approach this task is to look at different elements of each book and make a note of the things that are the same and the things that are different. These points can then be converted into questions, which will inform the children's research into the other annuals in the collection. For example, if the children note that both books have a contents page, this can be converted into a question like: *Does the book have a contents page?* One annual may have colour pictures throughout, while the other may only have black and white illustrations. Convert this into a question like: *Does the annual have colour pictures?* In response to the storyline, the children could ask: *What are the characters doing?* or *What are the characters saying to each other?* Make a list of the questions the children produce.

Ask the children to work in groups to look at two different annuals – preferably two of the same type, such as two comic annuals or two Blue Peter annuals. Explain that they should answer the questions to find out what they can about the content of each annual. Prompt them to look at incidental aspects of the pictures, such as fashion, everyday objects, types of activities, and any crazes relevant to that time.

Gather together at the end of the session to share what the children have found out. What do their answers tell them about the way children used to live? Ask, *Are there any clues in the content of the stories to what children's life used to be like?* (Depending on the annuals in your collection, they may answer *yes* or *no*.) You are likely to find out that they watched TV, and that some programmes were the same and others were not; that they read some of the same comics, as well as others. Differences will be identified in clothes, hairstyles, pop groups, fashion accessories and hobbies.

Evaluate how the questions help to guide the children's research to find out what life was like for children then, and the things they were interested in.

DIFFERENTIATION

Give lower attaining children the annuals that have pictures which show marked differences, such as characters wearing unfamiliar fashions and hairstyles, or children playing with outmoded toys. Draw the children's attention to items like watches and shoes, if they can be seen clearly. Model with them how they can use this information as a starting point to asking questions, and that they can find the answers to these in other books to learn more about how children used to live. Do this together, if necessary.

Give higher-attaining children less obvious annuals, such as comic books. Challenge them to think of questions about the activities that the characters are doing, as this often reflects the culture of the time. Evaluate with them how their list of questions helps them to find out more about the way children used to live.

WHERE NEXT

Display your list of questions for the children to use at other times to evaluate other books, magazines and posters.

ASSESSMENT

Most children will learn that aspects of annuals such as fashion, games, toys and the presentation of pictures and writing, can be used as a basis for asking suitable questions to find out about the past.

LEARNING OUTCOMES

Most children will learn to ask questions that will guide their research into finding out about what life was like for children in the past. Some will understand that the questions are based on particular aspects of the era that they want to find out about, such as toys and games, or fashion.

FURTHER HISTORY CHALLENGES
Comic characters

Look at two comics or annuals, one modern and one from the past. Talk about the similarities (perhaps the characters) and differences (perhaps the way they have been drawn). Choose one character and invite the children to note all the ways that the character is the same – in the way they look and behave, or the things they do. Note any differences in the same way. Challenge the children to convert the things they have found into questions, and to use these to find out about another character from the same comic or annual. List how the questions tell us something about what life was like for children in the past.

LIBRARY LOCATION

SUBJECT: GEOGRAPHY. QCA UNIT 6: INVESTIGATING THE LOCAL AREA.

LEARNING OBJECTIVE
To develop mapping and fieldwork skills.

THINKING OBJECTIVE
To define a problem.

THINKING SKILLS
The children will locate the nearest local library on a map and consider the difficulties people may face in trying to get there. This may be relatively easy if you live fairly close to one, so in this situation, ask the children to think about how difficult it would be if the library were in another town. They will then define the problem so that they can begin to find a solution to it.

WHAT YOU NEED
Leaflets with information about your local library; a map of the local area, large enough to see the location of the library and be able to identify the route and distance from the school – this may be a combination of a city or town plan and an OS map, depending on where you live; paper and pens.

WHAT TO DO
Look at the map of the immediate locality and locate features that the children know. You should also try to identify some with which they are less familiar. Ask the children if they know where the nearest library is. Ask, *Is it in the town where you live? Is it in a town or city nearby? How many of you do not know where the local library is?* Hand out the leaflets to the

children and encourage them to find out more about what the local library has to offer.

Discuss with the children how easy or difficult it is to get to the local library. Look carefully at the maps and locate where the library is, then draw the route from the school to the library and talk about how the children could get there. Ask the children to define the problem of how easy or difficult it is to get to the nearest library. Ask, *What difficulties do people face when they want to visit the local library? What is the distance? Can they walk or is it too far? What travel options do they have? If they drive, is there somewhere to park? Are there suitable bus routes, and if so, at what times do the buses run?* Calculate the distance (in miles, kilometres and metres) of the library from the school, a suitable car park and the nearest bus stop, using the scale on the map. Look again at the leaflets and note when the library is open. Identify any problems that these times would present to certain groups of people, such as the elderly, parents with small children, those who work full time, or children who go to school. Ask, *Do these opening times present any difficulties to different people? Is there a bus that runs at these times? Will they be able to get home fairly quickly, or do they have to wait a long time for the bus?*

Write a short description of the best way to get to the library and the best time to visit from the point of view of someone who goes to school, who works full time or who is retired.

DIFFERENTIATION
With lower attaining children, focus on the route and the different ways to travel. Challenge higher attaining children to think about geting to a specialist library – say, the British Library in London. Consider how the Internet can support such visits.

WHERE NEXT
Send a letter to the local town council about your findings on the difficulties people face when visiting their nearest library.

ASSESSMENT
Assess how well the children question the difficulties people face when they want to travel to the local library.

LEARNING OUTCOMES
Most children will be able to read a map and use the information to consider the difficulties people have visiting their nearest library. They will consider transport implications and the distance that they have to travel.

FURTHER GEOGRAPHY CHALLENGES
Mobile libraries
Talk to the children about how people who live in rural or more remote parts of the country can use a local library. Ask, *What problems do they face?* Tell them about the mobile libraries that visit more rural and remote parts of the country so that people can still access library facilities. If possible, ask the local library if a mobile library can visit the school so that the children can see the range of books and other lending items available.

The school library
Ask the children to think of a way to help younger pupils to look for a particular book in the library. Draw a plan of the school library, detailing where the different sections are. Ask, *How will you show the different sections? Will you colour them a different colour? Will you know just by looking at the colour where you would find a book about dinosaurs, for example? Will you need a key or will you label the different areas? How can you make it clear where to go? Which way round should the children hold the plan? Is that clear?*

BOOKSTANDS

SUBJECT: DESIGN AND TECHNOLOGY. QCA UNIT 3D: PHOTOGRAPH FRAMES.

LEARNING OBJECTIVE
To understand why it is important for structures to be stable.

THINKING OBJECTIVE
To evaluate information (judging usefulness).

THINKING SKILLS
The children will look at a number of different bookstands and consider what it is that makes them stable. This will include the strength of the materials used and the structure of the frame. They will then

evaluate the size and weight of the different books in the school library so that they can further evaluate the usefulness of the bookstands in terms of which books they can and cannot support.

WHAT YOU NEED
Books of different sizes; a range of different bookstands, including iron ones for cookery books, wooden ones in an easel style, plastic document display stands, and any other ornamental ones that are available; paper and writing materials.

WHAT TO DO
Tell the children that you want to design some new bookstands that could be used to display any of the books in the library, one at a time.

Evaluate the quality of the bookstands in your collection and their usefulness in terms of how well they suit their purpose. Start by looking at one of the bookstands in your collection and model the evaluation process for the children. Note how it is made and the material used, and then consider why this material has been used. Ask, *Why is the kitchen stand made from metal? Is it to make it fit in with the kitchen design? Is it because it can be painted with waterproof paint? What other material could it be made from? How is it made? If it were made from card or wood, would it be strong and stable enough?*

Divide the children into groups and give each group a bookstand to evaluate in the same way. Share the children's evaluations with the rest of the class after about ten minutes.

Challenge the children to use their evaluations to design a bookstand to display a book they have selected. They should choose a size of book that is commonly found in the library. Encourage the children to think about the size, weight and thickness of the book they have in mind before they start to plan. Remind them to label the design to show the structure, stability and the materials being used. They should give reasons for their choices that reflect their earlier evaluations of the collection of bookstands.

DIFFERENTIATION
Put different bookstands in the centre of the tables for the lower attaining children to refer to during their design task. Work alongside them, pointing out the different ways that the bookstands have been made stable. This could be by use of triangulation in a structure, the wide or different-shaped base of the stand, or added legs to hold the stand upright.

Higher-attaining children should think about the design styles, as well as the materials, structure and stability.

WHERE NEXT
Make a universal bookstand that is stable and strong enough to display most books in the school library.

ASSESSMENT
Note the children who use the information from the evaluations in their designs for bookstands. Assess how well they have labelled the different parts and materials for their design to show that they have thought about strength, stability and how the design fits its purpose.

LEARNING OUTCOMES
Most children will understand how evaluation of existing products will help them in their own designs.

FURTHER DESIGN AND TECHNOLOGY CHALLENGES
Big Books
Evaluate the stands used in school to display Big Books for whole-class literacy text work. Look in catalogues to see if there are different types, and consider whether the stands that hold large sheets of paper may be suitable. Evaluate the advantages and disadvantages of the stands used in school: *Does it give the book enough support? Is it large enough to stop the book falling over? Does it hold the pages at the bottom so that they do not flip over?*

Bookends
Challenge the children to design and make sets of bookends that fit in with the library design and are stable enough to hold a heavy book upright without any danger of it falling over. The children might like to design different ones for the various sections in the library, such as giraffes for the animal section, flowers or trees for the plant section, CD-ROMs for the computer section, and so on.

BOOK LOCATION

SUBJECT: ICT. QCA UNIT 3A: COMBINING TEXT AND GRAPHICS.

LEARNING OBJECTIVE
To learn how to import pictures into text and resize them to fit.

Thinking objective
To create ideas.

Thinking skills
The children will consider the books in the school library and how they are classified, before creating a poster to show other pupils in the school the system that has been used for this. When developing their ideas, they will consider which pictures it would be useful to include, and how they will use them. They will also consider how well their finished poster informs their schoolmates about where they can locate the book they need.

What you need
A computer and software with graphics and text.

What to do
Look at the books in each colour-coded section of the library and reflect on how they have been organised. Note the range of different sections within each colour-coded band – in science, for example, there may be space, machines and friction.

Start by choosing one colour-coded band and thinking together about all the attractive pictures you could choose to show the content of the books in this section. Show the children how to find some of these on a clipart package, either on a CD-ROM or on the hard drive. Choose one of the images and insert it into the screen, perhaps a picture of a planet and stars. Change the size of this, repositioning it in different places around the page until you have found a position you all like. Add the title of the section, for example 'Space', and the corresponding classification number (if appropriate). Evaluate whether this attracts attention, and make any changes to style, size or colour.

Repeat this for the next selection of books, for example 'Friction'. Choose a picture and move it to the spot you want. This could be directly underneath the first picture, to the right-hand side of the page, or at a diagonal angle. Let the children choose to help them develop their creativity.

Continue with this until you are sure the children understand how to use the ICT skills which will help them to create an attractive poster.

Organise the children to work individually or in pairs to create their own poster to help others find the book they want easily. Encourage the children to evaluate their work as they go along to improve their ideas. When everyone has finished their poster, print

them off and look at the range of different ideas that the children have used.

Differentiation
Encourage higher attaining children to explore how to move their pictures and symbols around the page to create different options from which they can choose. Offer lower attaining children some ideas to adapt by preparing a sheet of useful pictures and font styles from which they can choose.

Where next
Make any necessary improvements and display the posters in turn in the school library for other children to use when they are looking for books. Ask the children who use the library how useful they find them in helping them to locate the book they want quickly.

Assessment
Assess how well the children have used their creative ideas to make a practical guide to help others locate books quickly and easily. Note the children who have used pictures to support those who cannot read well and who have displayed these in a way that catches the reader's eye.

Learning outcome
All the children will have an opportunity to create a poster to help people locate books in the library. Some will make their poster user-friendly by using pictures.

Further ict challenges
Opening times
Make a leaflet that shows the opening times of the school library and the range of books available. Challenge the children to create ideas that will attract others to read the leaflet and thus go to the library.

Story-teller's visit
Organise a story-telling event for younger pupils and challenge your class to create a poster to invite them to the event. When developing their ideas, they need to consider how they can use colour and pictures to attract these younger children.

Loose covers

SUBJECT: ART AND DESIGN. QCA UNIT 4B: TAKE A SEAT.

Learning objective
To consider the style of chair that would be suitable for a story-teller.

THINKING OBJECTIVE
To think imaginatively.

THINKING SKILLS
The children will consider the needs of a story-teller and the most suitable style and height of chair required. They will then combine and contrast fabrics and other decorations to design and make loose covers to reflect the chair's purpose and make it look attractive. They will be encouraged to use their imagination to think about the different themes of stories, and the kinds of people who may tell these stories.

WHAT YOU NEED
Fabrics in a range of colours and patterns, including old curtains, throws, blankets and sheets; an old chair frame; frills and fringes; paper; writing and drawing materials.

WHAT TO DO
158
Think about the person who will sit in the chair. This could be a storybook character, a teacher, or some other adult who tells stories. Ask, *What sort of chair will they need? How high should the seat be? Will it have arms?* Think about the stories that the story-teller may tell. Ask, *Will this determine how the chair should be styled?*

Choose one story and, as a class, design a chair for a potential story-teller for this story. Consider the plot of the story and discuss whether the story-teller may dress up as one of the characters. Ask, *What style of chair would this person have?* Challenge the children to use their imagination to come up with several ideas for a suitable style of chair. Encourage them to think about how the chair will be constructed, and how it will be decorated.

Now ask the children to work in pairs or small groups to design a chair of any style and framework. Suggest that they choose a particular story, or a particular story-teller, and design with that in mind. When the children have finished these initial designs, look at a few together and make suggestions for improvements.

Choose one of the ideas together, preferably one where an immediate design is possible to achieve on a style of chair available in school or at home. Show the children the chair and suggest that it may be possible to use it to create the selected design. Explain how they can cover this chair with fabrics, using fringes and frills to add colour and pattern to make it look like their story-teller's chair.

Look at the fabrics you have in your collection. Explain that the children can choose any they like

to create a covering and decoration for the chosen design. Let the children use their imagination for their designs, combining two or three different fabrics to cover the chair, tucking and pinning them into place to make them safe. Make it inviting, as well as reflecting the character and function of the story-teller.

Dress up as the story-teller to tell the children stories at the end of the day.

DIFFERENTIATION
Work with lower attaining children to cover smaller chairs (found in many school book corners) with the different combinations of fabrics to evaluate the effects. Higher attaining children should be asked to think about other things they could use to add flair to the designs, such as bobbles, fur fabrics, tassels and ribbons.

WHERE NEXT
Change the style of the chair every so often, following some of the children's other designs.

ASSESSMENT
Note the imaginative ways in which the children combine colour and pattern to create covers for the chair.

LEARNING OUTCOMES
Most children will consider the character and purpose of the chair in their designs. They will think imaginatively, within a structure, to design a suitable covering for the chair.

FURTHER ART AND DESIGN CHALLENGES
Cushion comfort
Make a cushion for the chair for added comfort. The children should consider the pattern and colour of the cushion, and decide whether it should co-ordinate or contrast with the chair's cover.

MUSIC LIBRARY

SUBJECT: MUSIC. QCA UNIT 14: SALT, PEPPER, VINEGAR, MUSTARD.

LEARNING OBJECTIVE
To identify singing games to include on a tape that could be available for loan in the school library.

Thinking objectives
To plan research; to improve ideas.

Thinking skills
The children will plan how they can compile a tape of singing games for pupils to borrow from the school library. They will investigate the range of musical games that can already be borrowed from the local library and enlist the help of parents and grandparents in their search for material. They will then use this information to draw up a list of singing games to include on the tape. They will listen to and act out each game before choosing those that are most suitable. They will then improve upon their ideas by trying out their selected games with younger children, using the information gained from their feedback to look for additional material. This lesson focuses on making a collection of singing games to support younger children's history learning. The lesson works best if it is used to round off the QCA unit of work.

What you need
A collection of singing games for the children to learn and play, such as 'I sent a letter to my love' and 'The farmer's in his den'; a tape recorder.

What to do
Tell the children that you want to make a compilation tape of singing and playground games for younger pupils to borrow from the school library to support their learning in history. Ask, *Can you think how we might go about finding out what games are already available? How will we know whether the tape will be popular with the children?*

Plan the research together:

◉ *What do you need to do first?* (Collect all the games that they can.)

◉ *How will you go about doing this?* (By thinking of some they play themselves, looking at those available in the local library, and asking adults.)

◉ *What will you do with the information you collect?* (Choose some to make a draft tape of the games.)

◉ *How will you know whether they will be popular with the younger children?* (Play some of them together at playtimes and ask what they think.)

◉ *What will you do with the information?* (Improve the tape to include the games the children like best.)

Carry out the research plan. Listen to and learn a range of singing games over a few weeks. Think about the different types of games, clapping, skipping, and action songs. Invite a parent or grandparent to come in to play some of these with the children, or organise them as part of a lunchtime activity.

Now plan how you can go about making a tape to teach these games to the younger children. Ask, *What information do we need to have before we put the tape together?* (Knowing which ones the children like best, and find easiest to play.)

Suggest to the class that they could teach some of the games to the younger children in school at lunch-times. This would help them to find out which ones are favourites. Record versions of these onto a tape and ask their teacher if they may to listen to it during the day, or just before they go out to play, to remind them of the words and music. Ask the younger children what they think of the tape: *Is it interesting? Are there any games you like in particular? Why?*

Use their responses to improve ideas by putting together additional tapes for them to borrow, and/or by making videos to show them the skipping, clapping and actions that accompany each of these singing games.

Differentiation
Ask higher attaining children to think about games for children who are in Reception or P1. Make a tape and teach them the games. Lower attaining children should be encouraged to concentrate on one game at a time to include on the tape. This will help them to concentrate on improving their performance skills.

Where next
Research additional material by asking grandparents, parents and older members of staff for ideas. Make a videotape of some of the games.

Assessment
Assess how well the children plan their research to discover the most suitable games to include. Do they identify questions that include a full range of games? Do they focus on specific types of games? Do they find out which games the younger children prefer and how much they like each one?

Learning outcomes
All the children will be able to record at least one suitable singing game on tape for younger children to borrow. They will base this choice on research that they have planned themselves. They will consider how they can improve their ideas by adding to the collection and/or making additional tapes and videos.

Further music challenges
And – action!
Plan how to put together a videotape of the games, working in groups to plan the research. Ask, *Which*

ones will you include? Why? How will you direct the filming? Who will use the camera? Who will play and sing the games? How will you rehearse the film? How will you make sure you have used the best ideas and performed them as well as you can? Evaluate the games by trying them out with the younger children and make any improvements suggested by their feedback. Make sure there is enough variety for the children to enjoy.

PEOPLE OF IMPORTANCE

SUBJECT CONTEXT: RE AND PE

LEARNING OBJECTIVE
To make suggestions on books for particular library sections.

THINKING OBJECTIVES
To evaluate information; to suggest improvements.

THINKING SKILLS
The children will evaluate the quality and range of books available in the library to support learning in RE and PE, and will then look in catalogues, the local public library and Internet websites for additional relevant titles.

WHAT YOU NEED
A visit to the local public library; access to the Internet; paper and pens; lists of PE and RE topics.

WHAT TO DO
Look at the RE and PE sections in the library. Give each group of children a different RE or PE topic and a unit of work from your planned curriculum/scheme of work. Ask them to list all the titles they can find that support research and learning in these topics. Ask them to start by evaluating the overall range of books, deciding which aspects of the topic are not covered, or identifying areas where there is a limited selection of material.

Invite them to evaluate individual books next. Ask, How are you evaluating the quality of the books? Are you looking at the age and style of the pictures? How easy is it to locate the information inside? How helpful are the pictures and illustrations? Is the information easy to read? What topics does the book cover precisely? Are there any aspects of the topic that are not covered?

Ask the children to think of other ways they could research information on their given topics. Encourage them to think of all the other methods of research they could use, and then allow them to evaluate the CD-ROMs, videos and other materials that they have identified.

Use book catalogues and the Internet (for example, Abacus.com) to identify additional material that could be added to the collection.

DIFFERENTIATION
Give higher attaining children the job of evaluating whether the books available in the library are suitable for all ages. Organise them into pairs and give each pair a specific age to evaluate for in the different subjects. They should be encouraged to match the content to the topic, and to evaluate how easy and attractive the books are to younger and older readers. Disperse lower attaining children between the other groups, giving them a particular task such as ticking off a list the aspect covered by a particular section.

WHERE NEXT
Look at other subject sections to evaluate any gaps. Use this information to plan to purchase or borrow resources from the local library at specific times to support learning in these areas.

ASSESSMENT
Assess how well the children approach the evaluation task. Do they think about how they will evaluate the quality of the books and the value of the information to their particular topic? How well do they use the information to suggest improvements to the number, range and quality of books and other resources?

LEARNING OUTCOME
Most children will learn to evaluate the range and quality of books for gaining information about a certain topic. They will use this information to make suggestions for improvements to the range of materials available. Some will consider the quality of information for younger and older readers in terms of the style and content.

FURTHER RE AND PE CHALLENGES
Library books
Evaluate the books in the RE and PE sections and note how interesting and useful they are to different ages and genders. Ask, for example, Would a book about Hindus be more useful to you, or to older or younger pupils? Agree that it would be useful to them, as they study Hindus during the year. Ask, How about a book about football? Which group of children would be most interested in this? Identify any gaps in the RE and PE sections, in terms of their usefulness to the topic studied by the different year groups in the school, and their interest to different groups of children such as boys and girls.